POLITICAL ECONOMY

Political Economy

Public Policies in the United States and Britain

Edited by Jerold L. Waltman
and Donley T. Studlar

University Press of Mississippi
Jackson and London

This book has been sponsored
by the University of Southern Mississippi

The paper in this book meets the guidelines for permanence and
durability of the Committee on Production Guidelines for Book
Longevity of the Council on Library Resources.

Library of Congress Cataloging-in-Publication Data

Political economy.

   Includes index.
   1. United States—Economic policy.   2. United
States—Economic conditions—1945–   .   3. Great
Britain—Economic policy—1945–   .   4. Great
Britain—Economic conditions—1945–   .   I. Waltman,
Jerold L., 1945–   .   II. Studlar, Donley T.
HC106.P68   1987   361.6′1′0941   87-10425
ISBN 0-87805-313-1 (alk. paper)
ISBN 0-87805-314-X (pbk. : alk. paper)

British Library Cataloguing in Publication Data is available.

Contents

Preface ix

Policy Convergence? Political Economy in the United States 3
and Britain   *Donley T. Studlar*

Guiding and Making Policy: Ideas and Institutions 16
    John D. Robertson

Industrial Policy: Patterns of Convergence 44
and Divergence   *Jeffrey B. Freyman*

Labor Market Surgery, Labor Market Abandonment: 69
The Thatcher and Reagan Unemployment Remedies
    David B. Robertson

Changing the Course of Tax Policy: Convergence in Intent, 98
Divergence in Practice   *Jerold L. Waltman*

Energy Policy in the United States and Britain 120
    Joseph R. Rudolph, Jr.

Consumer Policy: Qualified Convergence 150
    Richard S. Flickinger

Do Policy Issues Determine Politics? State Pensions Policy 182
    Gary P. Freeman

Health Policy in a Period of Resource Limits 207
and Conservative Politics   *Beth C. Fuchs*

Housing Policy: Converging Trends, 233
Divergent Futures   *Nathan H. Schwartz*

The Strength of Policy Inheritance   *Jerold L. Waltman* 259

Notes on Contributors 270

Index 273

Preface

This book is designed to be complementary in several ways to our previous edited publication, *Dilemmas of Change in British Politics*, (University Press of Mississippi and Macmillan, 1984). That book dealt with institutions; this one is concerned with policy. The first focused on the politics of a single country; the second is more explicitly comparative. The earlier volume featured the collective talents of senior scholars; the present one relies heavily on younger contributors. In all of these ways, the two edited works reflect general trends in the development of political science. Whether this constitutes progress we leave for others' judgments.

The books are similar, however, in the dependence of the editors not only on the cooperation of the other contributors, but also on the goodwill of their families and the support of various academic organizations. Financial assistance to facilitate completion of the project was provided by the University of Southern Mississippi Faculty Grant Fund and the Centre College Faculty Development Fund. The papers included here were presented on panels at the following academic conferences: British Politics Group, Conference Group on Political Economy, Kentucky Political Science Association, Southern Political Science Association, and Western Conference on British Studies. The editorial staff of the University Press of Mississippi provided prompt and efficient services, including thorough critiques by reviewers.

Our families have sustained us throughout the toils of authorship and editorship. The contribution of our wives is reflected in our dedication of this volume to them. Our children have been supportive by being themselves.

POLITICAL ECONOMY

Policy Convergence? Political Economy in the United States and Britain

Donley T. Studlar

The United States and United Kingdom are probably the two most frequently investigated political systems in the world, and comparisons have often been made between them. Institutional analyses date from the beginning of political science.[1] Comparisons of political parties and political processes have also been a staple of the discipline.[2] More recently, frequent comparisons of policies have also been made.[3]

Three developments common to both the United States and Britain have made investigation of convergence theories especially appropriate for these countries. The first is the tendency, to paraphrase a British statesman, to see the United States as Rome to Britain's Greece. Similarities between the two polities, especially problems, are noticed and discussed. Samuel Beer summarizes this general perspective in the preface to his book *Britain Against Itself*:[4]

> When I asked a student recently why she was taking my course, she replied, "It was my father's advice. He said, 'Study England, a country on its knees. That is where America is going.' "

The most recent manifestation of this tendency has been to see many British and American policy problems of the 1970s and 1980s as similar, both in origin and response. After the long postwar economic boom and the emergence of consensus politics in both countries, matters have changed substantially in recent years. Economic performance in both countries has slumped; inflation and unemployment has increased; the 1973 oil crisis hit both hard; Keynesian economic prescriptions no longer appear to be a panacea for advanced industrial capitalism. The United States found itself, like Britain previously, buffeted by international economic forces beyond its control. In both countries, the role of the welfare state and more generally of big government in contributing to this economic predicament has been questioned.[5]

The decline of American economic hegemony has been accompanied by fears of loss of geopolitical standing. Few American politicians have viewed the idea of "America as an ordinary country"[6] with equanimity. Again, the experience of Britain as a declining great power is a natural reference point, and the linkage of economic and foreign policy decline has also been a preoccupation of the British themselves.[7]

Whether as cause or consequence of the economic and foreign policy problems, the postwar political consensus in the two countries has also been unravelling. The electorate no longer readily follows the leadership of two moderate parties. Instead, radical voices have been heard within the parties, extremist factions have flourished, significant minor parties have emerged, and electoral disenchantment and volatility have become norms in both Britain and the United States.[8] "Ungovernability" was a popular academic concept of the 1970s applied to both polities.[9]

The second trend of recent years encouraging research into American-British convergence was the advent of two ideologically conservative administrations within one year of each other, 1979 and 1980. Not only the surface similarity of their views, especially in regard to domestic socioeconomic policy, but also the expressed mutual admiration of the two leaders for each other has inspired various policy comparisons.[10] The *Economist* even refers to "Ronald Thatcher." The successful reelection of each to a second term of office assures that such comparisons will continue to be made, not only throughout the second terms but thereafter as well.

Third, more systematic comparisons of the party systems of the two countries have argued that convergence is occurring.[11] Even though these analyses do not agree on either the forms or mechanisms of convergence, the fact that independent academic examinations find a long-term institutional trend toward convergence, not limited to the Reagan-Thatcher years, is worthy of consideration.

Even if one accepts that some convergence of institutions is occurring, what is the impact on public policy? Our study will examine the applicability of convergence theory to a broad range of policies in political economy in the two polities.

CONVERGENCE THEORY: A REASSESSMENT

Political convergence is a term usually associated with the comparative study of the United States and the Soviet Union in the late 1950s and early 1960s. Two very different polities in origin and development were supposedly moving toward a general form of bureaucratized democratic socialism. Although not widely recognized, this was another application of the dialectic—thesis, antithesis, synthesis—to human affairs.[12] The idea of political convergence is not nearly so popular among scholars of the Soviet Union today.[13] Indeed, rather than converging with the West, Communist states themselves appear to be increasingly divergent from each other.[14]

In addition to Marx, cyclical theorists of history such as Spengler, Toynbee, and Sorokin were contributors to convergence thought.[15] Convergence emerged as a particular school of thought, however, with the publication of W. W. Rostow's *The Stages of Economic Growth: A Non-Communist Manifesto*.[16] Rostow postulated five stages of economic growth, culminating in what he called the stage of High Mass Consumption. Marxism, according to Rostow, was destined for the dustbin of history, a product of earlier stages of industrialization. At the stage of High Mass Consumption, a society had three economic options that it could pursue: a welfare state, consumption of individual durable goods, or advanced technology weapons. Different societies had somewhat different mixes of these three possibilities, but at this stage the evolution was similar. The United States was the first society to reach this stage, followed by, in order, Western Europe, Japan, and the Soviet Union. Rostow stated, "There are similar patterns of structural evolution in different societies as they go through the high-consumption phase."[17] The implication was that a similar pluralistic evolution in politics would also occur. Hence Rostow's view that Communism was an infantile disorder.

Less sanguine about the prospects for liberal democracy in convergence was A. F. K. Organski.[18] His four stages of political development were based on economic factors, although the interaction of these factors with social and political dimensions led to substantial variations within each stage. For the forthcoming "Politics of Abundance," however, he foresaw automation leading to mass unemployment, greater public-private cooperation, and a concentration of power.

> It remains a major question, however, whether a democratic system can be maintained in the face both of a tremendous concentration of political and economic power in the hands of a small elite and of a virtual guarantee that welfare measures will be continued even in the absence of democracy. It comes down to

this: if democracy is to be maintained in stage four of political development, it will be the result of conscious effort. The trends foreseen here all press in the opposite direction.[19]

The political implications of convergence were more explicitly developed and critiqued in Brzezinski and Huntington's *Political Power USA/USSR*.[20] These writers argued that the convergence theory was one linking economics to politics. Industrialization led to political liberalization, in four dimensions. First, industrialization gave rise to common culture, social forms, and politics across states—an anti-Soviet Marxism. Second, industrialization led to complications and diversity within states. Third, industrialization led to affluence and political pluralism. Fourth, industrialization resulted in mutual contact and influence (diffusion). Having put forth these four linkages between economic and political convergence, Brzezinski and Huntington then denied that such linkages were actually taking place. Archaic societies, they argued, may have had similar pastoral economies, but this fact did not lead to similar political structures. Even if the economic structures of the United States and the Soviet Union were becoming more alike, this did not mean their political structures would grow more similar.

Despite the fact that convergence theory would appear to be applied more reasonably to societies of greater superficial similarity than the United States and the Soviet Union, this has only rarely been done explicitly and systematically.[21] At least two implicit versions of the convergence theory, however, have flourished in the analysis of Western industrialized democracies, including the United States and the United Kingdom. The first version was the "end of ideology" thesis.[22] In essence, it was argued that the economic growth of the 1950s and early 1960s had created a politics of technical economic management. Subsequent increments of growth could be parceled out by groups competing for more or less, not all or nothing. Because the advanced economies were continually producing satisfactory rates of growth, there would be a decline in the tendency to engage in systematic criticism. The structure of politics would therefore become organized groups bickering over the distribution of the next increment. Conceptually, there are a number of difficulties with this thesis.[23] As for those bearing on convergence theory, the overriding salience of economic issues stands out. The politics of economic management would outweigh political conflict of all other types—linguistic, regional, cultural, ethnic. In essence, the harmony created by economic plenty would make economic, social, and political systems similar in the democratic societies of the West.

A recent attempt to combine empiricism with grand theory in comparative politics is the postindustrialism thesis. In some ways this idea is derived from the "end of ideology" school, as the pivotal role of Daniel Bell in each indicates.[24] Nevertheless, the differences between the two are considerable, at least beyond Bell. Rather than the decline of ideology, the proponents of postindustrialism argue that new cleavages and issues are arising to supplement and perhaps supplant older ones. The emphasis is on the changing economic-technical base of societies and how these changes are reflected in the attitudes of the rising generations.[25] So far, postindustrialism has been minimally concerned with policy, however, and has had little to say about distinctive patterns of postindustrial political institutions. Pomper, however, argues that it is social and economic changes in the form of postindustrialism that have led to changes in the British and American party systems.[26] In a similar vein, Waltman sees the judiciary as in danger of overload arising from postindustrial issues.[27] In short, despite the marriage of theory and data in postindustrial thought, it has not yet produced convincing evidence of systematic convergence.

Ironically, the explicit empirical investigation of convergence has continued to flourish among economists, who are more reluctant to talk about postindustrialism as a concept. A whole series of studies in recent years has investigated the similarities and differences among the economies of both industrialized capitalist and communist states, with varying results.[28] While some similarities are observable, continuing diversity is also found. Although not exploring politics systematically, some economists such as Kerr find formidable hurdles to further convergence in the political institutions and political beliefs of different societies.

> The most impenetrable barriers to convergence are the power and tenacity of the elites that lead the process, the inevitable eternal conflict over the highest economic and political goals, and the ingrained beliefs of the people. The second of these is probably the most persistent among, but also within, nations.[29]

Other scholars, however, have continued to deny that convergence is occurring, even in the economic sphere. The sociologist John Goldthorpe, for instance, a long-standing critic of convergence theory, argues that Western economies are increasingly divergent.[30] Rather than moving toward a general "pluralistic industrialism," capitalist economies are moving in two different directions, either toward corporatism (broadly inclusive labor-management-government bargaining patterns) or toward dualism (in which government allows management to split the labor market into sectors, often with large-scale unemployment and other social costs resulting).

CONVERGENCE AND PUBLIC POLICY

The controversy over classical convergence has continued in attenuated form in the work of scholars studying comparative public policy in advanced industrial societies. There are basically two schools of thought, the policy indicators approach and the politics of social choice theorists. Most of the policies examined by both of these groups are socioeconomic in nature—pensions, health, education, housing—and are usually limited to Western liberal democratic welfare states.

The first school is concerned with broad comparisons among Western industrialized states in regard to a few measurable policy indicators and usually emphasizes the influence of economic variables on the outcome.[31] Wilensky's conclusions are representative of the policy indicators group:[32]

> On the basis of a cross-sectional analysis of sixty-four countries, I conclude that economic growth and its demographic and bureaucratic outcomes are the root cause of the general emergence of the welfare state—the establishment of similar programs of social security, the increasing fraction of the GNP devoted to such programs, the trend toward comprehensive coverage and similar methods of financing.

Unlike some members of the policy indicators school, however, Wilensky qualifies this conclusion by noting that political and social factors influence which countries are leaders and which laggards in the welfare state. He specifically cites as important dimensions the degree of political centralization, ethnic heterogeneity of the population, social stratification and mobility, the size of the working class, and the influence of the military. Among countries, he notes a United States exceptionalism to many generalizations about the welfare state, a condition he attributes to the aforementioned qualifying factors.

Insofar as policy indicators theorists do leave the politics out of policy, such writing qualifies as an intellectual descendant of the "classical" convergence theory, in which economic factors were considered the primary influences on politics.[33] The role of economics in convergence did occasion, however, considerable debate in the 1960s.[34]

The "politics of social choice" school concentrates on in-depth investigations of the development of particular policies in certain countries, usually the United States and Western Europe.[35] These studies stress the roles of individual and group political actors, political institutions, and political cultures. They tend to emphasize differences among the states investigated, whereas the policy indicators approach usually stresses similarities. To some degree, of course, these differences of findings represent artifacts of the approaches themselves, in-depth case studies versus broad comparisons of a few indicators. As the proverb of the blind men and the elephant reminds us, a viewpoint near the object of study itself concentrates on differences while a perspective from a distance encourages similarities to be seen.

Nevertheless, social choice theorists agree on little with the policy indicators group except that United States exceptionalism exists. Scholars of this persuasion argue that politics is primary while economic and social conditions are secondary in explaining why even Western welfare states have different policies. But whose politics? And in what policy areas? Here differences within the school mount. Heclo argues that in forming social policy in Britain and Sweden, elites, especially in the bureaucracy, were more significant than masses.[36] King's more broadly comparative survey contends that the impact of ideas, both mass and elite, should not be underestimated in any consideration of differences in public policy.[37] In his view, ideas are more influential than elite structure, mass demands on government, interest groups, or political institutions. Like Wilensky and King, Heidenheimer et al.[38] are especially concerned to understand American exceptionalism across several policy areas. Their explanation attributes approximately equal weight to political institutions, ideology (ideas), and social conditions. The second edition of their book adds an explicit hypothesis about the conditions for convergence or divergence in socioeconomic policies, namely that in periods of economic prosperity capitalist democracies converge while during periods of economic decline they diverge.

It is easy to criticize Heidenheimer et al. and, for that matter, other writers in the politics of social choice school for their lack of precision and their tendency to conclude that every variable has some influence. Nevertheless, they are raising important questions for analysts to answer. Whose politics are significant—elites, masses, or both? How are these politics shaped by the available political institutions? What role does the political culture, elite and mass, play in policy formation? Are these patterns stable across policy areas, time, and different economic circumstances? Can countries be grouped according to the answers to these questions?

Another advantage of the work of the politics of social choice theorists is that it is closely linked to broader questions in the study of politics. One of these questions concerns the elitist-pluralist debate, which rages less fiercely now but is nonetheless important for democratic theory.[39] Another major consideration is whether policy sectors make a notable difference in evaluating how policy is made across countries. Research on how policy affects politics has been applied infrequently in the study of comparative politics,[40] but deserves more attention. Heidenheimer et al. find mixed results for the policy sectors approach in their brief survey of previous findings. Investigating the convergence theory, then, offers possibilities for addressing other large issues in the study of politics.

Donley T. Studlar

CONVERGENCE OR DIVERGENCE BETWEEN THE UNITED STATES AND BRITAIN?

If one returns to Brzezinski and Huntington's formulation of the convergence theory, their four propositions on the effects of industrialization—(1) common culture, social forms, and politics; (2) diversity within states; (3) affluence and political pluralism; (4) diffusion—seem less debatable in a comparison between the United States and the United Kingdom than in a comparison of the United States and the Soviet Union. Nevertheless it should be noted that while similarity of social structures and contact between states do sometimes lead to diffusion,[41] such processes do not necessarily guarantee mutual understanding, much less imitation.[42]

No clear answer has emerged about whether the United States and United Kingdom are converging, diverging, or remaining more or less in the same relative positions. Studies of postindustrialism have usually found both Britain and the United States fitting that classification although the United States has usually ranked higher on postindustrial indicators.[43] Moreover, attitudinal studies have found British respondents less likely to exhibit views characteristic of postindustrial society than Americans.[44] Obviously neither the United States nor the United Kingdom has achieved the end of ideology posited earlier, but the return of ideology to the politics of the two countries, in approximately the same form and at almost identical times, suggests that a more careful comparative examination of the role of ideology is needed.

Theorists of corporatism have tended to place the United States and Britain in the same category, that of pluralism (segmented economic interest groups) rather than corporatism (inclusive economic interest groups), even before the advent of Thatcher and Reagan.[45] Although he denies convergence, Goldthorpe sees both countries as developing dualist inclinations, allowing capitalist management to dominate labor and increasingly marginalize the latter's economic and political power.[46] In a widely cited study, Mancur Olson[47] argues that the relatively low postwar economic growth rates of both countries result from similar causes—entrenched economic interest groups benefiting from political stability but inhibiting economic dynamism.

The most detailed comparisons of United States and United Kingdom policies have been done by the politics of social choice analysts. Like their policy indicators counterparts, they have found the United States to be a laggard in several social policy areas. In fact, much of the previously noted conflict in this school over the impact of particular variables on policy stems from attempts to explain United States exceptionalism. While acknowledging that the United States is something of a deviant case, Heidenheimer et al. also distinguish between a continental European pattern of democratic corporatist policymaking and a more fragmented Anglo-American one.[48] However, they may be exaggerating the early success of the Reagan and Thatcher administrations in limiting and in some instances cutting established social welfare programs.

In sum, there are two different questions to be settled about convergence between the United States and United Kingdom. First, has there been convergence? In the area of public policies, our major concern, a careful comparison should yield a fairly straightforward answer. Second, why has convergence occurred or not occurred? Convergence could result from socioeconomic change generating political outcomes. If the political system is an epiphenomenon, then logically two societies having similar social and economic change should exhibit similar political outputs. Another possibility is that those in power choose similar paths for reasons of their own. That is, the state in this model exhibits autonomy, giving the authorities a large degree of discretion.[49] If the governors of the two societies choose to pursue convergent policies, for ideological reasons for example, the convergence is not causally traceable to socioeconomic change. An analysis of the mechanisms of choice and the political processes yielding specific policies is required when one proceeds along this line of inquiry.

On the other hand, if convergence is not occurring, the question of why remains equally interesting. Is it because of economic conditions, political culture, political institutions, or leaders' ideology? How likely, then, is it that convergence could take place?

PLAN OF THE BOOK

In this volume the contributors will compare Britain and the United States in several different policies—pensions, health care, housing, industrial policy, energy, taxation, consumer protection, and employment and manpower, all within a consideration of their general macroeconomic situations. These policies are related in that they all constitute aspects of what is called "political economy," the examination of the interrelationship of political and economic variables in a systematic fashion. Perspectives in this field vary widely, not only because of the complex subject matter, but also because of its broad scope—empirical *and* normative, behavioral *and* structural, international *and* domestic.[50] Nevertheless, limiting the policies analyzed to this particular area encourages closer comparison, especially since economic factors constitute an important aspect of the convergence theory. Not all facets of political economy are examined in this volume. Among the topics not extensively discussed are transportation, education, and the environ-

ment. Any generalizations found to hold for the policies covered can therefore be extended to examine these other policies. Overall, however, we have a
broad enough base of policies to justify confidence in any generalizations
emerging from the evidence.

Complaints are often voiced about books of collected essays that the
contributions do not cohere. There is virtue, however, as well as vice in
collections. If one adopts, as we do, the basic Heidenheimer et al. approach
of in-depth comparative case studies, the tendency, as noted earlier, is to see
the trees but not the forest, to emphasize diversity over uniformity.[51] This can
be counteracted, somewhat, however, by having a diversified group of
contributors, which Heidenheimer et al. do not. Narrowing the focus to a
particular policy area and utilizing experts in each policy to examine the
comparative data systematically provides for both analytical rigor and potential differences of viewpoint.

The analyses will consider the following questions: (1) *What* is happening
in this policy in each country (description of policy content)? (2) *Why* are
these things happening (explanation of policy content)? (3) *How* is the policy
made (policy process)? (4) Are the trends in the two countries basically
similar or different (convergence or divergence)? (5) What accounts for the
similarities/differences (explanation of convergence/divergence)? In each
instance, the individual specialist will discuss the portion of the history of the
policy concerned that is necessary for understanding the theoretical questions.

The traditional question underlying comparative political studies is how
similar or different two or more political systems are. Convergence theory,
however, argues that increasing similarity is the dominant trend. On the other
hand, divergence would mean that increasing dissimilarity of policies is
obtained. There could also be no direction of change either for convergence
or divergence. This empirical test of convergence theory across several
policies should improve our understanding of the politics of Shaw's "two
people separated by a common language."

NOTES

1. John W. Burgess, *Political Science and Comparative Constitutional Law*
   (Boston: Ginn and Co., 1890–91); James Bryce, *Modern Democracies* (New
   York: Macmillan, 1921).
2. Austin Ranney, *The Doctrine of Responsible Party Government* (Urbana: Univer-
   sity of Illinois Press, 1954); Kenneth Waltz, *Foreign Policy and Democratic
   Politics* (Boston: Little, Brown, 1967); Vernon Bogdanor, ed., *Parties and
   Democracy in Britain and America* (New York: Praeger, 1984).

3. Richard Rose, ed., *Lessons from America* (New York: Halsted Press, 1974); Richard Hodder-Williams and James Ceaser, eds., *Politics in Britain and the United States: Comparative Perspectives* (Durham: Duke University Press, 1986); Norman J. Vig and Steven E. Schier, eds., *Political Economy in Western Democracies* (New York: Holmes and Meier, 1985).
4. Samuel H. Beer, *Britain Against Itself* (New York: Norton, 1982), xi.
5. Samuel Brittan, *The Role and Limits of Government*, (Minneapolis: University of Minnesota Press, 1983); R. Emmett Tyrrell, ed., *The Future That Doesn't Work* (Garden City, N.Y.: Doubleday, 1977); Richard Rose and Guy Peters, *Can Government Go Bankrupt?* (New York: Basic Books, 1978).
6. Richard Rosecrance, ed., *America as an Ordinary Country* (Ithaca: Cornell University Press, 1976); Kenneth A. Oye, "International Systems Structure and American Foreign Policy," in Kenneth A. Oye, Robert J. Lieber, and Donald Rothchild, eds., *Eagle Defiant: United States Foreign Policy in the 1980s* (Boston: Little Brown, 1983), pp. 3–32.
7. Andrew Gamble, *Britain in Decline* (Boston: Beacon Press, 1982); Anthony Sampson, *The Changing Anatomy of Britain* (London: Hodder and Stoughton, 1983).
8. Ivor Crewe and David Denver, eds., *Electoral Change in Western Democracies* (London: Croom Helm, 1985).
9. Anthony King "Overload: Problems of Governing in the 1970s," *Political Studies* 23 (September 1975): 284–96; Richard Rose, "Ungovernability: Is There Fire Behind the Smoke?" *Political Studies* 27 (September 1979): 351–70; Michel Crozier, Samuel P. Huntington, and Joji Watanuki, *The Crisis of Democracy* (New York: New York University Press, 1975).
10. Joel Krieger, *Reagan, Thatcher and the Politics of Decline* (Oxford: Polity Press, 1986).
11. Samuel H. Beer, "Politics Without Precedent," *Times Literary Supplement* 183 (3 June 1983), pp. 563–4; Gerald M. Pomper, "An American's Epilogue," in Bogdanor, *Parties and Democracy*, pp. 255–74; Ivor Crewe, "Prospects for Party Realignment: An Anglo-American Comparison," *Comparative Politics* 10 (July 1980): 379–400; Donley T. Studlar, "Conclusion: A Crisis of Participation?" in Donley T. Studlar and Jerold L. Waltman, eds., *Dilemmas of Change in British Politics* (Jackson: University Press of Mississippi, 1984), 231–42.
12. John Kenneth Galbraith, *The New Industrial State* (Boston: Houghton Mifflin, 1967); Clark Kerr, *The Future of Industrial Societies* (Cambridge: Harvard University Press, 1983).
13. Daniel N. Nelson, "Political Convergence: An Empirical Assessment," *World Politics* 30 (April 1978): 411–31.
14. Archie Brown and Jack Gray, eds., *Political Culture and Political Change in Communist States*, 2nd ed. (New York: Holmes and Meier, 1979).
15. Pitirim A. Sorokin, *The Crisis of Our Age* (New York: Dutton, 1941).
16. W. W. Rostow, *The Stages of Economic Growth: A Non-Communist Manifesto* (Cambridge: Cambridge University Press, 1960).
17. Ibid., 91.
18. A.F.K. Organski, *The Stages of Political Development* (New York: Knopf, 1965).
19. Ibid., 208.
20. Zbigniew Brzezinski and Samuel P. Huntington, *Political Power USA/USSR* (New York: Viking Press, 1964).

14   *Donley T. Studlar*

21. Beth C. Fuchs, *Comparative Health Policy: A Humanistic Evaluation of Health Policy in Great Britain and the United States* (Unpublished Ph.D. dissertation, University of North Carolina, 1980).
22. Daniel Bell, *The End of Ideology* (Glencoe, Ill.: Free Press, 1960); Seymour M. Lipset, *Political Man* (Garden City, N.Y.: Doubleday, 1960); Seymour M. Lipset, "Some Further Comments on 'The End of Ideology,' " *American Political Science Review* 60 (March 1966): 17–18.
23. Joseph LaPalombara, "Decline of Ideology: A Dissent and An Interpretation," *American Political Science Review* 60 (March 1966): 5–16; Chaim Waxman, ed., *The End of Ideology Debate* (New York: Funk and Wagnalls, 1969).
24. Bell, *The End of Ideology*; Daniel Bell, *The Coming of Post-Industrial Society* (New York: Harper Colophon Books, 1976).
25. Ronald Inglehart, *The Silent Revolution* (Princeton: Princeton University Press, 1977).
26. Pomper, "An American's Epilogue."
27. Jerold L. Waltman, "The Courts and Political Change in Postindustrial Society," in Kenneth Holland and Jerold L. Waltman, eds., *The Political Role of Law Courts in Modern Democracies* (New York: St. Martin's Press, 1986), chap. 11.
28. Kerr, *The Future of Industrial Societies.*
29. Ibid., 87.
30. John H. Goldthorpe, "The End of Convergence: Corporatist and Dualist Tendencies in Modern Western Societies," in John H. Goldthorpe, ed., *Order and Conflict in Contemporary Capitalism* (Oxford: Clarendon Press, 1984), 315–43.
31. Francis G. Castles and R. D. McKinley, "Public Welfare Provision, Scandinavia and the Sheer Futility of the Sociological Approach to Politics," *British Journal of Political Science* 9 (April 1979): 157–71.
32. Harold L. Wilensky, *The Welfare State and Equality* (Berkeley: University of California Press, 1975), xiii.
33. Charles W. Anderson, "The Logic of Public Problems: Evaluation in Comparative Policy Research," in Douglas E. Ashford, ed., *Comparing Public Policies* (Beverly Hills: Sage, 1978), 19–41; M. Donald Hancock, "Comparative Public Policy: An Assessment," in Ada W. Finifter, ed., *Political Science: The State of the Discipline* (Washington: American Political Science Association, 1983), 283–308.
34. Rostow, *The Stages of Economic Growth*; Organski, *The Stages of Political Development*; Brezezinski and Huntington, *Political Power*; Galbraith, *The New Industrial State.*
35. Anthony King, "Ideas, Institutions and the Policies of Governments: A Comparative Analysis," *British Journal of Political Science* 3 (July and October 1973): 291–313; 409–23; Hugh Heclo, *Modern Social Policies in Britain and Sweden* (New Haven: Yale University Press, 1974); Arnold J. Heidenheimer, Hugh Heclo, and Carolyn Teich Adams, *Comparative Public Policy* (New York: St. Martin's Press, 1975); 2nd ed. (1983).
36. Heclo, *Modern Social Policies.*
37. King, "Ideas, Institutions, and the Policies of Governments."
38. Heidenheimer, et al., *Comparative Public Policy.*
39. Andrew Cox, Paul Furlong, and Edward Page, *Power in Capitalist Society* (New York: St. Martin's Press, 1985).
40. T. Alexander Smith, "Toward a Comparative Theory of the Policy Process,"

Comparative Politics 1 (July 1969): 498–515; T. Alexander Smith, *The Comparative Policy Process* (Santa Barbara: ABC-Clio Press, 1975).

41. Jerold L. Waltman, *Copying Other Nations' Policies* (Cambridge: Schenkman, 1980).

42. Richard E. Neustadt, *Alliance Politics* (New York: Columbia University Press, 1970).

43. Roger W. Benjamin, *The Limits of Politics* (Chicago: University of Chicago Press, 1980); John D. Robertson, "Further Implications of Post-Industrialism: A Cross-National Test of Nonincremental Expansion of the Public Economy," *Southeastern Political Review* 12 (Spring 1984): 237–60. For a dissent, see Bernard D. Nossiter, *Britain: A Future That Works* (Boston: Houghton Mifflin, 1978).

44. Inglehart, *The Silent Revolution*; Alan Marsh, "The Silent Revolution, Value Priorities, and the Quality of Life in Britain," *American Political Science Review* 69 (March 1975): 1–30.

45. See, for example, several of the contributions to Goldthorpe, *Order and Conflict in Contemporary Capitalism*.

46. Goldthorpe, "The End of Convergence."

47. Mancur Olson, *The Rise and Decline of Nations* (New Haven: Yale University Press): 75–117.

48. Heidenheimer, et al., *Comparative Public Policy*.

49. Eric Nordlinger, *On the Autonomy of the Democratic State* (Cambridge: Harvard University Press, 1981); Roger W. Benjamin and Stephen L. Elkin, eds., *The Democratic State* (Lawrence, Kan., University Press of Kansas, 1985).

50. Norman J. Vig, "Introduction: Political Science and Political Economy," in Vig and Schier, *Political Economy in Western Democracies*, 3–16.

51. The macroeconomic chapter is an exception to the comparative case study approach. Instead, it sets the general context of political economy for the other policy-specific chapters. A comparative case study of recent United States and British macroeconomic policy is available in Steven E. Schier and Norman J. Vig, "Reviving Capitalism: Macroeconomic Policies in Britain and the United States," in Vig and Schier, *Political Economy in Western Democracies*, 173–99.

Guiding and Making Policy: Ideas and Institutions

John D. Robertson

Before one can accurately assess whether British and American macroeconomic policies have been converging toward some common ground, we need to briefly explore the larger issue of macroeconomic policy itself. As an overview and introduction to British and American macroeconomic policy, this chapter will explore four aspects of macroeconomic policy: (1) its component parts; (2) the two principal intellectual traditions of macroeconomics; (3) the three major complicating factors affecting the selection and success of macroeconomic policy strategies; and (4) the comparative structures of macroeconomic policymaking in Great Britain and the United States.

WHAT IS MACROECONOMIC POLICY?

To understand what macroeconomic policy is, it is helpful to break the concept down into its component parts. Macroeconomics is the study of the overall performance of a country's economy. It deals generally with the aggregate patterns of exchange between those who produce goods and services, and those who consume these goods and services in society. The standard measure of the overall performance of the economy is the Gross

Domestic Product (GDP). This represents the sum total of all goods and services exchanged in society. Observing annual changes in the GDP allows economists and policymakers to monitor the health of the macroeconomy.[1] It should be noted that as the sum total of all individual exchanges in the entire economy, macroeconomics does not focus on the health of a particular group of sellers or buyers, nor on the motivations or the values that structure the decisions of these individuals. This is the purview of the microeconomy. Rather, the macroeconomy is assumed to be one giant industry, factory, firm, etc., and the study of it concentrates on the question of whether or not the current patterns of exchange in the national marketplace are contributing to the growth of the GDP. The student of the microeconomy, for instance, would want to know why the unemployment rate among workers in the automobile industry was growing or declining. He or she would also be interested in why the individual firms in the microcomputer industry were having so much difficulty in achieving sustainable profits.[2]

The macroeconomist, on the other hand, would be more concerned with why the *national* level of unemployment was growing or declining; or, why the sum total of the recorded profits of all firms in the national economy seemed to be growing or declining. To answer these sorts of questions, the macroeconomist would need to know something of the general macroeconomic condition (such as the strength of the overall Gross Domestic Product, or the national unemployment rate), since national macroeconomic conditions affect the individual firm or industry. The same applies to the macroeconomist who requires some knowledge about specific industries or firms if he/she is to accurately interpret and fully appreciate the macroeconomic trends observed.

Public policy is the use of public authority (for example, government) to allocate scarce values in a society. As such, it is the choice made by public authority between at least two values, or preferences. How public officials arrive at such choices, what factors influence their decisions, and what consequences such choices will have on society are the questions which students of public policy explore.[3]

Public policy and macroeconomics converge when the actions of public officials affect, either directly or indirectly, the choices and preferences of the consumers and producers of goods and services in society. The study of this interaction between the decisions of public officials and the patterns of exchange in the macroeconomy is called political economics; the how, what, and why of government decisions bearing upon these exchange patterns of the macroeconomy (the national economy, rather than specific industries) is the study of macroeconomic policy.

WHY MACROECONOMIC POLICIES?

Why do governments try to influence the macroeconomy? Why not simply leave the economy to the forces of private initiative, as classical liberal economists such as Adam Smith have suggested? Actually, there has never been a truly liberal economic system, in the classical sense.[4] Classical economists such as Adam Smith, Thomas Malthus, and David Ricardo were more interested in combining theories of liberal economics with appropriate policy descriptions to achieve the realization of these theories. Yet by the early twentieth century it was clear to many economists that the concept of the laissez-faire economy was tarnished by the increasing instability of private investments in capitalist societies, and the consequent costs to society in lost wages and capital. Simply put, it became evident to many that capitalism was not an adequate provider of employment stability. A change in philosophy was believed necessary. As E.H. Carr noted, "The great illusion of the nineteenth century was not about the contribution of that [laissez-faire] order to the wealth and welfare of mankind; these were, and are, unquestioned. The great illusion was that so transient and delicately poised a structure could remain permanent."[5] Since the 1950s, therefore, the governments of most democratic societies have come to play an increasingly significant role in shaping and influencing many of the exchange relationships which comprise the macroeconomy.[6] The challenge for policymakers and the public alike has been to devise the "right analysis of the [economic] problem to cure the disease whilst preserving efficiency and freedom."[7] The term given to public policies seeking to redress economic imbalances impairing economic growth is "stabilization policy." Since World War II, policymakers have relied on two basic strategies of macroeconomic policy to stabilize the economy.

THE STRATEGIES OF MACRO-ECONOMIC POLICY

In advanced industrial democracies, public officials may select between a fiscal strategy of stabilization or a monetary strategy of stabilization. The greater likelihood is that policy makers, over a course of time, will combine both of these.[8] Finding the right balance, though, between fiscal and monetary strategies has often proved to be more than a match for a number of incumbent governments in Europe and North America during the past 15 years. Few of these countries have experimented so openly with fiscal and monetary strategies of stabilization as have Great Britain and the United States.

Fiscal strategies involve the use of taxes and public expenditures to influence the aggregate supply and demand for goods and services in society. By raising or lowering taxes, and/or by expanding or contracting the amount of money spent by the public treasury, central governments can indirectly influence the preferences of individuals by manipulating the rates of private consumption in society.

Monetary strategies, as the name implies, seeks to influence aggregate demand and supply in the economy by controlling the availability of money in the national economy. Such instruments include (1) the government purchasing securities and bonds, (2) governments, working through central banks, manipulating interest rates, or (3) the imposing of strict guidelines and regulations on central banks in an effort to force the banks to store up liquid cash assets which can be drawn upon during periods of economic destabilization.[9]

THEORIES OF MACROECONOMIC POLICY

Since the Second World War, two intellectual traditions have been most prevalent among policymakers—particularly in Great Britain and the United States—and their economic advisors: the Keynesian and the monetarist paths to economic growth and stabilization. The choice between fiscal or monetary strategies have been determined largely by the arguments and merits of these two economic doctrines. Each has offered a justification for the appropriate instruments and targets of economic policy, as well as a simplified explanation of the economic environment confronting central government.

The Keynesian Tradition

In 1936, John Maynard Keynes published his classic study of economics, "The General Theory of Employment, Interest, and Money," ushering in what many have labeled the Keynesian Revolution in economic thought. Prior to Keynes's analysis, most students of economics and public policymakers were influenced by classical liberal notions of economic thought. These held that microeconomic decisions of investment by individuals were the best guarantee of economic growth and expansion. The assumption of the classical school of economic thought was that by allowing firms and individuals to buy and sell goods at prices which the market set, the individuals themselves could regulate occasional imbalances between supply and demand. Instruments of fiscal strategy, or for that matter, monetary strategy, were believed to distort the microeconomic forces at work in the economy by depriving private individuals and corporations of their maximum opportunities to pursue their economic interests. Under these conditions, the general growth of the economy and the capacity of individual producers and consumers to adjust to price inflation and unemployment would be severely hampered, because the use of fiscal or monetary instruments would constrain the options and restrict the freedoms of individuals to react to the changing levels of demand and supply. In short, according to this theory, government intervention in the form of fiscal or monetary strategies would only create "noise" in the system and undermine the strategies of private market forces which were believed to be far better suited to stabilize an imbalanced macroeconomy.[10]

The global scale of the Great Depression shattered the credibility of these classical notions. The resulting intellectual vacuum set the stage for the introduction of Keynes's novel prescription for capitalist societies. Keynes's contribution lay at two levels. The first level was academic: Keynes, like no economist before, suggested that economists realign their thinking about the relationship of demand for goods and services to expenditures on goods and services. Specifically, he reasoned that the total spending in the economy determined the national income in society; and it was national income which stimulated and regulated aggregate demand. If aggregate demand for goods and services could be accelerated, the unemployed could be returned to gainful employment as the "multiplier effect" took hold—that is, as the total increase in income accruing to society grew in proportion to the initial increase in expenditure within the economy.[11]

The second level of Keynes's contribution had a more dramatic and immediate impact on the daily lives of citizens in Great Britain and, later, the United States—the two countries where Keynes had the greatest appeal for public officials and professional economists.[12] Rather than waiting for prices to adjust to supply and demand, Keynes argued, the central government should actively and directly intervene in an effort to adjust its budget so as to directly influence aggregate demand in society. Keynes argued that "the outstanding faults of the economic society in which we live are its failure to provide for full employment and its arbitrary and inequitable distribution of wealth and incomes."[13]

The budget was now seen as an instrument to be manipulated by public authority to ensure the most effective and desirable level of public demand, in an effort to maintain national income at levels necessary to sustain economic growth. "Budgeting," as Alt and Chrystal note, "became an exercise of economic control, not balancing the books."[14]

Following the Second World War, Keynesian logic was extended to include specific prescriptions for achieving trade-offs between jobs and prices in society. With the development of the Phillips Curve in 1958, Keynesian logic was extended to hold that a precise level of inflation could predict an exact level of unemployment. Thus, governments could presumably locate the exact trade-off point where prices and jobs were "optimized"—in other words, where the most jobs could be had, given certain demand levels—for the least inflation. [15]

The Monetarist Tradition

The monetarists largely reject the Keynesian thesis that the economy can be "fine-tuned" through the central budget. They suggest instead that the Keynesian logic underestimates the importance of money to the overall stability of the economy. Altering the supply of this money—as happens when the public treasury spends more than its revenues allow—creates a destabilizing effect on the pattern of aggregate spending in society, thus destabilizing the supply of money. The consequence is disruption of the public's confidence in its own ability to predict the money supply in the system. The effect of this public anxiety is to raise the demand for money as people try to hedge against price increases, thus jeopardizing stable employment rates and exacerbating the inflationary spiral. The monetarist tradition of economic thinking holds that so long as the actual level of inflation, at any level of unemployment, remains higher than the level of expected inflation, individuals and firms in society will revise their expectations about inflation upward and set off on another round of inflationary demand for money.

Only when a "natural level" of unemployment is reached can the inflationary spiral be controlled, according to the monetarists. A natural level is achieved when the prices of goods and services meet expectations, thus stemming price anxieties in the public. However, if the unemployment level is below the "natural" level, further stimulus to aggregate demand would lead only to a new round of inflation. In such a circumstance, the only solution to further inflation is to sustain an uncomfortable but absolutely necessary period of unemployment in an effort to establish the natural level of unemployment in order to control the money circulation, so that the real prices of goods and services in society will match the public's expectations. [16]

In sum, therefore, the principal concern of the monetarist is price inflation, while for the Keynesian it is unemployment. No definitive resolution of the debate has occurred, as to which course is better for the macroeconomy. At best, there have been periods of Keynesian influence (such as in the 1960s in the United States and throughout the period from 1947 until the early

1970s in Great Britain), alternating with periods of monetarist logic (from
the mid-70s to the present in Great Britain, and from roughly 1979 to the
present in the United States), as well as periods when policymakers struggled
to have the best of both worlds (the 1970s in the United States and the
mid-1970s in Great Britain). Neither tradition has offered the policymaker—
especially in these two countries—a clear and smooth path to economic
stabilization and growth sustenance.

The Supply-Side Variant

A third path to macroeconomic growth and stability has recently come into
vogue with the 1977 Kemp-Roth legislative proposal for a $100 billion tax
reduction plan to be carried out over a three-year period. With the introduction of this piece of legislation, the American public and other capitalist
economies of the world had their first clear glimpse of "supply-side" economics. While the term itself is best understood as a rubric for several
different theories of macroeconomic supply-demand functions, the phrase—
first coined by Herbert Stein in 1976—commonly refers to a set of propositions which purport to explain how the macroeconomy can enjoy a burgeon-
ing tax revenue by simply reducing tax rates.[17]

Committed to the notion that government intervention into the economy is
detrimental to effective and efficient investment habits—that is, expenditure
decisions of private firms and individuals—the supply-sider theorists go
beyond the fiscal and monetary theories to hold that the role of the public
official is not merely a technical instrument but an act of aggression against
the wiser ways of the market itself. In short, they say, public expenditures
such as social security create disincentives in the economy, thus dampening
the necessary adventurous risk-taking spirit of a robust capitalist economy.
When the tax revenues which pay for such incentives are reduced, the supply-
side theorists have argued, more money will be invested into expansionary
programs through private funds, creating new jobs and hence expanding the
overall tax revenue.

There are two points to bear in mind when exploring the supply-side logic.
First, the theory is really neither a "liberal" nor a "conservative" philosophy,
and, as Herbert Stein reminds us, the validity of the logic cannot be demonstrated from positions resting on the traditional assumptions of either philosophical tradition.[18] Supply-side economics is an empirical theory, meaning
that the virtue of its logic must be supported by the existence of certain
quantities in the macroeconomy. This introduces the second cautionary note:
much more than either the fiscal or monetary tradition, the supply-side
"tradition" remains devoid of convincing empirical evidence to support its

propositions.[19] Yet it has become popular among respectable portions of the public, as well as many public officials, in both America and Great Britain. It is still too early to tell whether the supply-side theories actually herald a revolutionary departure from the ordinary alternatives offered by the traditional monetarist or fiscal strategies, or whether they are simply riding the ripples of Ronald Reagan's "economics of joy" message which has had such popular reaction in the United States.[20]

FACTORS COMPLICATING THE CHOICE AND THE SUCCESS OF MACROECONOMIC POLICY

The study of macroeconomic policy, then, is the study of what governments do to stabilize the overall economic performance of nations. The content of government policies is shaped in part by the intellectual tradition guiding the policymakers' interpretation of the economic situation. A Keynesian interpretation of the economic environment is likely to mean that central governments will pursue stabilization by manipulating fiscal instruments, such as taxation and public expenditure. If public officials in the central government interpret the economic condition through a monetarist lens, the instruments chosen for stabilization will be those believed best suited for controlling the money supply in society, such as the manipulations of interest rates, the purchasing of bonds and securities, and/or the regulation of cash reserves and liquid assets among central banks.

However, other factors beyond the intellectual preference of the policymakers can complicate both the choice of strategy and/or the overall success of the selected strategy. While these factors are quite numerous, three are most frequently seen by economists and political scientists as critical to the choice and success of macroeconomic policy strategy: the market complication, the political complication, and the international complication. As one surveys the development of British and American macroeconomic policy during the last decade, each of these complicating factors can be seen to have played a significant part in the final selection of strategy by policymakers, and/or to have affected directly the degree to which the strategy has been able to accomplish the macroeconomic goals defined by the policymakers.

The Market Complication

An ever present consideration of a policymaker faced with choosing a stabilizing strategy is what the market will do in response to the strategy, and what the independent action of the market will do to undermine or enhance

John D. Robertson

the success of the stategy. For instance, policymakers in central governments have before them a set of instruments which can be utilized to affect a particular target (for example, raising personal income tax rates by 5 percent to slow inflation believed to be generated by excessive consumer demand in society). Yet there also exists a range of virtually unlimited factors which can influence the ultimate effect the policy (tax increase) will have on the primary target (personal disposable income). Economists refer to this phenomenon as the *reaction function*.[21] This assumes that policymakers have some preferred or ideal economic condition which they seek to realize through a macroeconomic policy strategy. It is further assumed that to achieve this ideal, the policymaker must modify the existing strategy.

In the above example, for instance, the ideal is assumed to be some specified level of inflation, presumably one that is more politically palatable and economically less costly to the public. In this example, the relationship between aggregate demand and the nominal money supply is altered through the personal tax rate in order to adjust the current level of inflation to approximate the preferred level. The choice of the strategy has assumedly taken into account the reactions of the central banks, the producers, and the private consumers to the new strategy. In this simple example, the modification of the personal income tax rate by 5 percent may squeeze profit margins, which can affect the employment rate of particular industries or bring pressure to bear on the available money supply in the form of increased loan requests, thus pushing up interest rates and further threatening the profit margins and ultimately the employment rate. Additionally, the increased revenue in the public treasury as a consequence of higher tax rates could compel the central banks to raise interest rates, regardless of what private producers and consumers do, simply in expectation that more public revenue will eventually lead to more public expenditures and will destabilize the money supply. Of course, any strategy which threatens to alter interest rates also threatens an international market reaction in the form of an inflow of foreign currencies and a loss of foreign markets for domestic exporters, which shall be discussed below.

For the policymaker in this hypothetical example, the short-term payoff may be lowered inflation; the medium-term cost may be higher unemployment in certain sectors of the economy and a new round of inflation in reaction to the changing market structure. The point is, however, that the choice of the strategy and its ultimate success is affected by the action and reaction of the market.[22]

This important point can be further illustrated by moving from a simple hypothetical example to "real world" examples in Great Britain and the United States. An examination of the Thatcher government's efforts to combat inflation during the period 1979–82 is appropriate. Margaret Thatcher came to power in part on the pledge to pursue a more disciplined monetarist approach and rid the British economy of the devastating "stop-go" alterations between fiscal stimulation and monetarist restraint that had plagued the British economy during the 1970s. Nonetheless she sanctioned Sir Geoffrey Howe's first budget as a blend of both fiscal and monetarist strategy. Income taxes were effectively lowered, while the Value Added Tax was increased to build up revenue for the British treasury. Minimum interest rates were raised a few months later in November 1979 to 17 percent and the cabinet announced substantial cutbacks in public expenditures. In March 1980, the Thatcher government announced its Medium-Term Financial Strategy, designed to reduce gradually the supply of money in society, and to further reduce public expenditures. The plan called for a regime of fiscal discipline and restraint through 1984. However, market constraints to the strategy came in the form of a worldwide recession and resistance from British labor unions, as well as in reluctance by private industries to cut back on investment in expectation of substantial changes in the money supply and higher interest rates.[23]

By the end of 1984, inflation in Great Britain had certainly been curtailed relative to what it had been in 1979, declining from 18 percent in 1980 to approximately 3–4 percent in early 1985. But the proportion of the work force unemployed remained high at around 11–13 percent, and the British pound sterling was under extreme pressure from the U.S. dollar, thus threatening the 2–3 percent annual growth of the British Gross Domestic Product and raising the specter of another serious round of price inflation. Furthermore, the success of controlling inflation has to be weighed against the social costs inflicted by the Thatcher government's new strategy. For instance, between 1980 and 1984 Great Britain went through one of its worst bouts of economic recession, suffering record bankruptcies and huge cuts in manufacturing investments, which contributed to what many see as a permanent pool of unemployed manufacturing workers.[24] Additionally, British society has undergone what appears to be a substantial redistribution of wealth. According to data from Alt, only the wealthiest 20 percent of the British households saw their real income grow between 1978 and 1982, while the poorest 20 percent of the British households suffered through a 9.7 percent reduction in their real income.[25]

More recently, the Thatcher government has confronted yet another complication in the world oil market. The sharp decline in oil prices during 1985 and 1986 threatened the government's medium-term macroeconomic policy goal of gradually slowing the pace of monetary expansion in order to reduce inflation, running at under 3 percent as of August 1986. Yet lower oil prices—between $10 and $13 a barrel—threatened the Thatcher government's goal of maintaining a strong pound sterling, thereby further promising an increase in inflation (to match an unemployment rate at 13 percent in August 1986) and consequently reducing the revenues available to the public coffers. Indeed, the market complication for Thatcher and Lawson as of August 1986 was underscored by the fact that the latter as Chancellor of the Exchequer estimated oil prices to average $15 a barrel throughout 1986, fully $2-3 below actual price. The effect of this shortfall further threatened a one billion (pound sterling) deficit in projected revenue for Great Britain by the end of 1986, posing a major political and economic dilemma for Thatcher; to raise the level of public borrowing or to renege on her promises for continued tax cuts to British workers. Either course undermines and certainly complicates her government's monetary strategy.[26]

A slightly different illustration of the market reaction can be found in the recent American circumstance. While the reduction in taxes sponsored by the Reagan administration in 1981 had the *intended* effect of stimulating savings among corporations and individuals, thereby stimulating investment and capital construction, the *real* effect was something altogether different, largely as a result of independent market actions and, perhaps more important, market reactions to the macroeconomic policy strategy. During the course of the next two years, as the American economy moved through a recession (1981-83) and businesses were given tax incentives to invest and save, real business investment (controlling for inflation) rose by only 3.5 percent, compared to a 28.6 percent increase during the four years prior to the 1981 tax bill.[27] During this period, the public debt in the United States actually reached record levels, rather than being lowered, as was originally intended.

A further example of the market complications that can undermine macroeconomic policy is the recent travails of the American money markets. By the summer of 1986, the economic growth of the American economy was beginning to slow; projections by the Reagan administration for a 4 percent annual growth in the economy by the end of 1986 had been revised downward by the Federal Reserve Board to approximately 2.5–3.0 percent. To stimulate economic demand, the Reagan administration and the Federal Reserve Board chairman, Paul Volcker, agreed to a monetary policy strategy of reducing interest rates, thus making credit cheaper and providing an impetus to consumer demand. Yet the strategy, as of the summer of 1986, carried a certain degree of risk, primarily associated with the willingness of Japan and West Germany to adjust their macroeconomic policies to accommodate the American efforts designed to prevent the continuing decline of the exchange rate value of the American dollar and to revitalize American economic growth. If the interest rates of the German and Japanese markets were not simultaneously moved upward, the effect of the American monetary strategy would be to stimulate demand for foreign imported goods rather than for American domestic goods. The economic effect of such a consequence would be to expand the huge American trade deficit; the political consequence would be to further alienate those sectors of the American electorate most susceptible to foreign economic competition. Yet as of August 1986 neither the Japanese nor the German economic and monetary systems seemed, for political and economic reasons of their own, willing to accommodate the monetary policy strategy being shaped by the Reagan administration and the Federal Reserve.[28]

These examples point to the particular hazards posed by the market complication. The American examples highlight the fact that what the policymaker would like the market to do is not always what the sector for whom the policy was ostensibly designed will want to do. The British examples illustrate that while there may always be some short-term or perhaps even medium-term payoff to be had for the policymaker from a particular strategy, the longer-term costs of that policy may create a situation that renders the initial policy strategy less than effective in a relative sense. Of course, market complications do not always undermine the macroeconomic strategies of policymakers. Indeed, in 1985 Thatcher could look with pride on a substantially more stable price structure in Great Britain—no small feat for a country plagued for years with "imperial hangover."[29] Nonetheless, when one considers the course of British and American macroeconomic policy over the course of the past decade, the words of Denis Healy, the British chancellor of the exchequer from 1974 to 1979, seem to sum up the dilemma for the policymaker pondering strategic options: "On the whole, running the economy is more like gardening than operating a computer."[30]

The Political Complication

The second factor affecting the choice and success of an economic strategy is political, that is, the actual or expected political reactions to the choice of policy. The political complication facing elected officials formulating final decisions on strategy can be summarized in a basic question: Will a particular strategy ultimately enhance or weaken expected success at the next election? Harold Wilson captured this simple logic when he noted in 1968 that "all political history shows that the standing of a government and its ability to hold the confidence of the electorate at a general election depends on the success of its economic policy."[31]

Empirical evidence has tended to bear this out. Indeed, there are at least three political factors which not only complicate the choice of policymakers when fashioning a macroeconomic strategy, but may also affect its eventual success: (1) the ever present concern of the elected officials with the effect of the policy on the popularity of the incumbent government; (2) the ideological predisposition of the incumbent office holder; and (3) the proximity of the next expected electoral contest.

Since World War II, three economic factors have been the most critical in determining the popularity of the incumbent government: inflation, unemployment and disposable income.[32] Hibbs and Vasilatos report that Gallup poll data between 1973 and 1978 show that more than 70 percent of the American public identified some aspects of the economy as "the most important" problem facing the country in each year.[33] Mosley's analysis has shown that over the entire post-World War II era, the single most important economic factor determining the popularity of an incumbent government is personal disposable income.[34] However, his data also show that this relationship is highly unstable over time. During certain time periods, income may be less important than unemployment, while in other periods inflation may be more important to the popularity of the incumbent government than personal income, etc. On the whole, his data confirm the conclusions of Alt and Chrystal: Unemployment seems to be highly significant in shaping the popularity of an incumbent government only during those periods when there is a general unemployment crisis, while inflation is important to the popularity of the incumbent when there is an inflation crisis.[35] "In other words," concludes Mosley, "it looks as if changes in popularity are by no means stably related to economic conditions, but have to be triggered off by abnormal movements in the economy."[36]

The bottom line, however, remains that public officials must almost surely weigh the virtue of any strategy (in terms of its expected advantage for economic growth) with the popularity "costs" associated with the treatment itself. One implication of this is that monitoring public opinion polls can become as critical to the policymaker as monitoring the Gross Domestic Product's quarterly growth rate. Staying with the present macroeconomic policy strategy or devising a new one is a decision affected as much by how the opinion polls have moved as by the policymakers' assessment of what market reaction may develop in response to an existing strategy. More often than not, in fact, the two complicating factors work together, creating an even greater complication for the policy than each would by itself.

The strategy decision taken by the policymaker seems also affected by the ideological pressures bearing upon the incumbent. Edward Tufte has argued that "the single most important determinant of variations in macroeconomic performance from one industrialized democracy to another is the location on the left-right spectrum of the governing party."[37] Research by Hibbs and Cowart tends to strengthen the conclusion that ideology—that is, whether a government is "conservative" or "liberal" in its political outlook—will significantly complicate the decision of which strategy to follow, let alone the specific targets at which to aim the strategy.[38] Hibbs, for instance, has shown that when conservative governments are in office in democratic states, the macroeconomy is much more likely to be characterized by higher unemployment and lower inflation; when liberal governments hold office, lower unemployment is likely to exist concurrently with higher inflation. Cowart's research shows that conservative governments tend to stress monetary instruments for dealing with both inflation and unemployment, while liberal governments are more likely to mix their strategy, using monetary instruments to combat inflation and fiscal instruments to confront unemployment.[39]

Why does ideology seem to matter? The explanation has to do with the constituencies from which the incumbent government historically draws electoral support. Noted economist Paul Samuelson, for example, argues that in the case of the United States, it is a class difference: "The Democrats constitute the people, by and large, who are around median incomes or below. These are the ones whom the Republicans want to pay the price and burden of fighting inflation. The Democrats are willing to run with some inflation [to increase employment]; the Republicans are not."[40]

While one's class is not the only factor determining how a person will vote and what preference a person will have for a given political candidate, political parties remain closely identified with notably distinct economic strategies in large measure because of the electoral coalitions from which they draw their political support. For instance, the Labour party in Great Britain is closely associated with British labor unions, and this fact is widely believed to constrain the economic policy choices that would be available to the Labour party if it were to control the cabinet government of Great Britain.[41]

Finally, a third component of the political dimension complicating the policymaker's choice of economic strategy is the timing of the next general election. It is widely believed that as the next general election draws closer, the elected policy official will seek to "prime the pumps" of economic expansion in order to undermine opponents' criticism of the incumbent's macroeconomic performance. This synchronization of economic policy to general elections is referred to as the "political business cycle."[42] Basically, the concept of the "political business cycle" assumes that the voting public has a very short memory, and that decisions made one year will be largely forgotten two years hence. The result is that elected policymakers have substantial incentives to manipulate the economy in a cyclical fashion.[43] Tufte found that in 27 democracies, 19 had substantial increases in personal disposable income during election years between 1961 and 1972.[44] Powell found some evidence that this ability (or willingness) to manipulate the economy is probably more real for a country that has only one party in government (such as Great Britain and the United States), rather than a government where the executive cabinet is comprised of a two or more political parties in coalition (such as Italy).[45]

This trend suggests that in the case of the United States and Great Britain, the incumbent government would be in a strong position to manipulate the macroeconomy prior to an impending election. Indeed, data by Mosley support this assumption.[46] In the United States since World War II, in six elections out of nine through 1980, personal disposable income has increased during the twelve months prior to a presidential election. In Great Britain, where the government has the additional flexibility of calling a general election at the most propitious moment (though it must be within five years of the last election), real income has increased at above normal rates in six of seven elections through 1983.

The International Complication

The third factor complicating the choice and success of the macroeconomic policy strategy to be considered emerges from the international environment. As we have already seen, the international economy can impose serious effects upon domestic economic policy, as did, for instance, the oil embargo of 1973 and the ensuing world economic recession. However, international economics is more than simply the effect of world recession on domestic policies. At the core of the challenge posed by the international environment is the matter of accurately predicting the stability of prices of goods and services on the international market.

Consider, for example, a hypothetical case. Adjusting public expenditures can affect the total public debt of a country. Knowing this, an American president might decide to expand such a debt as a necessary cost in an effort to reduce unemployment or to achieve some other policy goal. However, this strategy may also drive up the price of money in the United States, as interest rates are adjusted to meet the new demand for money. As this demand for money becomes more intense, prices for American produced goods and services may also rise. This market reaction may also mean that American goods and services are too costly for foreign buyers, who must buy these goods with American dollars. Additionally, goods and services produced abroad become cheaper for American consumers to purchase than American-produced goods and services. This may serve to threaten the initial strategy of the policymaker by stimulating greater unemployment, thus closing off additional options for stabilizing the macroeconomy. Though much more complicated than this hypothetical example, the American economy has been affected by a similar international constraint since 1981.

Indeed, this example underscores one of the most important changes affecting the American macroeconomy in decades: the problem of international vulnerability. While Great Britain has long been subject to structural changes within its economy, such as a declining manufacturing sector and the loss of productivity and thus of international competitiveness, the United States has only recently had to face this challenge. The trend toward America's service economy has been spurred on by the substantial budget deficit and its related trade deficit.

As the American deficit pushes the cost of the dollar up, the cost of buying goods from abroad decreases, as explained above. The real world effect of this has been to generate a trade deficit of $123 billion by 1983 and over $150 billion by 1985. The trade deficit has itself contributed to a decline in manufacturing jobs and a rise in industrial unemployment. Between February 1985 and July 1985, a total of 221,000 manufacturing jobs were lost, many as a direct result of the cheaper foreign manufactured goods.

In response to these vulnerabilities, both political parties and chambers of Congress have moved recently toward a national policy of trade import restrictions. Just as the British government has implemented a more stringent labor wage restraint in an effort to improve the productivity and price competitiveness of British manufactured goods, so the American macroeconomy has had to consider policies which it traditionally could afford to ignore.[47]

While these examples illustrate how the reaction of the international market can constrain the choice and undermine the success of a macroeconomic policy strategy, they also suggest another side to the issue: Domestic strategies of one country can ultimately affect the choice and success of macroeconomic policy strategies in foreign countries. The actions of one state taken independently of the strategy at work in a second state increase the risk of policy failure for both countries.[48] Ironically, however, one country has little or nothing to say about the costs which its economy may bear as a result of the actions of the other country.

It was in this context, after the decade of the 1930s, that an international monetary system was created. In July 1944, forty-four countries met in Bretton Woods, New Hampshire to ratify an Anglo-American plan for stabilizing the international monetary system. At the core of the agreement was the desire to devise a system of fixed exchange rates among major world currencies. A foreign exchange rate is the price which a foreign unit of money costs in terms of the domestic currency. It dictates how costly it is for a country to purchase goods and services from a given foreign country, as well as how costly it is for the same foreign country to purchase goods and services in the other country's domestic market. The stability of exchange rates is determined by the international monetary order.

When one country buys goods and services from another country, the seller state must receive money in its own national currency. An unstable international monetary order exists when one country has too little of another country's currency. When this develops, the state in need of foreign currency has what is termed a "liquidity" problem. This requires the state to borrow from the country it wishes to purchase goods and services from in order to buy the goods and services. If the state in a liquidity shortage borrows too much of the foreign currency, it may find its own currency being drained to the producer country (or countries) from which it has borrowed the money. This will push up interests rates at home since demand for the currency becomes greater.

Higher prices in the domestic market will mean that the prices of the domestically produced goods are too expensive for foreign buyers to absorb; and higher domestic interest rates will mean that foreign goods are cheaper to buy, since the foreign currency will probably be lower relative to the domestic currency. This compounds the unemployment problem, putting greater pressure on domestic producers as foreign goods and services begin to cut into their markets. Tax incentives and direct state aid may be offered to domestic exporting industries in an effort to enhance the international competitiveness of these industries. Concurrently, tariffs and import quotas may be placed on all foreign goods being bought in the domestic market in an effort to discourage foreign consumption at home.

The ultimate result of this liquidity problem is the destabilization of the international financial market. Those countries which had previously depended on the domestic market of the country suffering a liquidity shortage will be severely hurt by the quotas and tariffs. Consumers in the country suffering the liquidity crisis will be hurt because opportunities to purchase foreign goods will be affected by the tariffs. A large-scale consequence of this reordering of exchange patterns is the internationalization of inflation and unemployment.

To avoid this crisis and preserve the stabilization of the international financial system, the Bretton Woods agreement created the International Monetary Fund and the World Bank, whose principal institutional responsibilities were to ensure that central banks in member countries would have enough reserve currencies on hand to manage temporary liquidity crises before the point of an international crisis was reached.[49] Because the U.S. dollar was the strongest and most secure currency immediately after World War II, it became the currency to which all other national currencies were "pegged," or fixed. In other words, all other major currencies had their international market value based on the strength of the United States dollar. Thus, a German Deutsche Mark was assigned a value relative to the dollar, and central banks in Germany were required to purchase American dollars with German DMs at this fixed, or pegged, price. This ensured enough U.S. dollars for the German central banks to cover the imports of Germany from any other country. Furthermore, the value of the DM was protected against overzealous monetary expansionist policies of the German government, because if the volume of DM was circulated in the German system faster than demand for it, the Bretton Woods agreement required the German central banks to repurchase the DM in order to keep its value in line with its "fixed" value to the U.S. dollar. Thus, domestic monetary policies of one country were far less likely to undermine either the international market place or the macroeconomic strategy success of a second country.[50]

The system worked relatively well until the 1960s. So long as the United States exercised monetary responsibility by not allowing its dollars to flow too freely out of the United States (to pay for imports)—that is, at a rate faster than their exports could reabsorb the dollars—the monetary system devised at Bretton Woods was secure. In the 1960s, however, the combination of the Kennedy and Johnson administrations' expansionary domestic programs, low tax rates, and the waging of the Vietnam War led to a situation where foreign central banks were buying with their own currencies more U.S. dollars than they could use in selling their domestically produced goods back to the United States. The dollar became a less secure currency than it had been in the late 1940s and throughout the 1950s.[51]

By 1971, extreme international pressure on the U.S. dollar forced the Nixon administration to "devalue" it. The devaluation had the effect of reducing the amount of a foreign currency needed to buy a U.S. dollar, thus easing the pressure on domestic currencies by making U.S. dollars cheaper to purchase.[52]

The devaluing of the American dollar ended the financial stability provided by the Bretton Woods arrangement. The immediate consequence was to create some confusion in the international monetary system. Many central banks in foreign countries at the time of the American devaluation held substantial reserves of U.S. dollars. Yet without the Bretton Woods agreement these banks were to hold onto these reserves.

To consume these reserves, some countries—Great Britain in particular—

decided to expand their domestic economy through abolishing the strict monetary discipline characteristic of the Bretton Woods years. Expansion, it was thought, would accelerate demand, thus allowing U.S. dollar reserves to be used to purchase American goods and services. In 1972 the Heath government introduced an expansionary budget, designed to expand the British economy and ease rising unemployment in the lagging British industry.[53] Yet the result was a dramatic rise in inflation in 1973, growing from 7.1 percent inflation in 1972 to 9.2 percent in 1973, 26 percent greater than the annual inflation rate for the OECD.[54] Following a brief respite from expansion, the Wilson government returned again to the expansionary policies in 1974, only to confront the OPEC oil price rise, bringing about Britain's greatest postwar inflation rate—24.2 percent—in 1975.

In short, for Great Britain, the ending of the Bretton Woods system and fixed exchange rates had two consequences. First, it contributed to a decision during the mid-1970s to expand the British economy at a time when it could ill afford inflationary pressure placed on the British pound sterling. Second, the effects of the spiralling inflation of 1974–77 contributed to a severe British balance of payments problem (the value of foreign imports of goods and services purchased exceeded the value of exports sold abroad), in part already fueled by the poor competitiveness of Britain's industry, due mainly to the lagging productivity of its labor force.[55]

The official ratio of foreign reserves held by the British central bank to the total value of imports of the British economy was 1:1.7 between 1974 and 1981, compared to the ratio of OECD members which was 1:2.5.[56] By 1976, as noted earlier, the British government was confronted with the extremely difficult and embarrassing circumstance of turning to the International Monetary Fund for loan assistance to confront rising prices, loss of economic competitiveness, and the soaring balance of payments crisis. Only the revenues brought in by the North Sea oil exports in the middle and late 1970s prevented the British economy from becoming a total captive of the shocks and buffets of the increasingly unstable and unpredictable international financial system left in the wake of the collapse of Bretton Woods and the weakening of the U.S. dollar.[57]

THE STRUCTURE OF ECONOMIC POLICYMAKING

Who makes macroeconomic policy in Great Britain and the United States? Who is primarily responsible for confronting the complicating factors outlined in the previous section? While the intellectual tradition and the various complicating factors are critical to shaping macroeconomic policy, such policy is also a by-product of the patterned interactions of formal institutions of public authority central to the macroeconomic policy process.

When comparing the American and British economic policymaking structure, one must begin by noting their two most important differences: the United States is a federal system while the British system is unitary; and the American system combines presidential leadership with the context of constitutionally separated powers existing between Congress and the Presidency, while the British executive arrangement is parliamentary and has no separation of powers between the executive and the legislature. In the American case, therefore, economic policy is more fragmented; the policymaking structure is divided among numerous component parts, each with some degree of control over the final form of the policy as well as the instruments of that strategy.[58]

The British structure of economic policymaking consists of two "circles" of elites: the inner circle of decision-makers composed of the Treasury (the Chancellor of the Exchequer) and selected cabinet ministers, the most crucial being the prime minister; and the "outer circle," consisting of the spending ministries (Defense, Education, Health, Social Security, Transport, Environment, etc.), the Bank of England—the "government's banker"—and the Inland Revenue, which, along with the Department of Customs and Excise, collects revenue and taxes for the Treasury and the cabinet.[59]

The core of economic policymaking resides in the inner circle, particularly under conditions of stress. Since its reorganization in 1975, the Policy Coordinating Committee (PCC), consisting of four permanent secretaries and a staff of nearly eighty individuals (up from only ten in 1960), has had the most crucial role to play within the Treasury regarding economic policy. As its name implies, the role of the PCC is to coordinate the forecasts of various departments and agencies within the Treasury, and to align these with the preferences of the Chancellor and cabinet.

Two forecasting rounds bring about this alignment: one in September-October, the other in December-January. Under normal conditions, the recommendations of senior civil servants within the Treasury will have a significant impact on shaping the final policy strategy selected by the Chancellor of the Exchequer. However, "normal" circumstances break down when, as we have seen, the market reaction to a policy differs from what was expected, and/or when the next election grows near. Under the first circumstance, conflicts between key cabinet ministers and their senior civil servants are more likely to surface as the pressure to treat an ailing economy becomes more intense. As Mosley has noted in the case of the sterling crisis of 1976, strict parameters of acceptable reaction to the falling British pound sterling defined what the Policy Coordinating Committee could reasonably recommend as remedies for the crisis.[60] Indeed, after the PCC had made its initial recommendation, it was virtually up to the chancellor and the prime minister to decide the final action to be taken. After this decision was made, of course, the next round included hard negotiations among various spending ministries on the one hand, and the prime minister and the Treasury on the other, over who would pay for the new policy designed to break the fall of the pound sterling. In the case of a proximate election, the PCC must alter its recommendations to accommodate the clear interests of the cabinet, which are now more likely to be firmly set in the face of political expediency.

In general, the British economic policymaking structure is much more centralized and coordinated than that of the United States. Since 1961 and the publication of the Plowden Report, the British government has provided an annual survey of public expenditure patterns which states clearly the objectives of these expenditures. Indeed, since 1969, these reports, in the form of a Public Expenditure White Paper published each March for public scrutiny, have laid out the five-year plan of spending for each of the major spending departments in the British government.[61]

While the interests and preferences of the various components of the British economic policymaking structure may not always align, achieving agreement and compromise policy is nonetheless facilitated by the fact that the British political system is far more centralized than the American system. Structurally, the two notable differences between the two systems are that in the United States the Central Bank of the United States (the twelve Federal Reserve Banks) are truly independent of the executive, unlike the relationship between the Bank of England and the British executive government; and second, the central legislature in the American system enjoys substantial control and scrutiny over all policy strategies preferred by the executive, including the use of specific instruments and the selection of various economic targets—again, unlike the British system where the House of Commons has only a very limited and informal check on the decisions of the prime minister.[62]

There are three notable sources of fragmentation within the American macroeconomic policymaking apparatus which complicate the ability of the policymaker to fine-tune and time accurately macroeconomic strategies for maximum political and economic impact. First, while the British prime minister has the advantage of a more subservient Bank of England, the American president must contend with a federal reserve system that is diffuse, decentralized, and independent of the president's power. The system consists of an appointed board of governors and twelve regional reserve banks, each having its own board of directors made up of private citizens. Each of the Reserve banks can set its own minimum lending rates (which in

Great Britain are centrally controlled by the Bank of England in line with the Treasury's wishes). Until the 1970s, there were only infrequent clashes between the president and the Federal Reserve. However, since 1974, differences have become much more common and pronounced. Thus, a monetary strategy in the United States is subject to the veto of many more actors than in Great Britain.

The ability of the president to set overall expenditure and revenue levels is also far more restricted than is the case with the British prime minister. The budgetary process in the United States is divided between two chambers of the Congress, each with its own budget committees, and each, as has been the case in the 1980s, could be controlled by different partisan majorities. In addition to this constraint, the coordination process of formulating the American budget proposal is divided between the Congressional Budget Office (CBO) and the executive's coordinating groups: specifically, the Office of Management and Budget (OMB), the Treasury, and the Council of Economic Advisors. Not only are there likely to be occasional differences over strategy between the CBO and the executive's forecasting agencies, but frequently such disagreement arises among and within the executive groups themselves. A third source of fragmentation in the American structure is the ease by which special interest groups can gain access to both congressional committees and executive agencies. The effect of such a pluralistic structure is to compound greatly the difficulty of quickly selecting and formulating macroeconomic policy strategy.[63]

Contributing to this problem is the fourth source of fragmentation in the American structure—the political party system. The decentralized nature of the American political party system, effectively characterized as fifty different party systems, and the growing localization of the House of Representatives complicate economic policymaking in the United States by expanding the range of issues on the macropolicy agenda and increasing the difficulty of compromise among various official actors in the arena of macroeconomic policy making.

What difference, however, does structure make to the success of macroeconomic strategy? As Cowart and Alt and Chrystal have noted, timing is critical to the success of an economic policy strategy.[64] For instance, manipulating the interest rates too soon can severely depress investment and economic growth, thus serving actually to push up inflation. Similarly, stimulating the economy through public expenditures too late can have the effect of straining the money supply in a system, thus pushing up interest rates and dampening investment. While neither the British or American policy structure can offer the president or the prime minister the means of perfect timing and controlled impact, the British system—with its reduced

fragmentation, greater policy centralization, and more legislative party discipline within the Parliament—affords the British executive more potential for
success than the American executive. Yet the uncertainty over domestic and
international market reactions, combined with the fact that information is
never perfect within the policymaking structure itself, acts to undermine
whatever coherency and consensus the centralized system of the British
might afford the economic policy making process.

CONCLUSION AND SUMMARY

In this chapter, we have considered four aspects of macroeconomic policy.
First, macroeconomic policy has been explained within the context of its
component parts: macroeconomics and central policymaking. Second, we
considered the common strategies of macroeconomic policy: fiscal and
monetary strategies. This led to a discussion of the two major intellectual
traditions of modern macroeconomics, Keynesianism and monetarism, and
a recent package, supply-side economics. Third, three factors complicating
both the selection and success of macroeconomic policy strategies were
reviewed. These were the market constraint, the political constraint, and the
international constraint. Finally we have considered the structure of economic policymaking in Great Britain and the United States.

While the British and American macroeconomies differ in many re-
gards—some of which have been outlined in this chapter—one common
feature is their complexity. This chapter has necessarily tried to simplify this
complexity for purposes of comparison and analysis, yet such compartmen-
talization unavoidably distorts the extraordinary challenges facing British
and American public officials responsible for shaping macroeconomic policy. Whether their respective current experiments in monetarism and supply-
side economics can result in substantial long-term gains, both of the macroeconomies depend in large part on the interplay of the factors outlined in
this chapter. As of mid-1986, no evidence yet suggests that either
Thatcherism or Reaganism is exempt from this tradition.

Ultimately the reader may be tempted to conclude that both the British and
American macroeconomic policies are converging toward some common
strategy and structural configuration. Yet while the evidence above would
lend itself to this observation, one must bear in mind the features of both
political economies which are sharply divergent in nature: a British centralization tendency and an American decentralization orientation; a strong
public sector experience in Britain contrasted with a more subtle suspicion of
the public sector still very active in the American polity; and a unique set of

challenges associated with a small, relatively resource-poor economy, contrasted with a huge, resource-wealthy economy still given to a faith in free enterprise and the virtues of private innovation. Declarations of convergence, in light of these considerations, must be carefully qualified.

NOTES

1. For instance, between 1960 and 1981 the average standardized annual percentage growth in the per capita GDP (the total value of all goods and services produced domestically in an economy, per person in society) for Great Britain and the United States was 1.8 percent and 2.2 percent, respectively. For the Organization for Economic Cooperation and Development (OECD), the corresponding value was 3.0. During the period between 1973 and 1979, however, the growth rates were 1.6, 1.4, and 1.9 percent, respectively. During the first two complete years of the Thatcher government in Great Britain, the average annual growth rate of the per capita GDP was -2.0 percent. All of this data can be found in OECD, *OECD Economic Outlook: Historical Statistics, 1960-1981* (Paris: OECD, 1983), 44. (The OECD was created in 1960 as an organization committed to coordinating data and information among the member states for the purpose of assisting the economic growth and development of the member states, which were originally Austria, Belgium, Canada, Denmark, France, West Germany, Greece, Iceland, Ireland, Italy, Luxembourg, the Netherlands, Norway, Portugal, Spain, Sweden, Switzerland, Turkey, Great Britain, and the United States. Japan joined in 1964, Finland in 1969, Australia in 1971, and New Zealand in 1973.)
2. Rudiger Dornbusch and Stanley Fischer, *Macro-Economics* (New York: McGraw-Hill, 1978).
3. Arnold J. Heidenheimer, Hugh Heclo, and Carolyn Teich Adams, *Comparative Public Policy: The Politics of Social Choice in Europe and America,* 2nd ed. (New York: St. Martin's, 1983), 1–20.
4. George Dalton, *Economic Systems and Society: Capitalism, Communism and the Third World* (Baltimore: Penguin Books, 1974).
5. E.H. Carr, *The New Society* (London: Macmillan, 1951), 39. See also G.V. Rimlinger, *Welfare Policy and Industrialization in Europe, America and Russia* (New York: John Wiley and Sons, 1971); Frederick Hayek, *The Road to Serfdom* (Chicago: University of Chicago Press, 1944); and Oskar Lange and Fred Taylor, *On the Economic Theory of Socialism* (Minneapolis: University of Minnesota Press, 1938).
6. There is a substantial literature on the phenomenon of government growth. See David Cameron, "The Expansion of the Public Economy: A Comparative Analysis," *American Political Science Review* 72 (December 1978): 1243–61; and Michael Lewis-Beck and Tom W. Rice, "Government Growth in the United States," *Journal of Politics* 47 (February 1985): 2–30. Broader surveys can be found in Charles Taylor, ed., *Why Governments Grow: Measuring Public Sector Size* (Beverly Hills: Sage, 1983); G. W. Nutter, *Growth of Government in the West* (Washington: American Enterprise Institute, 1978); Francis G. Castles, "The Impact of Parties on Public Expenditure," in Francis G. Castles, ed., *The Impact*

of Parties: Politics and Policies in Democratic Capitalist States (Beverly Hills: Sage, 1982), 21–96. and Richard Rose, *Understanding Big Government* (Beverly Hills: Sage, 1984).

   The growth of the public sector can be seen by examining the proportion of the GDP derived from government consumption. In the United States between 1960 and 1981 the average annual percentage of the GDP made up of government consumption was 18.1 percent, growing from 16.9 percent in 1960 to 18.1 percent in 1981, or a growth of 7.1 percent between 1960 and 1981. In Great Britain, between 1960 and 1981 the average annual proportion of the GDP composed of government consumption was 18.7, climbing from 16.6 percent in 1960 to 22.3 percent in 1981, or a growth of 34.3 percent between 1960 and 1981. The British growth between 1960 and 1981 is more than double that of the OECD's during the same period, which was only 15.3 percent. For all member nations in the OECD as a group, the average annual proportion of the GDP composed of government consumption was 16.2 percent. See OECD, *Economic Outlook,* 62.

 7. John M. Keynes, *The General Theory of Employment, Interest and Money* (New York: Harcourt, Brace, 1936), 380–1.

 8. See Charles Andrain, *Politics and Economic Policy in Western Democracies* (North Scituate, Mass.: Duxbury Press, 1980), 10–29.

 9. Incomes policy is a third kind of economic policy which has received substantial attention in recent years. The logic of incomes policy is to treat directly the aggregate demand by the use of governmental regulation of wages and prices. Modern Keynesians have espoused the application of incomes policy as a means of controlling rates of inflation so as to allow high growth rates and reduce unemployment without the consequent rise in prices ordinarily accompanying economic growth during the postwar era. Incomes policy in the United States and Great Britain has been only marginally effective. See Andrew Cowart, "Economic Policies of European Governments," *The British Journal of Political Science* 8 (July and October 1978): 285–311 and 425–39, esp. 287.

10. See Dalton, *Economic Systems.*

11. See James Alt and K. Alec Chrystal, *Political Economics* (Berkeley: University of California Press, 1983), 59–62.

12. Andrew Shonfield, *Modern Capitalism: The Changing Balance of Public and Private Power* (London: Oxford University Press, 1965), 64–5.

13. Keynes, *General Theory,* 381.

14. Alt and Chrystal, *Political Economics,* 61.

15. *Ibid.;* also see Alfred Eichner, *A Guide to Post- Keynesian Economics* (White Plains, NY: M. E. Sharpe, 1978).

16. A classic statement is Milton Friedman, *Capitalism and Freedom* (Chicago: University of Chicago Press, 1962).

17. Alt and Chrystal, *Political Economics,* 71.

18. Herbert Stein, *Presidential Economics: The Making of Economic Policy from Roosevelt to Reagan and Beyond* (New York: Simon and Schuster, 1984), 245.

19. Alt and Chrystal, *Political Economics,* 71–73; Stein, *Presidential Economics,* 240–49; and Michael Harrington, *Myth and Reality in the American Economic Policy Debate* (Bonn: Friedrich Ebery Stiftung, 1984).

20. For interesting "insider" interpretations and analyses of the Thatcher and Reagan supply side policies, see Alan Walters, *Britain's Economic Renaissance: Mar-*

garet Thatcher's Reforms, 1979–1984 (Oxford: Oxford University Press, 1986) and David Stockman, *The Triumph of Politics* (New York: Harper and Row, 1986).

21. Alt and Chrystal, *Political Economics, 129–30.*

22. For an excellent analysis and overview of the dynamics of the market constraint with particular attention to the recent economic strategies in the United States and Great Britain, see Steven Schier and Norman Vig, "Reviving Capitalism: Macroeconomic Policies in Britain and the United States," in Vig and Schier, eds., *Political Economy in Advanced Industrial Societies* (New York: St. Martin's, 1984), 67–70.

23. See Schier and Vig, "Reviving Capitalism," 178–81 and Paul Mosley, *The Making of Economic Policy: Theory and Evidence from Britain and the United States since 1945* (New York: St. Martin's, 1984), 67–70.

24. Schier and Vig, "Reviving Capitalism," 183.

25. Cited in Ibid., 22.

26. See *The Economist,* August 23, 1986, 45-46 and International Monetary Fund, *World Economic Outlook, April 1986* (Washington: IMF, 1986), 82-83.

27. Robert S. McIntyre, "Voodoo Incentives," *The New Republic,* February 25, 1985, 19-20.

28. See *The Economist*, 26 July, 1986, 7–72.

29. Sidney Pollard, *The Wasting of the British Economy: British Economic Policy 1945 to the Present* (New York: St. Martin's, 1982), 139.

30. Quoted in Mosley, *Making of Economic Policy,* 44.

31. Quoted in Ibid., 17.

32. Bruno S. Frey and Friedrich Schneider, "Recent Research on Empirical Political-Economic Models," in Douglass A. Hibbs and Heino Fassbender, eds., *Contemporary Political Economy: Studies on the Interdependence of Politics and Economics* (Amsterdam: North-Holland, 1981), 17.

33. Douglass A. Hibbs and Nicholas Vasilatos, "Macroeconomic Performance and Mass Political Support in the United States and Great Britain," in Hibbs and Fassbender, *Contemporary Political Economy,* 31–32.

34. Mosley, *Making of Economic Policy,* 33–34.

35. Alt and Chrystal, *Political Economics.*

36. Mosley, *Making of Economic Policy,* 33–34. See also Michael Lewis-Beck, "Economic Conditions and Executive Popularity: The French Experience," *American Journal of Political Science* 24 (May 1980); and Paul Peretz, *The Political Economy of Inflation in the United States* (Chicago: University of Chicago Press, 1983).

37. Edward R. Tufte, "Political Parties, Social Change, and Economic Policy," *Government and Opposition* 14 (April 1979): 35.

38. Hibbs, "Political Parties"; and Cowart, "Economic Policies."

39. Several empirical studies have explored the linkage between the partisan orientation of political parties and the likely course of economic policy. See, for instance, Richard Rose, *Do Parties Make a Difference,* 2nd ed. (Chatham, NJ: Chatham House, 1984); Manfred Schmidt, "The Role of Parties in Shaping Macro-Economic Policy," in Castles, ed., *The Impact of Parties;* Klaus Von Beyme, "Do Parties Matter? The Impact of Parties on Key Decisions in the Political System," *Government and Opposition* 19 (April 1984): 5–29; Michael Lewis-Beck, "Comparative Economic Voting: Britain, France, Germany, Italy,"

American Journal of Political Science 30 (May 1986): 315–46; and Castles, "The Impact of Parties on Public Expenditure."

40. Paul Samuelson, "Some Dilemmas of Economic Policy," *Challenge* 20 (March/ April 1977): 30.

41. Philip Norton, *The British Polity* (New York: Longman, 1984), 121–24.

42. See Willliam D. Nordhaus, "The Political Business Cycle," *Review of Economic Studies* 42 (April 1975): 169–90.

43. Alt and Chrystal, *Political Economics,* 103–125 contains a good discussion.

44. Edward R. Tufte, *Political Control of the Economy* (Princeton: Princeton University Press, 1978).

45. G. Bingham Powell, *Contemporary Democracies: Participation, Stability, and Violence* (Cambridge: Harvard University Press, 1982), 211.

46. Mosley, *Making of Economic Policy,* 183–6.

47. International Monetary Fund, *World Economic Outlook, 1985,* 40–47; and Ernest Conine, "Loss of Industrial Muscle Weakens U.S.," Louisville *Courier-Journal*, 25 July 1985.

48. James Alt, "Political Parties, World Demand, and Unemployment: Domestic and International Sources of Economic Activity," *American Political Science Review* 79 (December 1985): 1016–40.

49. Joan E. Spero, *The Politics of International Economic Relations* (New York: St. Martin's, 1977).

50. Alt and Chrystal, *Political Economics,* 92.

51. For a more detailed analysis of the causes and consequences of the collapse of the Bretton Woods arrangement, see Robert O. Keohane, *After Hegemony: Cooperation and Discord in the World Political Economy* (Princeton: Princeton University Press, 1984). For an overview of the structure and dynamics of international economic relations during the postwar period, see Spero, *The Politics of International Economic Relations.* For an in-depth discussion of the importance of a stable international monetary order for domestic macroeconomic strategies, see Benjamin J. Cohen, *Organizing the World's Money: The Political Economy of International Monetary Relations* (New York: Basic Books, 1977).

52. The effect of the devaluation of the U.S. dollar was abrupt. The value of the German DM to the U.S. dollar increased by 16.9 percent (from 3.7 DM to 3.5 DM per dollar); Japan's yen increased by 3 percent (from 360 yen to 349.3 yen per dollar), and the British pound increased by 1.4 percent (from .4167 British pounds to .4109 per dollar), during the course of the subsequent year. OECD, *Economic Outlook,* 19.

53. Alt and Chrystal, *Political Economics,* 74–77.

54. OECD, *Economic Outlook,* 83.

55. The annual percentage change in real value added in British industry (i.e., a measure of productivity) between 1973 and 1979 was only 20 percent of the OECD's average during the same period; its ratios for the real value added for manufacturing during the period 1973–79 was 25 percent of the OECD's; for services, they were 58 percent of the OECD. See William Lazonick and Bernard Elbaum, "The Decline of the British Economy: An Institutional Perspective," Boston University Department of Economics, discussion paper no. 105.

56. OECD, *Economic Outlook,* 108.

57. Sidney Pollard, *The Development of the British Economy, 1914– 1980,* 3rd ed. (Baltimore: Edward Arnold, 1983), 352–65.

58. Alt and Chrystal, *Political Economics*, 142–43.
59. Mosley, *Making of Economic Policy*, 45–47.
60. Ibid., 57–60.
61. See *Ibid.*, 46, as well as Douglas Ashford, *Policy and Politics in Britain: The Limits of Consensus* (Philadelphia: Temple University Press, 1981), 110; and Hugh Heclo and Aaron Wildavsky, *The Private Government of Public Money* (Berkeley: University of California Press, 1974).
62. This is not to suggest that the British prime minister faces no obstacle to policy from Parliament. An example of the assertiveness of the Parliament—rare as it is—can be found in the case of the Thatcher government's efforts in the autumn of 1984 to abolish the Greater London Council and the Metropolitan County councils as part of an effort to streamline public expenditures and lower pressure on the public debt. See *The Economist*, 10 November 1984, 16 and 24 November, 1984, 57–58.
63. See also Stein, *Presidential Economics* and Peter Riddell, *The Thatcher Government* (Oxford: Martin Robertson, 1983) for detailed and well-documented surveys of economic policymaking in the United States and Great Britain. For an excellent analysis of the particular decision making process associated with British monetary policy, see Geoffrey Wood, "The Monetary Decision Process in the United Kingdom," in Donald Hodgman, ed., *The Political Economy of Monetary Policy: National and International Aspects,* proceedings of a conference held at Perugia, Italy, July 1983; conference series no. 26, 93–113.
64. See Cowart, "Economic Policies," and Alt and Chrystal, *Political Economics.*

Industrial Policy: Patterns of Convergence and Divergence

Jeffrey B. Freyman

COMPARATIVE INDUSTRIAL POLICY

Industrial policy is governmental activity which influences the structure of a country's industrial base in a manner consistent with governmental priorities. Usually these priorities involve greater productivity, growth of output, and international competitiveness of national industrial enterprises.

The term "industrial policy" is used in a wide variety of ways. In its broadest sense, it refers to all activities of government which affect a country's industrial structure and performance. However, industrial policy is usually distinguished from such other economic policies as monetary or fiscal policy in its focus upon *long-term* improvement in the *supply* capacity through *microeconomic* interventions, rather than short-term movements in aggregate demand through macroeconomic manipulations. Industrial policy instruments include a host of government expenditure, taxation, and regulatory measures which influence the cost of productive inputs (capital and labor) and alter their distribution among firms and economic sectors. Virtually every government in the world has adopted some of these measures, often on an ad hoc and piecemeal basis. A number of scholars, however, deny that a multifarious collection of governmental interventions constitutes an industrial *policy*, reserving the term for an explicit, coordinated, and comprehensive national strategy for industrial development or revitalization.[1]

Varieties of Industrial Policy

Industrial policies in advanced capitalist societies can be distinguished by the type of industrial restructuring pursued as a strategic objective. First, the strategy may be oriented toward promoting the *transformation* of the country's industrial base from "basic" or "sunset" manufacturing industries (such as automobiles, shipbuilding, steelmaking) to "high-tech" or "sunrise" industries (such as computers, communications, precision castings, fine ceramics, aircraft). Basic industries tend to employ relatively standardized production technologies and relatively unskilled labor; they are at the mature end of their "product cycle" and are losing their comparative advantage in international competition to newly industrialized countries. High-tech industries, on the other hand, tend to employ state-of-the-art engineering and highly educated labor for which advanced societies retain a comparative advantage. A second orientation is the *adaptation* of basic manufacturing industries to stiffer international competition through the acquisition of more modern and efficient production techniques, production rationalization, and the shedding of "excess" labor, and through moving into product lines for which there is a more viable market. A related orientation is *adjustment*, easing the social and economic dislocations arising from market forces. This involves assisting firms, communities, and workers who have been adversely affected by economic change. A fourth orientation is *preservation*, attempting to avoid social and economic dislocations by constraining market forces through protectionist measures.

We may also distinguish among industrial policies on the basis of the role of government in pursuit of its objectives. Grant proposes three models of government involvement in industrial structuring.[2] The *social market model* takes the market "as generally efficient and, as far as humanly possible, a fair allocator of resources." Government intervention is intended merely "to facilitate the operation of the market . . . to correct market malfunction . . . and to offset some of the grosser social inequities produced by the operation of market mechanisms. . . ."[3] The *selective intervention model* seeks to substitute government discretion for market mechanisms in those areas where "the social costs which would be imposed by market operations are perceived as being too great," or where "the market is displaying a failure to work properly."[4] The *socialist model* seeks to supplant market mechanisms with political modes of collective choice. Rather than intervening indirectly through measures which restructure market incentives to persuade private firms to adopt certain actions, the socialist government would exercise direct control upon major enterprises. Of course, certain models of government intervention tend to be more consistent with certain objectives—transformation, adaptation, adjustment, preservation—than with others, but the relationship between them is far from deterministic.

Finally, industrial policies may be distinguished from one another by their institutional and functional arrangements for formulating, selecting, and implementing programs affecting national industries.[5] One type of institution (*consensus/informational*) is a tripartite body whose function is to build a consensus about industrial development among representatives from labor, capital, and government. This type of agency generally has no programmatic, regulatory, or policymaking responsibility. Rather, its job is to facilitate the convergence of interests and the sharing of technical information to improve production and commercial performance of national enterprises. A second type (*coordinating*) would direct programs and agencies affecting industrial performance in accordance with some comprehensive national industrial strategy. This type of institution is usually conceived as a vigorously activist cabinet-level agency, modelled after Japan's Ministry of International Trade and Industry. A third type (*financial*) provides public funding to targeted enterprises through subsidies, concessionary loans, loan guarantees, or purchases of equity.

Why do states *have* industrial policies? The international division of labor—whereby each national economy produces goods and services for which it possesses a comparative advantage—is commonly held to be optimal from the perspective of the world economy. Yet a given role in the international division of labor is often inconsistent with the interests of its constituent national units. Industrial policy is a response to the deleterious impact of a country's openness to world economic forces.

Industrial policy is all the more imperative in the postwar period because of the transformation of the international economic system. Since the second world war, the relatively independent national domestic economies increasingly often have been incorporated into an interdependent global economy. The increased exposure to the world economic system affects the distribution of costs and benefits within national economies. Economic changes often have social and political implications. Domestic political imperatives often entail state-directed restructuring of the domestic industrial base in order to influence the economic, social, and political consequences of world economic forces. Industrial policy is an attempt to reconcile these political imperatives with the requirements of the postwar liberalized international trade and monetary regime. In short, industrial policy is a sort of nonprotectionist neomercantilism.

The political-economic relationships among the state, the domestic economy, and the international economy constitute a country's industrial policy environment. Industrial policy is a political response to that environment—

either a positive response, seizing opportunities for national advancement, or a negative response, attempting to avoid national decline. Industrial policy in Japan and France in the postwar period represents a positive response, while in the United Kingdom and the United States it has taken on a less favorable aspect.

INDUSTRIAL POLICY IN THE UNITED KINGDOM

The Development of British Industrial Policy

The decade of the 1960s was a watershed in Britain's political economy. Aided by Marshall Plan dollars and an economic boom resulting from a rapidly expanding world market temporarily devoid of industrial rivals, the years immediately following the second world war were relatively successful in terms of the reconstruction of the economy. But Britain's postwar recovery peaked in 1951, and in 1952 the country suffered the first in a series of recessions precipitated by deflationary policies aimed at protecting the balance of payments. From the late 1950s, the rate of return on capital invested in Britain began to fall steadily. By 1960, the symptoms of the "British disease"—continuous inflationary pressures led by wage increases, labor unrest, recurring payments problems, and slow growth in productivity and output—were becoming marked. Amid a growing "mood of bewilderment and apprehension,"[6] the Conservative government of the day initiated an industrial policy approach by establishing the National Economic Development Council (NEDC), a tripartite (representing government, management, and labor) consultative and planning agency. NEDC had two implicit purposes: to serve as a countervailing bureaucratic power to the prevailing treasury orthodoxy on economic management, and to induce cooperation among trade unions over wage restraint.[7]

The period between 1964 and 1979 was marked by a pendulum swing of governments: first came the Labour governments of Harold Wilson (1964–70) after thirteen years in the political wilderness, then the Conservative rule of Edward Heath (1970–74), and then Labour again under Wilson and James Callaghan (1974–79). Each of these governments was, in one way or another, brought down by a confrontation with the nation's trade union movement. The electoral campaigns preceding the alternations of party rule were increasingly often characterized by class conflict and were ideologically polarized with regard to issues concerning the relationship between the state and the economy. Despite substantial ideological and rhetorical differences, however, when in office the two parties often adopted (or were forced to adopt) rather similar approaches to political economy. Although sometimes at variance with its own electoral manifesto and usually at odds with its most ideologically extreme activists and MPs, the industrial policies of Labour and Conservative governments during these fifteen years represented a latent partisan convergence on state-economy relations.[8]

At the core of this uneasy consensus lay an evolving national commitment toward discretionary and selective public financial assistance to noncompetitive industrial sectors and to enterprises located in distressed regions of the country. Such measures, regardless of the party in power, were usually justified in terms of promoting greater efficiency, productivity, profitability, and competitiveness of national industries in the name of achieving rapid and sustained economic growth. As publicly stated, the thrust of this policy orientation was to reinforce or correct, rather than resist, market forces by overcoming market imperfections and by assisting in the rationalization of industrial sectors and enterprises. Decisions emerged out of a process of tripartite discussion and negotiation. Objectives were pursued through making technical adjustments, thereby avoiding fundamental structural transformations which might upset the fragile postwar democratic-capitalist settlement between capital and labor. The policy was to be responsive to the interest of capital in its emphasis on promoting greater capital accumulation. It rested on the assumption that Britain's economic crisis was due to an undersupply of capital. The way to overcome this problem was to enhance opportunities and incentives for capital formation by restructuring the industrial base and by providing a favorable business climate. So, for instance, Labour governments established an Industrial Reorganization Corporation (IRC) in 1966 and a National Enterprise Board (NEB) in 1975 as institutional vehicles to provide public equity financing to promote mergers (in order to achieve economies of scale) and otherwise rationalize production (including the shedding of excess labor) within selected sectors of British industry.

But, despite the stated goals of industrial policy, the real motivation was often the political imperative of preserving "lame-duck" firms and the jobs that they provide. Ailing and endangered enterprises in declining basic industrial sectors—such as steel production, shipbuilding, or automobile manufacturing—were given substantial state financial support or were nationalized outright. Even Heath's Conservative government, which had extolled the virtues of the free market upon coming to power in 1970, found that economic exigencies were more potent than political ideology when it was compelled to nationalize Rolls-Royce in 1972 in order to forestall the company's impending bankruptcy. Nor is the Rolls-Royce case atypical of industrial policymaking in Britain during this period: measures were often adopted as ad hoc and incoherent responses to immediate economic and political crises regardless of their long-term consequences for the nation's economic performance.[9]

Even the most cursory examination of its performance since the initiation of industrial policy in 1962 leads one to conclude that Britain has not experienced revitalization of its industrial base. Quite the contrary: virtually all indications show a nation in economic decline relative to other advanced industrial societies. Why has Britain continued to do so poorly? Samuel Beer suggests a political explanation: industrial policy is itself the cause of Britain's disappointing performance. The policy, he argues, is a manifestation of "pluralistic stagnation," a consequence of the political contradictions inherent within the "new group politics" of the British collectivist polity.[10] Governments, he contends, have grown overly sensitive to the demands of powerful producer groups, such as business enterprises and trade unions, which have pursued their own economic interests to the detriment of the national economic well-being. An unrestrained pluralism has "fragmented the decision-making system as to impair its power of acting for the long-run interests of its members."[11] Industrial policy resulted in a mad "subsidies scramble" whose outcome, Beer argues, was "precisely the opposite of its goal. Aiming at greater efficiency, competitiveness, and economic growth, the subsidy strategy has encouraged inefficiency, complacency, and economic stagnation."[12] Political process, says Beer, has defeated political purpose.

Industrial Policy Under Thatcher

The incoming Conservative government of Margaret Thatcher, committed to market forces as the Heath government had been nearly a decade before, immediately abandoned Labour's "industrial strategy" and repealed virtually all provisions of the 1975 Industry Act. The new administration explicitly rejected the principles of British industrial policy previously adopted by the Labour and Conservative parties alike—namely, microeconomic, selective state intervention. The new approach to British industrial regeneration lay in controlling macroeconomic aggregates, especially the money supply. Reviewing its own philosophy and performance four years after taking office, the Thatcher government explained:

> Of overriding importance was the objective of controlling inflation and reducing the pressure on interest rates, as this would make a more substantial and lasting contribution to the improvement of industry's international competitiveness than 'fine tuning' by the instruments of industrial policy. The major means to that end was the determined control of monetary growth and public expenditure. . . . The

> Government's basic position was to work with the grain of market forces rather
> than to intervene to frustrate them, and to create a climate conducive to enterprise
> and growth by improving incentives and, wherever possible, reducing the burdens
> of taxation and legislation on industry.[13]

Despite its rhetoric, however, the Conservative government continued to provide substantial public funding to British industries. The Department of Industry budget for grants to industry through regional assistance and discretionary assistance to firms actually increased dramatically in its first two years in office. During these years, Thatcher ran financial rescue missions for several enterprises, including British Leyland, the British Steel Corporation, and ICL. Nevertheless, the focus of Britain's industrial policy under Thatcher after these initial years has shifted from the adaptive and preservative orientations of previous governments to a more marked transformative one. Basic manufacturing state-owned sectors such as the car and steel industries have undergone substantial labor-shedding rationalization. (A similar policy in the coal industry resulted in the most bitter strike in British postwar history.) The new thrust is toward promotion of high-technology, as the changing portfolio of a drastically overhauled NEB and its 1983 merger with the National Research Development Corporation in the British Technology Group (BTG) clearly indicates. The recently redefined mission of the BTG is to foster the transfer of technology from sources within the public sector to British industry as a whole. The government has begun to reduce subsidies to basic industries significantly (in part because major former loss-makers such as BL and BSC have been restructured and are approaching commercial viability) and has concentrated instead on providing scientific and technical support schemes combined under the rubric of "Support for Innovation" in 1983. Promotion activities have also shifted from large enterprises to small businesses—through a loan guarantee scheme, a business expansion scheme, and a small engineering firm's investment scheme—and from a sectoral basis to a horizontal basis (i.e. a particular technology) for providing financial assistance. The government's efforts have especially emphasized the development and application of information technology.[14]

In addition to its reorientation of support for industry, the Thatcher government has adopted two other industrial policy initiatives. Beginning in 1980, specific depressed urban areas have been designated as "enterprise zones" in which business enterprises are provided with investment incentives through various tax benefits and relaxed regulatory enforcement.[15] The government has also begun to privatize state-owned industrial assets in order to release economic resources for more productive utilization, to reduce the government's deficit (the public sector borrowing requirement, or PSBR), to increase competition and efficiency, and perhaps also to weaken the industrial power of organized labor. The government has already sold off at least part of its holdings in some fifteen state-owned enterprises, including British Petroleum, Britoil, Cable and Wireless, British Aerospace, Jaguar, Enterprise Oil (a division of British Gas), and British Telecom. Privatization has been gathering momentum, with net proceeds of £ 313 million in the 1979–80 fiscal year, £ 495 million in 1981–82, £ 1.2 billion in 1983–84, and £ 2.50 billion in 1984–85. (These figures do not include over £ 6 billion raised through the sale of local authority housing during this period.) In all, as many as 400 thousand workers (or approximately one-quarter of those employed by state-owned industries) have been moved to the private sector through privatization. The government plans an additional £ 7 billion sale of assets by 1988.[16]

The Thatcher government has treaded softly in the area of statutory limitations on organized labor. The government has enacted several pieces of legislation (the Employment Acts of 1980 and 1982 and the Trade Union Act of 1984) which have progressively constrained trade union immunities, but it has hesitated to enforce them in the courts. Instead, it has relied on monetary restraint, and the unemployment thereby produced, to discipline organized labor.

Thatcher's "social market" assault on the principles of industrial policy as practiced by preceding governments has been mirrored by the "alternative economic strategy" of the Labour party.[17] Derivative of the economic analysis found in the party's 1973 and 1976 programs, this theory ascribes Britain's economic decline not to technical problems or market imperfections to be overcome through tripartism but rather to a fundamental reality of capitalist economics—namely, the mobility of capital. According to this perspective, the decision by British capital to invest abroad rather than domestically (the "strike of capital") has impeded the nation's capital formation and productivity growth, contributed to its declining international competitiveness, exacerbated its balance of payments, and undercut the industrial and political power of labor as a sociopolitical force. Labour's prescriptions are essentially neomercantilist. It proposes a fundamental realignment of Britain's political economy. Internationally, this would entail selective import controls (tariffs and quotas), capital controls (sterling would cease to serve as an international exchange currency and would no longer be freely convertible), and nationalization of assets of foreign multinationals in Britain (to be financed from the sale of British overseas portfolio investments). Domestically, the "alternative economic strategy" would rely upon Keynesian demand expansion to achieve growth and full employment; the control of prices, wages, and interest rates; the extension of public ownership to the twenty-five (or so) largest manufacturing companies and financial institutions; the implementation of compulsory planning agreements; and the redistribution of economic resources through a more progressive income tax and a wealth tax. The Labour party is also committed to the renationalization of privatized industries "without speculative gain" for shareholders. Since the 1983 electoral debacle, the alternative economy strategy has been fudged under the phrase "social ownership," but many of the elements remain.

The nation's two major parties have, each in its own way, rejected earlier industrial policy—the Conservatives because of the means employed and Labour because of the ends pursued. While accepting the goal of capital formation, the Conservative party under Thatcher rejects in principle the strategy of selective state intervention oriented toward the adaptation or preservation of Britain's basic manufacturing industries. The Labour party's "alternative economic strategy," while espousing the instruments of industrial policy, rejects their use in the promotion of capitalist accumulation.

It is perhaps ironic that during the same period—the late 1970s—which Britain's two major parties began to reject conventional industrial policy, advocates for such a policy began to emerge in America.

INDUSTRIAL POLICY IN THE UNITED STATES

The Coming of the American Debate

A report prepared by the Congressional Budget Office has suggested, "The term 'industrial policy' represents not so much a policy as a debate over the best way to address America's long-term industrial problems."[18] It is commonly argued that the United States does not have an industrial policy. But as former Assistant Secretary of Commerce Frank Weil told a congressional panel investigating industrial policy, "We have an industrial policy in this country; the policy is that we do not want an industrial policy."[19] In a similar vein, Wildavsky has written, ". . . there is no such thing as not having an industrial policy. Action and inaction alike affect the conditions of industry."[20]

But it would be wrong to suggest that the United States has been inactive with regard to its industries. Since Hamilton's *Report on Manufactures* and Clay's "American System," the nation has throughout its history adopted programs influencing industrial development. Postwar industrial policy measures have aimed at export promotion, regional development, adjustment assistance, stimulation of technological innovation, and small business promotion. By far the most important mechanisms of industrial policy have been government procurement and tax incentives for capital formation.

Perhaps the distinction made earlier between *an* industrial policy and a collection of uncoordinated measures affecting industry is useful here. It is generally agreed that United States industrial programs—certainly in the postwar era—have been ad hoc in their intention and often contradictory in their effect.[21] Rarely if ever have these programs been promulgated with explicitly economic objectives. They have rather been implemented in the name of social welfare or, more often, national security. The debate is precisely over these related issues: should the government engage in explicit and coherent policymaking and, if so, which economic goals (transformation, adaption, adjustment, or preservation) should such a policy pursue? These issues became pressing by the late 1970s with the growing public awareness that America had lost its economic supremacy.

The United States was clearly dominant in the international capitalist economy during the first twenty years of the postwar period. America emerged from the war accounting for over one-half of the world's gross product. As a national economy, it possessed a near monopoly in domestic and world markets in large part because of the devastation of its primary industrial rivals, especially Germany and Japan. America's postwar economic problem was not international competition but international liquidity. The successful resolution to the world's liquidity problem was in part the nation's economic undoing. In 1958 the United States began to run permanent deficits in its balance of payments, and the world's "dollar shortage" became a "dollar glut." A dollar overvalued under the Bretton Woods international monetary regime in the context of the relatively free trade regime of GATT, the outward foreign investment of American multinational firms which undercut domestic reinvestment, and the inevitable industrial resurrection in Europe and Japan—all interacted to threaten United States industrial and commercial hegemony. By the late 1960s, the American economy had begun to evince the major symptoms of the "British disease."

The ratio of United States exports to imports of manufactures had been falling since 1964, and in 1971 the country's trade balance in manufactures moved into deficit (and has remained there almost permanently). This year marked a turning point for American political economy. The Nixon administration's "New Economic Policy," which undermined the Bretton Woods currency regime and imposed a freeze on wages and prices in the United States, was a significant retreat from the country's traditional commitment to economic liberalism. The demarche "amounted to a sort of mercantilist revolution in domestic and foreign policy," declares Calleo, in response to an increasingly hostile international economic environment.[22]

Changes in the international economy had a dramatic impact upon American economy and society during the 1970s. Most important was the growing perception of national "deindustrialization," that is, a trend toward reduced levels of employment, output, and exports in manufacturing sectors. The declining international competitiveness of American manufacturing firms obviously was an important factor in explaining this trend. So too, ironically, was the "post-industrial" transformation of the United States economy from basic manufacturing to services or to high-technology industries. This decline in American manufacturing had obvious social and political import. One of its consequences was the migration of investment, employment, and population from the "rustbelt" states of the Northeast and Midwest to the "sunbelt" states of the South and West or abroad to foreign "production platforms." This geographical relocation of capital had a severe impact on communities in the predominantly manufacturing regions in terms of their employment opportunities, tax bases, public revenues, and public expenditures. And the decreased ability to provide social services and to maintain infrastructure, in turn, stimulated further capital relocation. By the end of the 1970s, numerous stories emerged of business enterprises playing off desperate communities against one another for greater concessions toward providing a positive business climate. A concomitant phenomenon was the weakening of organized labor in the United States. Increasing unemployment and insecurity, replacement of unionized manufacturing jobs by non-unionized high-tech or service jobs, migration of employment to right-to-work states or abroad, and the increasing pressure on unions to make concessions or face runaway shops combined to put the American trade union movement on the defensive industrially. The decade of the 1970s saw the emergence of a union-backed political agenda to defend American manufacturing industries and industrial workers. It is in this context that one must understand the emergence of industrial policy as a national issue in the last two years of the Carter administration. However, the momentum behind the initiation of industrial policymaking generated in these years was abruptly halted with Carter's defeat.

Industrial Policy Under Reagan

The fundamental assumptions of the Reagan administration's strategy for recovery of United States manufacturing were largely antithetical to industrial policy. The administration ascribed the decline in American manufacturing primarily to short-run, cyclical forces (that is, the recession) rather than long-run structural problems in the country's industrial base. What structural problems did exist could be overcome by market-oriented policies to stimulate profits, savings, and investment. Government intervention in the market, according to this view, was the cause, not the cure, of industrial decline. Like Thatcher, Reagan felt that government could best aid industry in removing the barriers to profitability, savings, and investment by reducing taxes (particularly on corporations and wealthy individuals who have a greater propensity to save), reducing regulations on enterprises, and reducing the government deficit, which affects interest rates or the cost of capital. Also like its British counterpart, the current American administration rejected in principle a strategy of microeconomic, selective state intervention, relying instead on a macroeconomic and nonselective approach to industrial re-generation. Administration officials have stated publicly their continued opposition to the idea of industrial policy.[23]

Probably the cornerstone to the Reagan industrial strategy has been in the area of tax policy. The 1981 Tax Act had a number of provisions meant to enhance savings and investment. It aimed at stimulating savings of personal incomes through a flat-rate reduction in marginal tax rates and through deferment of taxes on Individual Retirement Account (IRA) contributions by individuals participating in other pension arrangements. Its "Accelerated Cost Recovery System" sought to offset the increase in the cost of physical capital assets due to inflation by significantly shortening the tax lives of those assets. The Act also provided that the 10 percent investment tax credit (ITC) for qualified investments (primarily machinery and other equipment) could be carried forward or backward fifteen years for tax purposes. The "Safe Harbor Leasing Program" provisions allowed firms with insufficient tax liabilities in effect to sell their ITC and other depreciations to other firms. The 1981 law also instituted a 25 percent tax credit on incremental research and development outlays above the previous three-year average base level. A Congressional Budget Office study released in May 1985 indicated that Reagan's tax measures had reduced the average tax rate for all American corporations from 43.8 percent in 1980 to 21.9 percent in 1984, the lowest figure in over fifty years. In a significant reversal of policy, however, recent administration tax reform proposals would allow less generous write-offs than current law for plants and equipment and would abolish ITC. (The proposals also call for a three-year extension of the research and development tax credit and a cut in the maximum capital gains rate, which favor high-technology firms.)[24]

Nontax measures intended to stimulate profits, savings, and investment have included the price-and-entry deregulation of specific industries and the reduction of social regulations in the fields of the environment, consumer protection, occupational health and safety, equal employment, and antitrust activity across the entire economy. The administration also removed barriers to exportation by relaxing enforcement of foreign corrupt practices laws, relaxing United States insistence on human rights records in selling military and nonmilitary products to third-world nations, and reducing tax burdens for American citizens working abroad. In the area of adjustment assistance, the administration sponsored the Job Training Partnership Act of 1982, which replaced more generous provisions of the 1974 Trade Act and placed federal assistance to displaced workers under the rubric of the "new federalism."

The administration has in principle opposed government assistance to specific sectors or firms. Its 1985 budget proposals, for instance, called for the abolition of the Small Business Administration and the elimination of direct loans for the Export-Import Bank. The administration also planned a significant reduction in federal funding for community economic development, and it proposed to abolish the Economic Development Administration and the Appalachian Regional Commission. Reagan's policy initiative in the area of community economic development has been to support legislation establishing "enterprise zones."[25] These are intended to facilitate investment in selected depressed urban areas by offering reductions in income and property taxes, tax credits for hiring eligible residents, reductions of capital gains tax on new investments, and reductions in various regulations (including minimum wage restrictions). The enterprise zone idea was borrowed explicitly from a similar program adopted by the Thatcher government.

The president, however, has not been entirely consistent in a free market approach. His position, like Thatcher's, has been more "social market" than "pure market" in orientation. In part because of congressional pressure, he has been selectively interventionist and protectionist in issues of trade policy, including raising duties on motorcycles and placing quotas and duties on specialty steel (both actions following recommendations of the International Trade Commission), tightening restrictions on textiles, reintroducing quotas on sugar, obtaining voluntary export quotas on Japanese automobiles, and negotiating export quotas with European steelmakers. And although opposed to industrial policy in principle, Reagan attempted to sidestep the industrial policy issue prior to the 1984 election by appointing a Commission on Industrial Competitiveness (composed of academics and chief executive officers of major corporations, but with no representation of organized labor)[26] and by proposing a cabinet-level Department of International Trade and Industry which would incorporate a variety of already existing agencies (including the Office of U.S. Trade Representative). Meanwhile, the greatest efforts in selective intervention have been in those industrial sectors important to the administration's defense buildup and modernization program, particularly aerospace, information technology, and telecommunications.

Toward an American Industrial Policy

Numerous comprehensive industrial policy proposals were advanced throughout Reagan's first term, primarily by congressional Democrats.[27] Legislation was introduced to establish various institutional frameworks, including a national council on economic cooperation (a triparite body of representatives from capital, organized labor, and government to discuss national industrial objectives), an economic development financial institution (modelled upon the Reconstruction Finance Corporation of the New Deal period), and a cabinet-level agency responsible for the coordination of the nation's industrial programs and for the formulation of a comprehensive industrial strategy or plan.

Proponents differ on the general orientation which industrial policy should take. Lester Thurow has advocated a policy of "picking winners and losers" so as to promote the transformation of the United States economy from its reliance on basic manufacturing industries toward high technology.[28] Felix Rohatyn identifies the need for an American policy to enable basic manufacturing industries to adapt to international competition.[29] Without denying the importance of industrial adaptation, Robert Reich emphasizes the role of adjustment assistance (in the form of human-capital investment) to national revitalization.[30] And Barry Bluestone argues that because America's problem lies in the mobility of capital and the immobility of labor, direct controls upon private investments must be placed in the hands of government and the workers themselves.[31]

Although proposed as an alternative to Reagan's economic policies, industrial policy shares a fundamental assumption of conservative "supply-side economics." Both reject a heretofore almost exclusive reliance on Keynesian demand-management techniques for economic stabilization and growth. Both view America's economic woes as arising from supply-side, rather than demand-side, weakness—in particular, a shortage of investment capital. Whereas Keynesianism postulates that short-term stabilization will provide an environment most conductive to long-term growth, proponents of industrial policy and supply-side economics see sustained growth as the prerequisite for stabilization. And both agree that economic growth results from increased productivity brought about by greater incentives and opportunities to work, save, and invest. George Gilder has noted that industrial policy is nothing more than "a new supply-side microeconomics of the left."[32] Bob Kuttner argues,

> [L]iberal economics is at an ideological dead end because it has accepted the central premise of conservative economics. That is the alleged crisis of capital

supply. In a capitalist economy, not surprisingly, the main source of capital is private capitalists. If America truly is suffering mainly from too little private investment, then most of the conservative prescription of rewarding the rich and reducing the state follows logically enough. The difference between the liberal supply-siders—the advocates of industrial targeting—and the conservative supply-siders—the advocates of tax cuts and deregulation—is really minimal. Both accept the capital supply view. The only issue is government's competence to supply capital: whether government is a better friend of industry by subsidizing it more or by taxing it less. But both major parties have become the party of business.[33]

Aside from the merits of recent industrial policy proposals in terms of the performance of American industry, these proposals must also be understood as a political phenomenon, for they serve as a vehicle for political, and especially electoral, mobilization. Put simply, industrial policy represents an attempt by the American left to redefine "liberalism" in the context of the perceived failure of Keynesianism and a prevailing conservative consensus on political economy.

PATTERNS OF CONVERGENCE AND DIVERGENCE

It is time to draw together the disparate threads of the discussion. A word of caution is in order. Any discussion of industrial policy in the United States is prey to terminological confusion because of the ambiguity of "industrial policy" described earlier. One may speak of American industrial policy (rather than *an* American industrial policy) in the sense of a collection of government programs which, even if only implicitly, affect industrial performance and structure through microeconomic interventions. If, however, one reserves the term for an explicit, coordinated, and institutionalized industrial strategy, then it can be said that America lacks an industrial policy. Unless otherwise stated, the term will be used here in the first, more inclusive, sense.

What general comments can be made about industrial policy convergence and divergence in the United Kingdom and the United States? Three rather paradoxical conclusions emerge. First, both countries have experienced similar political-economic dislocations resulting in, and exacerbated by, their decline relative to other advanced capitalist economies. Second, despite similar policy environments, their postwar industrial policy responses have been very different in terms of institutional-functional arrangements, strategic objectives, and models of government involvement. Third, the two countries have converged during the Thatcher-Reagan period, ironically, in their explicit rejection of the fundamental principles of industrial policymaking. Each of these propositions, however, needs some qualification.

The Postwar Policy Environment

Britain and America have suffered similar structural problems in relation to the international economic system in the postwar period. Both countries emerged from the second world war with their industrial bases relatively intact, and the governments of neither country immediately perceived a need for a comprehensive strategy for postwar reconstruction. As leading postwar economies, however, both have experienced a relative economic decline as formerly dependent and peripheral economies have emerged as industrial rivals. This process has been furthered by massive capital outflows from America and Britain, which undermined domestic industrial performance by lowering savings and investment in the two core economies.[34] Declining international competitiveness has been exacerbated by the inflationary conditions associated with Keynesianism—full employment and deficit financing of the welfare state.

The incompatibility between Keynesianism at home and the liberal international economic order was particularly significant for the United States and Britain because of the role of their currencies in the international monetary system. For the United States, the dollar's role in the Bretton Woods gold-exchange standard precluded the automatic exchange-rate adjustments existing under a classical gold standard to restore its international payments equilibrium.[35] In Britain, government policy in the postwar period continued to be committed to an overvalued pound for reasons of national prestige, reflecting as well the influence of the City (Britain's financial center) on economic policy.[36] The overvalued dollar and pound hurt national exports, sucked in imports, and stimulated further outward foreign investment—all of which undercut capital formation and productivity growth in America and Britain.

These underlying, structural problems of political economy have manifested themselves in similar ways in the United Kingdom and the United States. Compared to other major advanced industrial democracies, both countries have been plagued by: low rates of capital investment, low investment in research and development of new nonmilitary technologies, slow productivity growth, declining competitiveness in manufactures, import penetration of domestic markets, loss of international market share, balance of payment deficits,[37] and relatively slow economic growth. These symptoms constituted a vicious circle of economic decline which Keynesian techniques apparently failed to arrest. Keynesianism appeared unable to cope with the increasingly severe (and politically sensitive) domestic economic problems of simultaneously rising levels of inflation and unemployment. According to Keynesian theory, inflation and unemployment represented policy trade-offs. That is, governments could always achieve lower levels of one by allowing higher levels of the other. The condition of stagflation, in which both inflation and unemployment grew at the same time, did much to discredit the prevailing Keynesian orthodoxy both theoretically and politically. The growing disillusionment with Keynesian prescriptions in Britain (in the early 1960s) and America (by the late 1970s) led to serious consideration of alternative strategies for economic revitalization. Industrial policy seemed to offer such an alternative. Whereas Keynesianism depended upon short-term movements in aggregate demand through macroeconomic manipulations, industrial policy focused upon long-term transformations in the supply capacity through microeconomic interventions.

Yet some significant differences exist in each country's relationship with the international environment. Whereas Britain's experience with industrial decline has been a long-term phenomenon (beginning perhaps in the last century),[38] America's eclipse is relatively recent (beginning in the mid-1960s). Despite increasing foreign commercial competition, the United States economy remains far less vulnerable to international economic forces than does the British economy, which must "export or die." And while the reality of Britain's industrial decline has been almost universally acknowledged by both expert and mass opinion in the nation, the reality of American industrial decline has been a subject of much disagreement.[39] For these reasons, the environmental stresses upon the United States have been neither sufficiently chronic nor sufficiently acute to precipitate a political crisis. Had the 1980–82 recession assumed crisis proportions in the United States by virtue of greater severity or duration, it is arguable that Reagan would have lost the 1984 presidential election to Mondale; as a consequence of this, the United States would have initiated some form of explicit industrial policy.[40]

Postwar Policy Response

The differing degrees of political-economic stress in Britain and America may partially explain the differences in their postwar policy experiences. Britain established an institutional framework for industrial policymaking in the 1960s. America, on the other hand, has yet to acknowledge the necessity of an explicit industrial policy, much less to establish an institutional framework or a consensus about its proper objectives or models of state intervention.

The degree of coordination in British industrial policy should not be overestimated, however. In fact, its programmatic and institutional discontinuities are perhaps as evident as its continuities.[41] In terms of the commitment of public funds, British programs throughout the postwar period have tended to center on regional development (assistance to depressed regions) and the preservation of major loss-makers (usually in nationalized basic industries such as steel, automobiles, and shipbuilding). This direction has been changed somewhat by the Thatcher administration, which has downplayed aid to traditional industries and has attempted to transform the economy by promoting the development of high-tech enterprises. Antitrust measures were emphasized during the first twenty years of the postwar period, but by the mid-1960s the government took the view that mergers should be encouraged to achieve economies of scale which would enhance the international competitiveness of British firms. The Thatcher government has reintroduced an emphasis on intranational competition, arguing that this would promote the rationalization of British enterprises and thereby enhance their international competitiveness.

Industrial policy programs in the United States have been fairly consistently maintained during the postwar period. Public financial support has generally been focused upon defense and agricultural sectors and upon assistance to small businesses. It is perhaps ironic that this continuity has been achieved despite the absence of an established institutional framework or an explicitly formulated national policy.

In fact, one is tempted to hypothesize that programmatic consistency may be due to the incoherence of the industrial policy process in the United States. Industrial policy in America is largely *distributive*. Such policies minimize public contestation because there are few political actors which are specifically and directly disadvantaged by another's reception of benefits. As a result, opposition to the continuation of distributive programs is generally weak. Industrial policy in Britain, on the other hand, is primarily *redistributive*.[42] This policy process tends to be highly politicized and ideologically polarized, making it more difficult to sustain a broad-based and long-term support for (or acquiescence in) specific programs. Redistributive policies are salient to the mass electorate and often are used as "position issues" by political parties. Thus Britain's experience in industrial policymaking has been characterized by explicit, and often ideological, formulations by political parties and by concomitant discontinuities because of alternating party governments.

A number of structural variables help to explain broad differences in the nature of British and American industrial policymaking in the postwar period.[43] As we have already seen, different *economic conditions* are related to their respective policy evolution. Unlike its British counterpart, the American economy remains relatively independent—although increasingly less so—from international market exigencies. Thus the environment pressures giving rise to a consensus on the need for a comprehensive and coordinated state industrial policy have not been as compelling in the United States.

A second structural variable is America's *pervasive liberal ideology*, which culturally conditions a limited role for the state in social and economic spheres. "[T]he State plays a more limited role in America than elsewhere," King states, "because Americans, more than other people, want it to play a limited role. In other words, the most satisfactory explanation is one in terms of Americans' beliefs and assumptions, especially their beliefs and assumptions about government." King summarizes these ideas "in a series of catch phrases: free enterprise is more efficient than government; governments should concentrate on encouraging private initiative and free competition; government is wasteful; governments should not provide people with things they can provide for themselves; too much government endangers liberty; and so on."[44] In contrast to British corporatist[45] and collectivist[46] traditions, the American cultural legacies of individualism and populism are arguably inconsistent with the requirements of comprehensive industrial policymaking.

A third variable is the *structure of political institutions* in the United States. The fragmentation, decentralization, and diffusion of power and authority throughout the American political system vitiates the process of comprehensive and coordinated policymaking by government officials. The system provides multiple access points for groups to effectively veto government policies which negatively affect their interests. Institutional features such as federalism, the separation of executive and legislative powers, the role of legislative committees, and the absence of disciplined national political parties are often cited in this regard. These institutional features are clearly different from the unitary, centralized, parliamentary arrangements of the United Kingdom. Perhaps more important, institutional differences exist between the two countries specifically in the field of economic policymaking. These include the more comprehensive role of the Treasury in Britain compared to America, the insulation of economic policymakers in Britain compared to the United States, and the existence of a substantial nationalized industries sector in the former, but not in the latter.[47] These arrangements institutionalize a greater coherence, autonomy, and scope of authority for economic decision-making in British government—attributes which are essential for a coordinated industrial policy.

Recent Policy Convergence

The political economies of the Thatcher and Reagan administrations are predicated upon principles which are antithetical to industrial policy as microeconomic, selective state intervention. Both Thatcher and Reagan believe that such interventions, by distorting market forces, are counterproductive to reversing industrial decline. Both espouse a macroeconomic, nonselective approach to economic regeneration. This convergence of political economy in the two countries points clearly to the important role of political leadership and of the ideological commitments of policymakers in the policy process.

The rejection of the principles of industrial policy by the two conservative administrations is a specific case of what Gary Marks has referred to as a "revival of laissez-faire" in the United States and Great Britain in the 1980s.[48] After decades of increasing government intervention in the economy, both countries have recently witnessed a trend toward the re-separation of state and economy, in which the state comes to exercise less authority than previously over the allocation of scarce economic resources. Marks explains the return to laissez-faire primarily in terms of two political similarities in Britain and America. First, in contrast to other advanced industrial democracies, the conservative parties of both countries have a traditional commitment to laissez-faire. Marks attributes this commitment to distinctive characteristics of the Republican and Conservative parties, specifically the absence of a significant Catholic political influence (which, in the countries of central and southern Europe, is often linked with "antiliberal and anti-capitalist values") and the unitary representation of the political Right (which obviates the need for coalitional politics and political compromise on issues of political economy).[49] Second, again in contrast to other advanced industrial democracies, the governments of the United States and Britain are compelled toward laissez-faire because of political constraints upon alternative approaches to state-economy relations. Economic interest groups in Britain and America possess the political power to resist or to distort the impact of state intervention in the economy, while they lack the requisite organizational centralization and mutual trust to engage effectively in cooperative state-capital-labor arrangements of economic management. The inability of British and American governments effectively to formulate and implement economic strategies without producer group support leaves these governments no alternative other than to rely upon market forces for regulating the national economy.[50] Thus for Marks the distinctive characteristics of their conservative parties and of their pluralist political process have led to a convergent revival of laissez-faire in both the United States under Reagan and Great Britain under Thatcher.[51]

The similarity between their approaches to industrial regeneration should not be overdrawn, however. A distinction between the *direction* and the *content* of policy may be useful here. In terms of policy direction, the two conservative leaders are agreed that their respective nations should move away from the prevailing politics of government intervention toward greater reliance upon market forces. But the characteristics of the politics of government intervention prevailing in the two nations, to which Thatcher's and Reagan's policies are reactions, are rather different. Britain has a legacy of explicit industrial policymaking; America has not. Britain has a substantial nationalized industries sector; again, America has not. Thatcher's conservative revolution began in the context of a very different set of institutions and programmatic commitments than did Reagan's. That is, a similar direction was taken from very different starting points. So despite similar orientations, the content of the two governments' approach to industry remains divergent. Thatcher has begun to reorient and reduce the financial assistance of the British government to industrial enterprises and geographic regions, but the level of direct government support and the explicitness of the government's transformative objective remain much higher than in America.

The differing legacies also mean that, despite their mutual acceptance of macroeconomic and nonselective approaches, the two leaders have adopted different specific instruments. Thatcher has relied primarily upon (1) controlling the growth of the money supply and the public sector borrowing requirement, and, increasingly often, (b) privatization of state-owned industrial assets. Reagan's economic regeneration program has centered upon (a) personal and corporate tax cuts and (b) deregulation. The two strategies are in some ways analogous, but in other ways they entail quite divergent fiscal consequences.

Despite the ideological and rhetorical similarities between the Thatcher and Reagan administrations on the issue of state assistance to industry, significant aspects of the actual policies adopted by government are rather dissimilar in the two countries, reflecting the very dissimilar policy legacies from which each emerged. Policy is historically conditioned: it is a product of its own evolution from a given configuration of institutional and programmatic commitments whih constrain future policy options and define the modalities which future policy will take.[52]

CONCLUSIONS

Let us return to the generalizations with which we began this section on the patterns of convergence and divergence in Anglo-American industrial policy. First, although both countries have experienced industrial decline relative to other advanced capitalist economies, such dislocations have been of greater severity and duration in Britain than in America. Second, in addition to the degree of political-economic stress arising from the hostile international environment, differences in political culture and institutional structure account for divergent industrial policy regimes in Britain and the United

States in the postwar period. Differences in policymaking, however, should not be exaggerated. Although explicit, British policymaking has experienced institutional and substantive discontinuities with successive governments; American policymaking has been implicit but fairly consistent over time. Third, the Reagan and Thatcher approaches to state-industry relations have been convergent on certain issues and divergent on others. But despite their ideological and rhetorical similarities, each approach reflects the very different policy context from which it derives.

NOTES

1. See, for instance, Chalmers Johnson, "Introduction: The Idea of Industrial Policy," in Johnson, ed., *The Industrial Policy Debate* (San Francisco: Institute for Contemporary Studies, 1984), 10–11.
2. Wyn Grant, "Comment: Analysing Industrial Policy," *Public Administration Bulletin* 32 (1980): 50–55; and Grant, *The Political Economy of Industrial Policy* (London: Butterworths, 1982). For additional typologies, see John Pinder, "Causes and Kinds of Industrial Policy," in Pinder, ed., *National Industrial Strategies and the World Economy* (Totowa, N.J.: Allanheld, Osmun, 1982); and F. Gerald Adams and C. Andrea Bollino, "Meaning of Industrial Policy," in Adams and Lawrence R. Klein, eds., *Industrial Politics for Growth and Competitiveness: An Economic Perspective* (Lexington, Mass.: D.C. Heath, 1983).
3. Grant, "Comment," 51.
4. Ibid., 52.
5. This typology is presented in Congressional Budget Office, *The Industrial Policy Debate* (Washington, D.C.: GPA, December 1983), 52–56.
6. Michael Shanks, *Planning and Politics: The British Experience 1960–76* (London: George Allen and Unwin, 1977), 17.
7. The two purposes were interrelated. The government hoped that it could convince the unions to accept an incomes policy in return for a government commitment to faster growth. On this point, see Shanks, *Planning and Politics*, 21, and Leo Panitch, *Social Democracy and Industrial Militancy* (Cambridge: Cambridge, 1976), 47–52.
8. On the history of industrial policy during this period, see Michael Stewart, *The Jekyll and Hyde Years: Politics and Economic Policy Since 1964* (London: Dent, 1977); Panitch, *Social Democracy*; David Coates, *The Labour Party and the Struggle for Socialism* (London: Cambridge, 1975); Coates, *Labour in Power? A Study of the Labour Government 1974-1979* (London: Longman, 1980); and Michael Hatfield, *The House the Left Built* (London: Gollancz, 1978).
9. See note 41 below.
10. Samuel H. Beer, *Britain Against Itself: The Political Contradictions of Collectivism* (New York: Norton, 1982), chap. 1, passim.
11. Beer, *Britain Against Itself*, 4.
12. Ibid., 74.

13. Memo to the NEDC, 21 September 1983. Quoted in *Survey of Current Affairs* 3 (November 1983): 379.
14. Such as the Alvey Program for advanced information technology.
15. It is argued that despite its rhetorical thrust, the "enterprise zone" program is actually an experiment in selective intervention rather than a free market strategy. Michael Keating, et al., "Enterprise Zones: Implementing the Unworkable," *Political Quarterly* 55 (January 1984): 78–84.
16. Annual figures are computed from Samuel Brittan, "The Politics and Economics of Privatisation," *Political Quarterly* 55 (April 1984), table 1 on 111. For slightly different figures, see "Privatisation in Britain: Making the Modern Dinosaur Extinct," *The Economist* (23 February 1985): 76–78.
17. For statements of the "alternative economic strategy," see Stuart Holland, *The Socialist Challenge* (London: Quartet, 1974); Cambridge Political Economy Group, *Britain's Economic Crisis* (Nottingham: Spokesman, 1975); Geoff Hodgson, *Socialist Economic Strategy* (London: Labour Party, 1979); CSE London Working Group, *The Alternative Economic Strategy* (London: CSE, 1980).
18. Congressional Budget Office, *Industrial Policy Debate*, xiii.
19. Congress of the United States, House Committee on Foreign Affairs, *Government Decision-Making in Japan: Implications for the United States*, 97th Cong., 2nd sess. (Washington, D.C.: GPO, 1982), 92.
20. Aaron Wildavsky, "Squaring the Political Circle: Industrial Policies and the American Dream," in Johnson, ed., *The Industrial Policy Debate*, 28.
21. Organization of Economic Cooperation and Development, *The Aims and Instruments of Industrial Policy* (Geneva: OECD, 1975); Robert F. Westcott, "U.S. Approaches to Industrial Policy," in Adams and Klein, eds., *Industrial Policies*; "The Reindustrialization of America," special issue of *Business Week* (30 June 1980); Ira C. Magaziner and Robert B. Reich, *Minding America's Business: The Decline and Rise of the American Economy* (New York: Random, 1983).
22. David P. Calleo, *The Imperious Economy* (Cambridge, Mass.: Harvard, 1982), 82.
23. Ronald Reagan, "America's New Beginning: A Program for Economic Recovery," presidential message, 18 February 1981; statements by Edwin L. Harper (domestic policy advisor to the president), quoted in Stuart Auerback, "White House Hits Industrial Policy Idea," *Washington Post* (16 June 1983); statement by William E. Brock (then U.S. Trade Representative) in Hearings Before Subcommittee on Economic Stabilization (House of Representatives), *Industrial Policy*, part 5, (Washington, D.C.: GPO, 1984); Donald T. Regan (then Secretary of the Treasury), "Industrial Policy." address at the University of Kansas (J.A. Vickers Lecture Series), 14 October 1983.
24. As of this writing (August 1986), the U.S. Senate and House of Representatives have not yet agreed on a final version of the reform legislation. It appears that these provisions will be included in the new tax law.
25. First introduced in 1980, the administration-backed Kemp-Garcia bill has been repeatedly passed by the Senate but has failed to clear the House Ways and Means Committee.
26. On the issue of the commission's membership and the general policy orientation of its chairman, see the testimony of John A. Young in Hearings Before Subcommittee on Economic Stabilization, *Industrial Policy*, part 5. Its report was presented to the president after the 1984 election and avoided recommending the

adoption of comprehensive industrial policymaking institutions or orientations. See the Report of the President's Commission on Industrial Competitiveness, *Global Competition: The New Reality* (Washington, D.C.: GPO, January 1985), vol. 1.

27. A comprehensive list of legislative proposals introduced during the 98th Congress can be found in Wildavsky, "Squaring the Political Circle." See also: Sidney Blumenthal, "Drafting A Democratic Industrial Plan" *New York Times Magazine* (28 August 1983), 31–63; Special Task Force on Long-Term Economic Policy, Democratic Caucus/U.S. House of Representatives, *Rebuilding the Road to Opportunity: Turning Point for America's Economy* (September 1982); Industrial Policy Task Force, Senate Democratic Caucus, *Jobs for the Future: A Democratic Agenda* (16 November 1983); Study Group on Industrial Policy, *Restoring American Competitiveness: Proposals for an Industrial Policy* (Washington, D.C.: Center for National Policy, January 1984); *Deindustrialization and the Two Tier Society: Challenges for an Industrial Policy* (Washington, D.C.: Industrial Union Department, AFL-CIO, 1984); *International Trade, Industrial Policies, and the Future of American Industry* (Washington, D.C.: Labor-Industry Coalition for International Trade, April 1983).

28. Lester Thurow, *The Zero-Sum Society* (New York: Basic Books, 1980).

29. Felix G. Rohatyn, "Reconstructing America," *New York Review of Books* (5 March 1981).

30. Robert B. Reich, *The Next American Frontier* (New York: Time Books, 1983).

31. Barry Bluestone and Bennett Harrison, *The Deindustrialization of America* (New York: Basic Books, 1982).

32. George Gilder, "A Supply-Side Economics of the Left," *The Public Interest* 72 (Summer 1983): 30.

33. Bob Kuttner, "The Left's Recovery," *The New Republic* (13 February 1984), 26.

34. Robert Gilpin, *U.S. Power and the Multinational Corporation: The Political Economy of Foreign Direct Investment* (New York: Basic Books, 1975).

35. Calleo, *Imperious Economy*, 63.

36. Stephen Blank, "Britain: the Politics of Foreign Economic Policy, the Domestic Economy, and the Problem of Pluralist Stagnation," in Peter J. Katzenstein, ed., *Between Power and Plenty* (Madison: University of Wisconsin, 1978).

37. Masked by North Sea oil revenues in the United Kingdom.

38. E.J. Hobsbawm, *Industry and Empire: The Making of Modern English Society, vol. 2, 1750 to the Present Day* (New York: Pantheon, 1968); E.H. Phelps Brown, et al., "The 'Climacteric' in the British Economy of the Late Nineteenth Century: Two Interpretations," in Barry E. Supple, ed., *The Experience of Economic Growth: Case Studies in Economic History* (New York: Random House, 1963), 205–25.

39. Not only from those on the right. See, for instance, Charles L. Schultze, "Industrial Policy: A Dissent," *The Brookings Review* 2 (Fall 1983): 3–12; and Robert Z. Lawrence, *Can America Compete?* (Washington, D.C.: Brookings, 1984).

40. Industrial policy did not become a major issue in the 1984 presidential election, in part because of the dominance of the "Brookings view" (see note 42) in the Mondale campaign, with the central role given to Walter Heller and George Perry in economic affairs. See "Relying on Some Familiar Faces to Counter Reagonomics," *Business Week* (30 July 1984), 28.

41. Linda Hesselman, "Trends in European Industrial Intervention," *Cambridge Journal of Economics* 7 (1983): 203; Michael Davenport, "Industrial Policy in

the United Kingdom," in Adams and Klein, eds., *Industrial Policies for Growth and Competitiveness*; R. James Bell, "Industrial Policy in the United Kingdom," in Michael L. Wachter and Susan M. Wachter, eds., *Toward a New U.S. Industrial Policy?* (Philadelphia: University of Pennsylvania, 1981); Aubrey Carter, ed., *Industrial Policy and Innovation* (London: Heinemann, 1981); P. Mottershead, "Industrial Policy," in F.T. Blackaby, ed., *British Economic Policy, 1960–74* (Cambridge: Cambridge University Press, 1978).

42. "Distributive policies are characterized by the ease with which they can be disaggregated and dispensed unit by small unit, each unit more or less in isolation from other units and from any general rule . . . these are policies that are virtually not policies at all but are highly individualized decisions that only by accumulation can be called a policy." Redistributive issues "cut closer than any other along class lines and activate interests in roughly class terms." Theodore Lowi, "American Business, Public Policy, Case Studies and Political Theory," *World Politics* 16 (July 1964): 690, 707. On the distinction between distributive and redistributive policy, see also Lowi, "Decision Making vs. Policy Making: Toward An Antidote For Technology," *Public Administration Review* 30 (May/ June 1970): 314–25; T. Alexander Smith, *The Comparative Policy Process* (Santa Barbara, Cal.: ABC-Clio, 1975).

43. This analysis derives *mutatis mutandis* from Arnold J. Heidenheimer et al., *Comparative Public Policy: The Politics of Social Choice in Europe and America* (New York: St. Martin's, 1975), chap. 9.

44. Anthony King, "Ideas, Institutions and the Politics of Governments: a Comparative Analysis," *British Journal of Political Science* 3 (July and October 1973): 418.

45. Keith Middlemas, *Politics in Industrial Society: The Experience of the British System Since 1911* (London: A. Deutsch, 1979).

46. Samuel H. Beer, *British Politics in the Collectivist Age* (New York: Knopf, 1965).

47. On the British policy process, see Hugh Heclo and Aaron Wildavsky, *The Private Government of Public Money: Community and Policy Inside British Politics* (Berkeley: University of California Press, 1974); and Samuel Brittan, *Steering the Economy: The Role of the Treasury* (London: Penguin, 1964). On the American policy process, see Lawrence L. Pierce, *The Politics of Fiscal Policy Formation* (Pacific Palisades, Cal.: Goodyear, 1971), and Aaron Wildavsky, *The Politics of the Budgetary Process* (Boston: Little, Brown, 1964).

48. Gary Marks, "The Revival of Laissez-Faire," in Richard Hodder-Williams and James Ceaser, eds., *Politics in Britain and the United States: Comparative Perspectives* (Durham, N.C.: Duke, 1986).

49. Ibid., 34–40.

50. Ibid., 40–52.

51. It should be noted that Marks reaches conclusions somewhat at variance with those of this chapter. To some extent, this reflects the different comparative perspectives taken in the two analyses. Marks's finding of substantial similarity in U.S. and British economic policy flows from his broader analytic focus, which includes virtually all advanced industrial democracies; compared to them, of course, the U.S. and Britain are more similar than they are different.

52. The evolutionary nature of policy is argued in Hugh Heclo, *Modern Social Politics in Britain and Sweden* (New Haven; Yale University Press, 1974).

Labor Market Surgery, Labor Market Abandonment: The Thatcher and Reagan Unemployment Remedies

David B. Robertson

Within a year after they secured dramatic budget cuts, the Thatcher and Reagan governments faced double-digit unemployment rates, levels not experienced in either Britain or the United States since the 1930s. While both conservative administrations had resolved to slash government programs, both came under enormous political pressure to respond aggressively to the growing pain of the jobless. These pressures included pleas to increase, not reduce, government labor market intervention in the form of public training programs and subsidized jobs.

Confronting similar grave problems and given similar ideological predispositions and policy remedies, one would expect Thatcher and Reagan to move their national governments' employment policies closer to one another. The two governments indeed took some similar actions in response to high unemployment. Despite strong pressures to converge, however, these conservative administrations pursued remedies sufficiently different in spirit and outcome to preclude acceptance of the convergence thesis. In important respects, the two regimes widened the gulf between American and British labor market policies because each pursued a different conservative strategy in attacking joblessness.

These conclusions are drawn in a telling policy area, for across labor market policy in industrial states fall the shadows of a government's economic strategy and its conception of social welfare. Unexpectedly high or low unemployment confounds economic policy. The former strains budgets by raising public compensation for the jobless while decreasing tax collections; the latter may create skills bottlenecks or high wage settlements and may fuel inflation. During this century, American and British officials of all ideological persuasions have embraced public initiatives to "fine-tune" labor markets. At the same time, many citizens depend on such programs, along with unemployment compensation, as essential to their survival and advancement in economies subject to uneven and rapid change. Historically, labor market policies provide an early indicator of a welfare state's strategy. Public labor exchanges and unemployment insurance were the earliest of Beveridge's legacies in Britain, and the United States government's emphasis on education and on grants-in-aid to states surfaced in its vocational education policy as early as 1917.

PRESSURES TO CONVERGE

The growing resemblance of the factors shaping British and American labor markets makes the convergence thesis quite plausible with respect to employment policy. By the early 1980s, similar socioeconomic trends, policy limitations, and ideological beliefs exerted strong pressures on both central governments to move toward similar projects.

Labor market deterioration created the most insistent of these pressures. Compared to other industrial democracies, unemployment levels in Britain and America between 1965 and 1980 were neither extremely high nor extremely low.[1] As Table 1 reveals, Britain's jobless rate hovered at the OECD average until 1980, while the United States rates ran above that average until 1984. Both nations experienced sharp rises in unemployment in the early 1980s.[2]

Unemployment worked against convergence only after 1983. British joblessness drifted upward to ever more excruciating levels, reaching devastating proportions in the northern industrial centers. Among OECD nations, the British unemployment rate was second only to Spain's in early 1986. American unemployment rates began to recede early in 1983. These rates settled to just above 7% by early 1986, high by the standards of the 1970s but low enough to relieve the Reagan administration of many of the pressures that

TABLE 1:   *Unemployment Rates in the OECD, United Kingdom, United States,*
            1972–1986 (Standardized to OECD Concepts)

Year	OECD Average	United Kingdom	United States	Difference, U.K.–U.S.
1972	3.6	4.0	5.5	− 1.5
1973	3.2	3.0	4.8	− 1.8
1974	3.5	2.9	5.5	− 2.6
1975	5.1	4.3	8.3	− 4.0
1976	5.2	5.6	7.6	− 2.0
1977	5.3	6.1	6.9	− 0.8
1978	5.1	5.9	6.0	− 0.1
1979	5.0	5.0	5.8	− 0.8
1980	5.7	6.4	7.0	− 0.6
1981	6.6	9.8	7.5	2.3
1982	8.0	11.3	9.5	1.8
1983	8.6	12.5	9.5	3.0
1984	8.2	12.8	7.4	5.4
1985	8.1	13.0	7.1	5.9
1986[a]	8.0	13.1	7.0	6.1

[a] January through March.

SOURCE: Organization for Economic Cooperation and Development, *Quarterly Labour*
          Force Statistics, 2 (1986): p. 78.

continued to build in Britain. The differences in the level of unemployment
help explain why Margaret Thatcher's popularity plummeted while Ronald
Reagan's reached unprecedented levels in the mid-1980s.

Changing economic structure exacerbated the employment problems of
displaced industrial workers and youth. On both sides of the Atlantic, the
demand for service workers outpaced the need for agricultural, mining,
construction, and manufacturing employees. The decline of industrial employment in Britain has been especially marked, and the British and American labor markets are more structurally similar now than in 1960 or even
1975 (table 2).

In both nations, regions once heavily dependent on mines and factories for
jobs have disproportionately long jobless queues. As it shrinks, industry does
not as easily absorb a large proportion of new, unskilled secondary school
graduates, a problem particularly acute in Britain, where fewer students
continue into higher education. Youth unemployment, about three times
greater than adult unemployment throughout the 1970s, has long been a

TABLE 2:   *Percent Distribution of Employment by Economic Sector, 1960–82.*

	AGRICULTURE[a]			INDUSTRY[b]			SERVICES[c]		
	U.S.	U.K.	U.S.–U.K.	U.S.	U.K.	U.S.–U.K.	U.S.	U.K.	U.S.–U.K.
1960	8.5	4.1	(4.4)	33.4	47.3	(15.9)	58.1	48.6	(9.5)
1975	4.1	2.7	(1.4)	29.5	39.2	(9.7)	66.4	58.0	(8.4)
1982[d]	3.6	2.9	(.7)	27.2	33.8	(6.6)	69.2	63.3	(5.9)

[a] Agriculture, forestry, hunting, and fishing
[b] Manufacturing, mining, and construction
[c] Transportation, communication (public utilities, trade, finance, public administration, private household services, and miscellaneous services)
[d] Figures for the U.K. are estimates.
SOURCE: U.S. Bureau of Labor Statistics, May 1985.

the United States. In Britain, the ratio increased from twice to three times the adult rate between 1971 and 1976.[3] Of these jobless youths, more and more were inner city ethnic minorities—a target of American job programs since the War on Poverty of the 1960s.

Policymakers in both central governments found that they could apply only a limited set of policy techniques to rectify directly these employment problems; these similar technical limitations created a second source of pressure for policy convergence. In the 1960s and 1970s, top American and British officials viewed unemployment mainly as a macroeconomic problem amenable to Keynesian demand management. More aggregate spending would generate jobs. Neither government developed the extensive micro-economic tools used in France to intervene in industries or in Sweden to manage the labor market. Rising unemployment throughout the OECD cast doubt on the Keynesian consensus beginning in the mid-1970s. Those doubts gave credence to the conservative, free market diagnoses of Milton Friedman, Keith Joseph, and Arthur Laffer.

Beginning in the 1960s, both governments initiated small if ambitious job training initiatives to adapt workers to structural changes and economic expansion. Both governments consolidated these efforts in 1973. America's Comprehensive Employment and Training Act (CETA) drew together several job training programs into a federal-local grant arrangement, authorized funds for publically subsidized jobs, and lodged oversight responsibility in the Department of Labor's Employment and Training Administration (ETA).[4] Britain's Manpower Act created a tripartite Manpower Services Commission (MSC) answerable to the Employment ministry and responsible for employment and training schemes.[5] Both the ETA and the MSC had absorbed unexpected expansion in their activities and budgets by the end of the 1970s.

Moreover, the employment and training programs of this period left a similar record of ambiguous results and controversy in both countries. The goals of labor market policy remain complex and only superficially consensual. While few would quarrel with the aspiration to help the jobless obtain work, proponents of these programs often differed on tactics and measures of success. An example familiar to experts in both countries is "creaming" (that is, selecting the most job-ready candidates eligible for services) practiced by public employment offices, job training organizations, and subsidized employers. Creaming improves performance and placement statistics, but it excludes those for whom job services are most desperately needed, and for whom benefits could most dramatically exceed program costs. In addition, studies of job training showed graduates with rather modest gains in income, and revealed high dropout rates. Efforts to subsidize job creation, whether in private industry, nonprofit organizations, or local government, often lead to the substitution of subsidized employees for those on payrolls and thus fewer net jobs created. Sometimes fraud and political abuse accompanied subsidized employment.[6] By 1980, British and American labor market schemes had proved anything but unambiguous, indisputable successes in both nations.[7]

The press of unemployment coupled with inflation (and the limited effect of central government efforts to reduce these problems) contributed to the accession of the Thatcher and Reagan administrations, ideologically committed to radically conservative diagnoses and remedies for economic ills. The broad ideological similarity of these administrations exerted a third pressure favoring policy convergence. Both condemned unemployment, but officials in both governments gave more immediate attention to inflation than to joblessness.[8] What distinguished their ideology from conservative predecessors was the evocation of their nations' industrial adolescence as a model for economic renewal. When governments exercised less influence in markets, argued the two leaders, productivity and growth accelerated and those who truly sought work could find it. Government itself had become a major obstacle to full employment in an inflation-free economy by erecting barriers to broader market forces. Such interference maintained artificially high wages, reduced entrepreneurs' incentive to create jobs, and as a consequence restricted job creation.

These leaders preferred private initiative to public effort. Writers with the ear of the two governments damned the faults of predecessors' policy in strikingly similar language. The Employment and Training Administration, according to the influential Heritage Foundation, was "one of the poorest managed, confused, and directionless agencies in the government."[9] The secretary of state for employment in the new Thatcher government, wrote the *Economist*, should rein in the "extravagent and unemployment creating" Manpower Services Commission.[10] Keith Joseph ridiculed public job creation as "counting lamp posts,"[11] while CETA jobs were described as "leaf-raking." Both governments, then, promised drastic cuts in existing programs and institutions; what remained, they said, would promote entrepreneurship and the private sector.

These similar economic, technical, and ideological forces pressed American and British policymakers in the same direction in 1979–80. Despite such pressures to converge, the two governments pursued remarkably different remedies for labor market failure.

GREAT BRITAIN: LABOR MARKET SURGERY

Few in 1979 would have predicted that the Thatcher government would exert so much effort to govern British labor markets. One could have discerned in the Thatcher diagnosis of joblessness the need for intensive labor market surgery as a complement to the tenacious pursuit of monetarism. High joblessness spurred an active government stance that added millions of pounds to the Manpower Service Commission's budget and tried to restructure the MSC's employment schemes. All of these efforts emphasize private sector initiatives, the softening of wages, and the creation of a more flexible (even malleable) workforce.

For Thatcher loyalists such as Keith Joseph, Keynesian policies of demand stimulation had been a major cause of inflation, the "certain source of all conceivable economic, social, and political evils," including unemployment.[12] Too much money had circulated in Britain. A restriction of the money supply and a reduction of government interference in markets would set the economy right.

Well before the 1979 election, these Tories hinted that a shift from active to passive demand management would require a shift from a relatively passive to an active labor market policy. Paradoxically, the creation of "free" markets in late twentieth-century Britain depended on the government's ability to discipline the labor force.[13] Joseph specifically counted "the efficiency of the labor market [and] the rewards to work, enterprise, innovation and efficiency" as essential to a healthy economy. Britain's employment, welfare, and training laws had hardened Britain's economic arteries, preventing the lower wages that create employment. "[G]roups of workers can price themselves out of jobs," said Joseph in the mid-1970s.[14] The Conservative party election manifesto of 1979 promised to restore the "will to work." The manifesto notably broke with the postwar consensus by refusing to promise that a Thatcher government would seek full employment.[15]

The government doggedly held to its Riccardian analysis of high wages as the cause of unemployment. For Geoffrey Howe in 1981, the remedy was obvious: British employment could not improve without a lower standard of living.[16] Howe's successor, Nigel Lawson, blamed continuing high unemployment rates on the steady growth in real wages. Lawson held up Hong Kong, with low wages, little unionization, no unemployment insurance, and low taxes, as a model for a fully employed Britain.[17] The 1985 White Paper, *Employment: Challenge for the Nation,* sought a policy that would alter labor markets "so that people are neither prevented from pricing themselves into jobs nor deterred from taking them up."[18]

The diagnosis implied several remedies. Monetarism and privatization would in general make labor markets more competitive and eliminate artificially high (and often protected) wages in nationalized industries. British circumstances, though, included a highly unionized work force and many laws protecting jobs and wages. These circumstances compelled true monetarists to attack labor market "rigidities" head-on. The government energetically assaulted the unions in legislation and confrontations. The Employment Acts of 1980 and 1982, and the Trade Union Act of 1984 cumulatively undermined union power. Combined with the recession, the government's attack indeed placed British unions on the defensive, particularly after the Labour Party's 1983 election defeat.[19]

The government's labor market policy was delegated to Thatcher's most dedicated and capable lieutenants. Until the fall of 1981, the moderate Tory James Prior headed the Department of Employment. As a prominent "wet," his public reservations about the second Employment Act and his pressure for expansive MSC budgets contributed to the loss of his post in the 1981 Cabinet shake up.[20] His successor, Norman Tebbit, has proved in contrast "the most outspoken and agile Conservative hawk." Tebbitt served until late 1983, building a reputation as Thatcher's heir apparent.[21] Tom King succeeded Tebbit, and Kenneth Clark succeeded King.

The choice and subsequent career of David Young as chair of the Manpower Services Commission even more clearly illustrates the high priority of labor markets in the Thatcher government. Sir Richard O'Brien, MSC chair appointed by James Callaghan a month before the 1979 election, resisted Conservative suggestions of budget cuts very vigorously. In late 1981, several months before the completion of O'Brien's term, Tebbit (in a characteristic move) leaked his choice of Young to replace O'Brien, causing heated

76 *David B. Robertson*

TABLE 3: *Manpower Services Commission Expenditures, 1975–76 to 1987–88*

Calendar Year	Unemployment Rate	Fiscal Year	MSC Expenditure (millions of £)	Employment and Training Outlays as % of GDP[a]
1974	2.9	1974/75	125	0.15
1975	4.3	1975/76	249	0.23
1976	5.6	1976/77	430	0.35
1977	6.1	1977/78	544	0.39
1978	5.9	1978/79	641	0.41
1979	5.0	1979/80	727	0.41
1980	6.4	1980/81	869	0.43
1981	9.8	1981/82	1111	0.51
1982	11.3	1982/83	1337	0.57
1983	12.5	1983/84	1769	0.69
1984	12.8	1984/85	2066	0.76
1985	13.0	1985/86	2262[b]	n.a.
1986	13.1	1986/87	2375[c]	n.a.
		1987/88	2405[c]	n.a.

[a] Column 4 plus Mobility Allowances paid through National Insurance; Gross Domestic Product measured on an expenditures basis for calendar year beginning three months prior to budget year. Using GDP measured on an incomes basis yields effort that ranges from .47 in 1979–80 to .87 in 1984–1985. For income-based GDP, see below, Central Statistical Office, table 14.1.
[b] Estimate, MSC
[c] Estimate, 1985 Public Expenditure White Paper

SOURCES: Table 1: Frank Coffield, "Is There Work after the MSC?," *New Society*, 26 January 1984: 128–130; *Manpower Services Commisson Annual Report, 1983/84* (London: MSC, 1984), 35, and *1984/85* (London: MSC, 1985), 40; *Manpower Services Commssion Corporate Plan, 1985–1989* (London: MSC, 1985), 8; Central Statistical Office, *Annual Abstract of Statistics* (London: HMSO, 1986), table 3.5; OECD, *Quarterly National Accounts* 1985, no. 4, 136.

complaints about Tebbit's secret, unilateral decision style. Young, who, like Tebbit, had advised Keith Joseph, drew fire as Tebbit's "hatchetman." Young proved far more conciliatory than many feared, softening Tebbit's tough stands and even resisting MSC staff cuts. Like Tebbit, Young significantly advanced his standing in the government through his contributions to labor market policy. In the fall of 1984 he was made a life peer, and Lord Young became minister without portfolio responsible for the government's employment program. Bryan Nicholson, of Rank Xerox corporation, succeeded Young.[22]

The government placed an increasing share of the nation's income in these officials' hands. Table 3 shows that spending on "active" labor market measures approached 1% of GDP in the mid-1980s, a trend in striking contrast to the austere fiscal policy of the Thatcher government. As a share of GDP, spending on these "active" measures grew four times faster than spending on "passive" unemployment insurance and supplemental benefits between 1981 and 1984.[23] The 1986-87 budget added even more to these projections, increasing the MSC budget £195 million in 1986–87 and £290 million in 1987–88.[24]

Prodded by persistent high unemployment, the government invested this money and talent in restructuring British labor markets. It attacked some institutions, shifted job training and job creation in the direction of Thatcher's ideology, and produced experimental schemes consistent with the goals of lowering wages, increasing entrepreneurship, and expanding the MSC's jurisdiction.

The assault on existing labor market institutions was more radical in intent than result, as cuts in the Industrial Training Boards (ITBs) demonstrate. Created in the mid-1960s to manage apprenticeship and training on an industrywide basis, two dozen such boards existed in 1980 (examples include the Engineering ITB and the Hotel and Catering ITB). The Boards' income included a levy on employers and a £51 million subsidy. ITBs had long been a target of right-wing Tories; Enoch Powell in 1971 decried the ITBs for "igniting a prairie of fire of bureaucracy and profligate spending"[25]. Prior announced plans to end their subsidy in 1980 and Tebbit enthusiastically pursued these cuts during his first months in office. While the Labour Party and some sections of the CBI rallied to the ITBs' cause, their defense proved less than fervent. The MSC thinly veiled its suspicion of the boards, nominally under its control, as bureaucratic competitors. The continuation of a government grant to seven of the larger boards owed much to the Confederation of Business and Industry, which disappointed Tebbit by objecting to voluntary, industrywide apprenticeship agreements that would permit some employers to undercut the wages of the larger firms.[26]

The Department of Employment overhauled and expanded other preexisting programs, also with modest success. The Youth Training Scheme (YTS) is by far the most often discussed and most expensive of the results. Reportedly, the prime minister viewed apprenticeship and vocational training in West Germany as a model for a more productive Britain,[27] and sought to recast the British system in a German mold. This impulse dovetailed with the social crisis brought on by urban riots, especially in inner cities with high youth unemployment rates. As rioting broke out in South London and Liverpool in June 1981, Prior announced a £51 billion package of employment measures guaranteeing a job to each unemployed teenager.[28] The 1981

White Paper, *A New Training Initiative*, reaffirmed the government's intent to expand programs and guarantee all young persons under eighteen the opportunity for continued full-time education or work experience and training.[29] By 1986–87 the government budgeted more than £850 million for the YTS.[30]

If the cost of this commitment and the very notion of a government guarantee strike an uncharacteristic note for the Thatcher government, the provisions of the schemes suited the government well. Enrolling youths in job training reduced the unemployment count and mitigated the government's most serious political difficulty.[31] Beyond the political benefits, such programs as the YTS illustrate the marriage of neoliberal ideology with aggressive labor market intervention. The program resembled a predecessor in that it was planned to pay stipends and training costs for unemployed sixteen- and seventeen-year-old school leavers. As announced, however, it would compel youths to participate, at the risk of losing supplemental unemployment benefit. Also as announced, youths would not receive a stipend of £23.50 a week as had been the case in an earlier program, but £15 a week, approximately the same as unemployment benefit.[32]

Withering criticism (the Trades Union Congress called the program "conscription") and the moderating influence of David Young caused Tebbit to back down in mid-1982, permitting the higher wage and requiring a much less draconian penalty for those refusing to sign on. Tebbit never relinquished the vision of YTS as a vehicle for a low-wage, productive Britain. The employment secretary in the fall of 1982 conducted discussions with several firms on the use of YTS trainees as surrogates for third-world labor. As Tebbit explained, "Britain is assembling components made cheaply in Korea and Taiwan"; in factories staffed by YTS participants, Britain "will now be able to make [components] itself at Korean and Taiwanese prices."[33] To achieve the goal of adequate YTS opportunities for all British youth by 1983, the MSC enlisted many local governments as well as private firms as trainers; but in 1984 the MSC drastically cut the same subsidies to local government, allocating these slots to the private sector over howls of local government and union protest. By the end of 1984, Prime Minister Thatcher again proposed to deny supplemental benefits to unemployed young persons refusing to enroll in the YTS.[34]

The Tory expansion and revamping of job creation is even more striking. The budget for 1979–80 produced by the government soon after the 1979 election contained no such expansion; it pared the Labour budget for job creation from £87 million to £54 million, and restricted the scheme to areas with the worst joblessness. In 1980 James Prior announced a new nationwide effort to direct private sector work subsidies that would encourage "sponsorship of projects involving community benefit." Prior's plans to expand job creation projected £122 million in 1982–83 and 1983–84. Tebbit added to the employment budget in late 1981.[35] Spending for MSC job creation schemes in fact rose to £86.6 million in 1981–82, £177 million in 1982–83, and exploded to a projected £625 million in 1987–88.[36]

As in the case of youth training, the government used these resources to deflect the political costs of rising unemployment and recast labor market governance. In March 1982, Geoffrey Howe's budget proposed a new scheme that created a furor. Howe's plan would channel £150 million into employers' overhead costs for any long-term jobless individual voluntarily willing to work for the equivalent of unemployment benefit plus £15 a week for expenses. Union leaders, particularly in local government, damned the effort as a source of cheap labor and lowered wages. The tripartite MSC backed a simple expansion of existing programs. In May and June, the MSC and Tebbit worked out a compromise: a new program that would emphasize part-time employment, but at a wage well above unemployment benefit. The MSC approved the new Community Programme in July, but its Trades Union Congress (TUC) representatives withheld their full endorsement. In the fall, some public employee unions and voluntary groups advised their members, who controlled many jobs which would be subsidized, to boycott the plan.[37] The MSC, now chaired by Young, considered "covert methods of circumventing the influence of trade unions and local authorities opposed to the programme."[38] By late 1983, two-thirds of the places in the Community Programme were part-time rather than full-time.[39]

The Thatcher government, then, enjoyed some success in redirecting youth training and job creation efforts in Britain, although necessary compromises limited original right-wing Tory impulses. Fewer obstacles restricted the smaller MSC schemes that more clearly reflect Thatcherite employment strategy of lowering wages and disaggregating the work force. Alan Walters, special economic advisor to the prime minister, designed a Young Workers Scheme that would subsidize (up to £15 a week) employers hiring unemployed youth, provided the employers held the wages paid these workers under £40 per week. This scheme sought to reduce youth wages and directly challenged Wages Councils, which generally set wage levels at £40 per week in the service industries (such as restaurants) that hire young persons in large numbers.[40] Ultimately the government exempted eighteen- to twenty-one-year-olds from Wages Council rates. After phasing out the Young Workers Scheme, the government introduced a similar scheme for older workers in 1986.[41]

Another example of neoliberal labor market activism is the Enterprise Allowance Scheme (EAS). For individuals with £1000 to invest in a business of their own, the EAS provided a weekly payment of £40 in lieu of unemployment benefit. This program consistently had more applicants than funds to serve them. As the prime minister noted in endorsing the expansion of this effort, most "people on the scheme continue to practice the trades from which they were made redundant."[42] Such a pattern suggests that the program may facilitate the "contracting out" of services by firms; rather than hire a window cleaner at full wages and benefits, for example, a firm can contract with a self-employed window cleaner at a lower cost. The extent of this practice in the Enterprise Allowance Scheme is unclear. The trend toward self-employment in Britain is marked. One in ten British workers was now self-employed in 1985, the highest percentage since 1921.[43]

Finally, the growth of MSC jurisdiction indicates the willingness of Thatcher loyalists to use government more actively as a labor market manager. When Employment Secretary King termed the MSC a "national training authority" in early 1984, he blessed a much more active MSC role in education. During 1984, the Employment Department transferred £65 million in vocational education funds from the control of local authorities to the MSC.[44] David Young thrust the MSC into the education of fourteen- to eighteen-year-olds with the Technical and Vocational Education Initiative, a pilot project begun in 1983. Young developed this initiative—in contrast to the YTS—without consulting the local education authorities (which the Thatcherites viewed as excessively autonomous), unions, or other participants. Despite implementation difficulties stemming from the MSC's unfamiliarity with education policy, and despite calls to refuse the grants dangled before local education authorities, 80 percent of these authorities had applied for the grants by the end of 1984. Two years later Young announced that this Education Initiative would be expanded nationwide.[45]

The Thatcher government committed money, talent, and the state's attention to active labor market manipulation. Three forces—unemployment, politics, and the technical limits of policy—helped to force the central government to act, but also held its radical propensities in check.

By August 1980, more than half of Britain's citizens believed that unemployment was the most serious problem facing the country. With the exception of the Falklands war, unemployment remained the public's top concern into 1986.[46] The urgency of the jobs problem, fueled by civil disorder, backbench Tory revolts, partisan attacks, and press coverage of all these, made pressure on the government difficult to resist. But the nature of the problem made the more theoretical Tory remedies impracticable. The government had to hold out jobs or the promise of jobs. The need for a direct response to the problem ruled out unorthodox, indirect wage-lowering policies without any demonstrable, immediate impact on joblessness.

Politics, both partisan and institutional, further hemmed in the more radical impulses of the Tory policymakers. A private sector strategy requires private sector cooperation, but the CBI had interests that sometimes diverged from those of the government. To create jobs, however low the wages, the MSC required the cooperation of organizations willing to give people jobs to do: business, unions, local government, voluntary organizations. The MSC itself would not unanimously endorse proposals unacceptable to the TUC representatives. The government compromised with these organizations and pursued programs less radical than it would have liked in order to assuage the sense of crisis and reduce its vulnerability to its opponents. As important as any accomplishment of the special measures, at least to officials in power, was the fact that these measures kept 350,000 persons off the jobless rolls by the spring of 1983, just before the general election.[47]

Finally, the limited range of unemployment remedies, and the ambiguous results they yield, have channeled the government's more radical impulses. Job training and community service jobs are obvious, direct solutions to unemployment. While the conservatives renamed and modified these programs, there is good evidence that endemic technical problems haunt them. Her Majesty's Inspectorate gave YTS a mixed verdict in mid-1984, noting the tendency for trainees to drop out prematurely, a lack of information about skills in demand, and a lack of integration among the institutions that implement the program. Researchers described as a "high pay-off" their finding that, of the jobs subsidized by the Young Workers Scheme, only 20 to 25 percent were "net new jobs," that is, jobs that would not have existed without a public subsidy. Fraud in the Community Programme made headlines in 1986.[48]

The perception of an unemployment crisis, political pressure to respond directly to the problem, and the inherent limitation of the techniques of direct response were at work in Washington as they were in Whitehall. In America, though, policymakers pursued a substantially different strategy.

THE UNITED STATES: LABOR MARKET ABANDONMENT

As a cure for unemployment and other maladies of the American economy, President Reagan prescribed less government. During his presidency, White House policymakers have displayed little faith in federal efforts to improve labor markets. Instead, the administration instinctively tried to terminate policies even as joblessness rose to record levels. When Congress insisted on action, the administration compromised, achieving greater policy devolution (as in the case of Job Training Partnership Act) or ensuring that federal efforts would be short-lived. With unemployment dropping after mid-1983, the administration returned to its early posture, trying to terminate old programs and blocking new ones.

In Reagan's view, the 1980 election confirmed a simple diagnosis of national economic problems. "Our government is too big and it spends too much," he told Congress in a dramatic speech after recovering from the attempt on his life.[49] Cutting the federal budget and the taxes raised to maintain it would overcome the economy's problems, according to the supply-side economists invoked as authorities by senior administration officials. George Gilder's *Wealth and Poverty* became a bible for such policymakers as David Stockman. For Gilder, increasing tax rates discouraged work effort and entrepreneurial drive, and therefore job creation. Budget and tax cuts would reverse this psychology, for these actions would galvanize risk-takers, who would invest capital, create new enterprises, and expand employment. Accepting the Republican presidential nomination, Reagan explained that "[w]e cannot have jobs unless people have both money to invest and the faith to invest it"; budget director Stockman echoed that view, saying that "[t]he whole thing is premised on faith," as he planned cuts in federal spending.[50]

In this analysis and in contrast to Thatcherite views, direct federal labor market manipulation remained largely irrelevant as an unemployment remedy. Certainly the public service jobs provided through the Comprehensive Employment and Training Act clashed with the Reagan view. Reagan was not alone in identifying CETA as the kind of discredited social policy effort that the government could drop. By 1981, CETA public jobs programs were an easy target for budget cutters. Few defended CETA in city halls, the media, or in Congress.[51] A more subtle point is that the supply-side approach does not prescribe a federal assault on wage levels, in contrast to Thatcher officials' repeated public complaints about high pay. Even for a glib president, exhortations to lower the standard of living could hardly be reconciled with carefully drawn images of national pride and prosperity, or with an economic theory premised on faith. Gilder mentioned minimum wages as an obstacle to employment in America, but viewed them as a mere symptom of a much more fundamental problem, high taxes.[52]

The Reagan administration's determination to return policy to state and local governments complemented its lack of enthusiasm for federal labor market intervention. Reagan sought greater state authority over social programs as California's governor. During his first year as president, federal grants to the states were pared and state and local discretion was increased. The unemployment rate of 8.9 percent at the end of 1981 did not deter devolution. Reagan's 1982 state of the union address emphasized the revolutionization of federalism, an emphasis that shaped the job training proposals made public several weeks later.[53]

The administration's personnel and budget decisions put these beliefs into practice in employment policy. In agencies such as the Department of Labor, and especially in subcabinet positions such as the Employment and Training Administration, appointees were carefully screened for their willingness to implement these principles. Unlike the labor economists, lawyers, and trade union leaders who had served in recent Republican and Democratic administrations, the new labor secretary Raymond J. Donovan had little expertise in employment policy. A construction executive, Donovan had chaired the 1980 Reagan campaign in New Jersey. Much of Donovan's term was devoted to fending off charges of improper actions, which contributed to his eventual indictment. The assistant secretary of labor in charge of the Employment and Training Administration, Albert Angrisani, managed the Reagan campaign in New Jersey. A management expert and a former vice-president of the Chase Manhattan Bank, Angrisani occupied himself with improving the reduced operations of his agency until resigning in late 1983.[54] Both officials served during the period of greatest concern over joblessness. A moderate Republican, William Brock, replaced Donovan in 1985.

These officials prepared to implement the deep budget cuts that Stockman planned for the Labor Department even before Reagan's inaugural. By March 1981, the Office of Management and Budget's revised budget for fiscal year 1982 included deeper cuts in the Labor Department (from $34.5 billion to $26.7 billion) than in any other agency. Even with unemployment at its peak (nearly 11 percent) in January, 1983, the Administration introduced a fiscal year 1984 budget that reduced the Employment and Training Administration's funds, proposing cuts in summer jobs for youth and in the Job Corps, a residential job training program created by the Great Society.

Table 4 shows that the Reagan administration's efforts proved successful. The Carter administration at first had expanded employment and training to stimulate the economy, but spending on such programs began to decline gradually after 1978. In spite of rising unemployment in 1983, the Reagan budgets dramatically accelerated this reduction. As a share of gross domestic product, these expenditures fell by two-thirds between 1980 and 1985.[55] The slight increases in 1985 and 1986 indicate funds carried over from preceding years, not new commitment. During the first Reagan term, Angrisani slashed the jurisdiction and personnel of the Employment and Training Administration and "in countless strong actions asserted his ideas throughout the agency."[56]

Events, particularly congressional pressure to respond to rising joblessness, tempered the administration's laissez-faire inclinations. The president

David B. Robertson

TABLE 4:   *Federal Employment and Training Expenditures, 1975–1988*

Calendar Year	Unemployment Rate	Fiscal Year[a]	Employment and Training Outlays (millions of $)[b]	% GDP[c]
1974	5.5	1975	4063	0.25
1975	8.3	1976	6288	0.39
1976	7.6	1977	6877[d]	0.49
1977	6.9	1978	10784	0.54
1978	6.0	1979	10833	0.48
1979	5.8	1980	10345	0.41
1980	7.0	1981	9241	0.34
1981	7.5	1982	5464	0.18
1982	9.5	1983	5295	0.17
1983	9.5	1984	4644	0.14
1984	7.4	1985	4972	0.13
1985	7.1	1986	5221[e]	0.13
1986	7.0	1987	4467[e]	n.a.
		1988	4357[e]	n.a.

[a] 1975–1976, ends June 30; 1977–1986, ends September 30

[b] Budget Function 504; includes job training, public service employment, Older Americans Employment in Department of Labor; Work Incentive (WIN) program in Department of Health and Human Services. Excludes tax expenditure through Targeted Jobs Tax Credit ($305 million in fiscal 1981 and an estimated $420 million in fiscal 1986). See Sar A. Levitan and Isaac Shapiro, "Federal Policies Affecting American Workers," unpublished mimeo.

[c] Gross Domestic Product, expenditures basis, preceding calendar year (in 1977–1986, calendar year and fiscal year overlap between October and December).

[d] An additional $1.9 billion was spent in the "transition quarter" (July–September, 1976).

[e] OMB estimate, 1987 budget document

SOURCES: Table 1; U.S. Office of Management and Budget, *Historical Tables, Budget of the United States Government* Fiscal Year 1987 (Washington: GPO, 1986), table 3.3; OECD, *Quarterly National Accounts* 1985, no. 4, 34.

approved new job training legislation in late 1982, two job creation programs in the following months, and a package of structural measures in early 1983. In each of these cases, the programs that emerged reflected the Reagan priorities.

The Job Training Partnership Act of 1982, the only significant labor market initiative approved in Reagan's first term, illustrates the administration's ambivalence towards a continued federal labor market role.[57] Preparing a new budget in 1981, Stockman "zeroed out" the remainder of the CETA program, thus proposing to terminate all federal funds for job training (at the time about $3 billion). Pressed too far, Labor Department officials secured a compromise from the Office of Management and Budget: in return for eliminating CETA, they could retain a reduced job training program. No administration bill appeared until March 1982. The bill authorized a $2.4 billion block grant to the states. Each state would establish a business-dominated council that would allocate the money. No federal funds could be used to provide stipends to trainees. Unenthusiastic Senate Republicans introduced it in the upper chamber as a courtesy. No Republican could be found to introduce it in the House of Representatives.[58]

Working closely with a wide range of experts and interest groups, the Senate and House subcomittee chairmen with jurisdiction over CETA had been crafting their own proposals for months. Republican Senator Dan Quayle of Indiana (a Midwestern state with acute employment difficulties) sought a consensus on job training and produced a bill cosponsored by Edward Kennedy as well as by very conservative Republicans. The Quayle bill authorized $3.9 billion a year and increased state and private sector participation while retaining a role for local governments. Quayle's House counterpart, Democratic Representative Augustus Hawkins of Los Angeles, represented a black, inner city area. His bill authorized $5 billion and guaranteed local government control, though it increased the advisory power of states and the private sector. The House proposal provided stipends to trainees; the Senate proposal severely restricted such payments to those receiving training.[59] Both houses agreed to protect certain programs such as the Job Corps, a favorite of Senator Orrin Hatch, the Utah Republican who chaired the full Senate Labor Committee.

In the three-way negotiations that ensued, and in implementing the Job Training Partnership Act after its passage in October 1982, the administration shifted the program toward a block grant. Bargaining on disputed provisions proved arduous. Stockman, anxious to approve employment legislation before the mid-term elections in November, helped persuade other administration officials to accept severe restrictions on stipends rather than an outright ban. In the final law, 70 percent of the funds were available only for job training.[60] While all sides agreed to increase business's role in job training (through local, business-dominated private industry councils with a potentially active local role), restrictions on stipends further enhanced the program's dependence on business, which could provide wages as well as skills to participants through on-the-job training.

Although the Senate and the House did not consider the program a block grant, the administration frustrated Congress by treating it as one. In preliminary guidelines prepared before the president's signature, the ETA as-

serted that "[t]he delivery system will reflect the block grant features of the
New Federalism . . . [t]he States will be given the maximum degree of
authority and discretion permitted by the law."[61] When the ETA proposed
minimal regulations in 1983, the Office of Management and Budget rejected
even those as too restrictive, prompting a congressional hearing. Robert
Guttman, who headed Quayle's subcommittee staff, conceded that "we did a
miserable job of explaining what we meant" in detailing the states' role and
its limits.[62]

If the Job Training Partnership Act reflects the Reagan administration's
disinterest in federally led labor market innovation, the job creation programs it accepted in 1982 and 1983 show that the administration took little
interest in reconstructing American labor markets. The administration's job
creation compromise took the form of accelerating public works projects and
funding block grants not controlled by the Labor Department. Democratic
candidates' successes in the 1982 elections eroded the objections of Congressional Republicans to job creation programs. The president remained
steadfast, at least in principle. While Reagan attacked past federal job
creation efforts in mid-November, he almost immediately endorsed a Department of Transportation plan to increase gasoline taxes, raise $5.5 billion, and
accelerate road and bridge repair projects. The administration insisted that
this program focus on highways, not jobs. Given the high cost of materials in
such public works projects, this claim contains a good deal of truth. By
August 1983, the Transportation Department estimated that the program had
created about 90,000 jobs, less than 1 percent of the number of unemployed.[63]

With unemployment nearing 11 percent and a more Democratic Congress
insisting on positive action in January 1983, the administration embraced job
creation, but on its own terms. These terms surfaced in the press within a
month: the acceleration of "already scheduled federal construction projects
that President Reagan says he favors," more humanitarian aid for the jobless
(through shelters and soup kitchens), and additional programs "to stimulate
jobs through the building of roads, airports, and other projects to improve the
flow of commerce." For their part, the Democrats were "eager to pass some
legislation, however limited, that the president can sign."[64] The Emergency
Jobs and Recession Relief Act, signed in March, provided $4.6 billion for job
creation.

The law funded a variety of public works projects, and authorized a billion
dollars worth of public works and public service employment through the
Community Development Block Grant Program (managed by the Department of Housing and Urban Development rather than Labor). The law
provided temporary funding for existing programs, bypassing the Employ-

ment and Training Administration. Moreover, the Housing and Urban Development officials spent the billion dollars for community development very slowly. Asked a year later about the expenditure, a HUD official conceded that it had spent $19 million in fiscal 1983, and "probably less than 20 percent" through March 1984. HUD's inspector general criticized the agency in the fall of 1984 for lax implementation. While HUD claimed its money had created 69,000 permanent jobs, the report found that 99 percent of these jobs were either nonexistent or substitutes for jobs that previously were locally financed.[65]

Not until two years into its term, under political pressure to act on joblessness, did the Administration present a set of measures designed to loosen labor market structure. Labor Department officials had disappointed Republicans in Congress in 1981 with a most ambivalent endorsement of a youth subminimum wage. As late as November 1982, the administration remained reluctant to press for such a measure.[66] Responding to the changed political calculus of 1983, Reagan proposed his own Employment Act, which included enterprise zones, the youth subminimum wage, and a plan to permit the unemployed to use jobless benefits as a "voucher" which private businesses could use to reduce their tax liability. Reagan, in a public comment, correlated rising teenage unemployment with increases in the minimum wage ($3.35 an hour in 1983), a rare and notably selective criticism of wage levels. The proposal for a summertime youth minimum wage of $2.50 an hour arrived stillborn in Congress. Unions and Democrats predictably opposed it, but so did influential congressional Republicans. The administration failed to persuade even the American Retail Association (a trade association that presumably would benefit) to rally to its cause. Its priorities elsewhere, the Reagan administration did not devote its best efforts to an active conservative policy to loosen labor markets. Ironically, the moderate William Brock took up the issue again after taking office in 1985, again with little success through 1986.[67]

With the decline in unemployment that began in early 1983, White House officials again took the offensive on budget and program cuts. As it had in previous budgets, the Office of Management and Budget called for terminating the Job Corps and training for workers displaced by international trade.[68] It also sought to end the Work Incentive (WIN) program (providing job training for welfare recipients) in the Department of Health and Human Services. In 1983, the administration proposed the transfer of a public jobs program for older Americans from the Labor Department to Health and Human Services, a change that would reduce the Employment and Training Administration budget by another $300 million.[69] Just prior to the 1984 election, Reagan did not hesitate to veto a three-year, $225 million scheme to employ young people in conservation projects. This American Conservation Corps created "make-work, dead-end" jobs in his view and constituted a "discredited approach to youth unemployment."[70]

In contrast to the Thatcher government, the Reagan administration refused to make new, long-term budgetary or program commitments to labor market management. Instead, American officials tried to disengage the federal government from labor markets. As in Britain, economic conditions, politics, and policy techniques moderated this strategy.

As unemployment rose in 1982, peaking at year's end, the sheer weight of the problem and public demands for action caused officials to retreat— temporarily—from single-minded budget cutting and devolution. At the beginning of 1983, three out of four Americans favored a federal jobs program even if it enlarged the budget deficit, and more than half the public disapproved of Reagan's performance as president.[71] Rhetoric alone would not mask or deflect the problem. Even David Stockman conceded the necessity of costly action. Given that imperative, these officials made the best of the situation, claiming as much credit as possible for programs they had originally opposed (for example, the Job Training Partnership Act). They made certain that new programs would reduce federal power over labor markets.

These officials faced a more daunting array of political obstacles than their conservative counterparts in the United Kingdom, for Congress and the Republican party are less compliant than Parliament and the Conservative party. Republican Senator Dan Quayle championed a restructured job training system rather than none at all. Fellow Republican Senator Orrin Hatch supported the Job Corps and helped ensure its survival. Even with its loyal political appointees, the Labor Department chafed at the prospect of losing its authority entirely. The natural inertia of American political institutions worked against the creation of small, controversial programs. While sluggish policymaking helped the AFL-CIO to suffocate the subminimum wage, few conservatives were willing to risk a "logrolling" agreement to establish a youth subminimum wage that would also raise the minimum wage for all adult workers. Within these institutional constraints, the Reagan administration maximized state discretion and minimized the role of the Labor Department, both as a job training manager and as a conduit for job creation funds.

Compelled by economic conditions, public opinion, and an anxious, independent Congress to deviate from the path of benign neglect, the administration found its technical options limited. Two decades of federal employment policy had created an extensive bipartisan network of employment professionals who would inevitably implement new legislation. Beyond the issues of state autonomy and stipend payments, the administration took in the Job Training Partnership Act what the experts gave it. Early evidence from the program suggests that job training in the new system operates about the way it did under CETA. In the area of job creation, the administration pursued the course of least resistance, accepting the simple temporary expansion of existing federal programs designed for other purposes. Reagan officials have characteristically not shown great interest in technical innovations that have yet to be tested. Rather, they have permitted states the discretion to experiment with new employment initiatives (and some have done so).

CONCLUSION: DISTINCT POLICY STRATEGIES

The similarity of the tone and policy attitudes of the Reagan and Thatcher governments strike any casual observer of recent American and British employment policy. Each administration viewed unemployment as one of a constellation of economic difficulties aggravated, not assuaged, by the employment initiatives of previous governments. Each criticized public jobs for the jobless, and praised the work ethic for welfare recipients. Each sought to transfer more responsibility for solving unemployment to the private sector from government; each sought to emulate business practice in remaining government responsibilities. High unemployment in the early 1980s compelled each to respond, and gave each the opportunity to translate its views into policy.

The policy responses of the Reagan and Thatcher government are similar enough to make the convergence hypothesis plausible. Each government installed top policy administrators generally loyal to its ideals and these officials made a public show of tightened management and strict performance measurement. Each has made ambitious cuts in those programs inconsistent with its ideology, such as CETA in the United States and the ITBs in Britain. Both governments tested the idea of taxing unemployment benefits and floated other proposals shocking in the context of extraordinarily high joblessness. Both tried to force the work ethic on welfare recipients. The Reagan administration did so by permitting the states to require many on welfare to work for these benefits. The Thatcher government encouraged those on the dole to work for voluntary agencies while drawing benefits. Education being less objectionable to conservatives than public jobs, both embraced job training. The best evidence for the convergence hypothesis is that both governments overhauled job training policy and created major, new, ostensibly permanent training schemes consistent with conservative views: the British Youth Training Scheme and the American Job Training Partnership Act.

Alone, this evidence suggests that American and British employment policy has converged since 1980. These facts, however, are not strong enough to counter evidence to the contrary. Even with both governments controlled by resolute free-market conservatives, Britain and America have responded to joblessness in different ways. British and American government policies grew notably more divergent in several respects by 1986. The British Manpower Services Commission expanded its budget and jurisdiction in the early 1980s, while the American Employment and Training Administration lost both authority and financial resources. Influential, skillful, and rapidly rising Tories crafted British employment schemes, while the Reagan administration relied on loyal but undistinguished amateurs to extract the federal government from labor market governance. The Thatcher appointees overhauled existing programmes, creating a Youth Training Scheme and a Community Programme molded more closely to its views, and experimented with a Tory version of an "active" labor market policy, creating the Young Workers' Scheme and Enterprise Allowance Scheme among other innovations. The Reagan administration resisted new programs. Forced to accept a new Job Training Parntership Act (JTPA) and a jobs creation program, it put little effort into managing or monitoring these initiatives.

Such differences undermine the convergence thesis, which holds that the Reagan and Thatcher years have made American and British unemployment policy more similar. Rather, these facts sustain the alternative view that the two governments have followed basically different conservative strategies for improving labor markets. At least three sets of circumstances help explain how similar principles could yield such distinct strategies.

First, unemployment rates of American proportions were a novel and shocking problem for Britain in the late 1970s and early 1980s. As a result, the perceived pressure for government intervention in Britain exceeded that at work in the United States, particularly when riots erupted in London and Liverpool but not in Detroit or Watts. Furthermore, British policymakers, committed to monetarism and economic austerity, had little evidence that high jobless rates would be short-lived. They were proved correct as unemployment rose relentlessly into the mid-1980s. In America, in contrast, unemployment declined in 1983 and 1984 to rates which, while high in comparison to 1972 and 1979, appeared mercifully low and a confirmation of laissez-faire. In its coupling of monetarism and increased labor market attention, the Thatcher government resembles not the Reagan administration but the Nixon-Ford administrations in 1974. In America, expecting unprecedentedly high joblessness, Federal Reserve Board chairman Arthur Burns in August of that year called for monetary and fiscal austerity and for a $4 billion federal job creation program.[72]

Second, British labor market policy, far more than American, shares many characteristics of policy in other Western European nations. This fact poses special policy constraints and opportunities for British conservatives. British labor law, pressed and defended by relatively powerful unions, closely governs apprenticeship, restricts dismissals, protects union activity, and explicitly requires such employer actions as notification of expected redundancies. By European standards, in one expert's view, American businesses "continue to have . . . an extraordinary freedom to lay off workers when orders shrink"; Western Europe has stressed job security over job mobility, while North America has emphasized job mobility.[73] At the same time its membership in the Common Market provides the British government with a source of funds for employment initiatives. The European Social Fund provided Britain with £321 million for employment measures in 1983, a larger share than any other member nation received.[74] Finally, continental nations, especially Germany, have provided model programs admired even by the prime minister and partially incorporated into British initiatives. In contrast, American initiatives such as JTPA owe virtually nothing to foreign models and everything to past lessons of success and failure.

Third, different political structures offered each conservative administration a different mix of opportunities and constraints. The Thatcherites took the helm of a relatively expeditious and centralized policymaking apparatus. The government could and did exercise discipline by preempting the independent influence of local government and quangos. Seen in this light, the expansion of the MSC into local education is part of the same fabric as the elimination of the Greater London Council. In contrast, the Reaganites faced a strong and still independent Congress, including a Senate that demanded a response to unemployment. In any event, the federal system offered American conservatives an alternative to centralized Toryism. American federalism is especially effective at braking social policy effort and at blocking impediments to business autonomy.[75] By devolving authority for social policy to the state governments, conservatives understood that federal employment funds would become part of the economic development "war between the states" to lure and keep business. Imprisoned in their own "common market" with borders that cannot be sealed against business flight and budgets vulnerable to recession, American states are disinclined to follow the defiant path of the GLC. The Reagan administration insisted on just those few legal provisions in JTPA that would prevent it from becoming an income maintenance program rather than a state-run business subsidy.

These circumstances grew no more similar between 1979 and 1986, and there is no evidence that they will grow more similar in the future. However, there is evidence of a shift in the nature of industrial capitalism itself, and consequently in the distribution of quality jobs. Increasing numbers of workers in jobs that are temporary, part-time, nonunion, low-paying, and insecure underscore the trend toward economic "dualism" in industrial democracies. Such jobs are located in the "secondary" sector of the economy in contrast to the "primary" sector, where jobs are secure and high-paying, and where workers are often unionized.[76] The Thatcher government held up the secondary labor market as an ideal solution for the jobless and essential for a more productive Britain. The prime minister invested considerable surgical effort to transform primary sector jobs into secondary sector jobs. By abandoning labor market governance, the Reagan administration has merely tolerated the growth of the secondary labor market and the erosion of government protections.[77]

By the mid-1980s, American policy entrepreneurs more aggressive than Raymond Donovan were attracted to elements of the Thatcher strategy, notably the Enterprise Allowance Scheme.[78] Stung into moderation by conservative successes, American policymakers may respond to future unemployment problems with programs sufficiently similar to those of the Thatcher government to merit another test of policy convergence.

NOTES

A preliminary version of this chapter was presented at the 1985 Meeting of the American Political Science Association. The author thanks Alfred Diamant, Jeremy Moon, Neil Mitchell, Jerold Waltman, Donley Studlar and two anonymous reviewers for generous comments on earlier drafts of this paper. Remaining errors and misinterpretations remain the author's responsibility.

1. David Cameron, "The Politics and Economics of the Business Cycle," in Thomas Ferguson and Joel Rogers, eds., *The Political Economy* (Armonk, NY: M.E. Sharpe, 1984), 237–62.
2. Similarity in rates masks differences in absolute numbers of unemployed, because the American labor force is more than four times larger than that of Great Britain. Using OECD figures, 8.7 million persons were unemployed in the U.S. in the first quarter of 1986, and 3.3 million were unemployed in Britain. At the American recession's peak in the first quarter of 1983, twelve and a quarter million Americans were jobless. OECD, *Quarterly Labour Force Statistics* 1986, no. 2, 13, 61.
3. Constance Sorrentino, "Unemployment in International Perspective," in Brian Showler and Adrian Sinfield, *The Workless State: Studies in Unemployment* (Oxford: Martin Robertson, 1981), 167–214.
4. Roger Davidson, *The Politics of Comprehensive Manpower Reform* (Baltimore: Johns Hopkins University Press, 1972).
5. P.J.C. Perry, *The Evolution of British Manpower Policy* (London: British Association for Commercial and Industrial Education, 1976); David J. Howells, "The

Manpower Services Commission: The First Five Years," *Public Administration* 58 (Autumn 1980): 305–32.

6. The technical problems of British programs are noted in S.D. Smith, "Evaluation of MSC Special Programmes," in Andrew McIntosh, ed., *Employment Policy in the United Kingdom and the United States* (Cambridge, MA: Abt Books, 1980); F.F. Ridley, "The Job Creation Programme: Administrative Problems of Implementation," *Public Administration* 58 (Autumn 1980): 261–85; and London *Sunday Times*, 6 July 1980, 62. For the U.S., see William Mirengoff and Lester Rindler, *CETA: Manpower Programs under Local Control* (Washington, D.C.: National Academy of Sciences, 1978); Grace A. Franklin and Randall B. Ripley, *CETA: Politics and Policy, 1973–82* (Knoxville, TN: University of Tennessee Press, 1984).

7. While liberals tend to exaggerate the accomplishments of employment programs, conservatives often overstate their failures. In his widely read book, *America's Hidden Success* (New York: Norton, 1983), John Schwarz offers evidence that CETA job training programs significantly boosted the earnings of trainees (50–3). He concedes, though, that a major study by the National Academy of Sciences yielded mixed results (54). These ambiguous evaluations permitted policy architects to use identical data to support and to question such programs. For example, Robert Guttman, a key Senate staff member who contributed to the design of the Job Training Partnership Act, had no quarrel with Senator Edward Kennedy's statistics on the CETA program; instead, Guttman viewed the results as too insubstantial to justify continuation of the status quo. See note 57.

8. Peter Riddell, *The Thatcher Government* (Oxford: Martin Robertson, 1985), pp. 57 ff.; Isabel V. Sawhill and Charles F. Stone, "The Economy: The Key to Success," in John L. Palmer and Isabel V. Sawhill, eds., *The Reagan Record* (Cambridge, MA: Ballinger, 1984), 69–106.

9. Charles L. Heatherly, ed., *Mandate for Leadership* (Washington: Heritage Foundation, 1980), 476.

10. *Economist*, 12 May 1979, 13.

11. *Daily Telegraph*, 12 April 1979, 1.

12. Keith Joseph, *Stranded on the Middle Ground?* (London: Centre for Policy Studies, 1976), 55.

13. Andrew Gamble, "The Free Economy and the Strong State: The Rise of the Social Market Economy," *Socialist Register* 16 (1979): 1–25, and *Britain in Decline* (London: Macmillan, 1981). Cf. Gary Marx, "The Revival of Laissez-Faire," in Richard Hodder-Williams and James Ceaser, eds., *Politics in Britain and the United States: Comparative Perspectives* (Durham, NC: Duke University Press, 1986), 28–54.

14. Joseph, *Stranded on the Middle Ground?*, 40, 52.

15. Jock Bruce-Gardyne, *Mrs. Thatcher's First Administration* (New York: St. Martin's, 1984), 28–29.

16. London *Times*, 16 October 1981, 1; cf. Riddell, *The Thatcher Government*, 66–68.

17. London *Times*, 3 October 1984, 19; *Sunday Times*, 5 August 1984, 45.

18. *Employment: Challenge for the Nation*, Cmnd. 9474 (London: HMSO, 1985), p. 14.

19. Riddell, *The Thatcher Government*, 186–91; cf. David Deaton, "The Labour Market and Industrial Relations Policy of the Thatcher Government," in David S.

Bell, ed., *The Conservative Government, 1979–1984: An Interim Report* (London: Croom Helm, 1985).

20. London *Times,* 11 August 1981, 1.
21. London *Times,* 17 October 1983, 1; 7 May 1984, 22.
22. *Sunday Times,* 12 February 1982, 4; 27 February 1983, 65; and April 10 1983, 62; London *Times,* 14 September 1984, 18.
23. Calculated by the author from the sources listed in table 3. Spending on unemployment-related benefits was £5008 million in 1983–84 (equal to 1.67 percent of GDP), still more than twice the sum devoted to active employment policies.
24. London *Times,* 19 March 1986, 22.
25. Perry, *Evolution of British Manpower Policy,* 276.
26. *Employment Gazette* 88 (August 1980): 821, and 89 (February 1981): 51; London *Times,* 3 August 1980, 18.
27. London *Times,* 2 December 1981, 1.
28. London *Times,* 8 July 1981, 1; 16 July 1981, 2.
29. *A New Training Initiative,* Cmnd. 8455 (London: HMSO, 1981).
30. *Manpower Services Commission Corporate Plan, 1985–1989* (London: MSC, 1985), 12.
31. In 1983, *Time Out* magazine published documents of the Central Policy Review Staff that indicated that the "essence of the [training guarantees] is to reduce the size of the labor force by raising to 17 the age of entry into the normal labor market," a move that would reduce registered unemployment (London *Times,* 19 May 1983, 2).
32. Jeremy Moon, "Policy Change in Direct Government Response to U.K. Unemployment," *Journal of Public Policy* 3 (August 1983): 301–10; Patricia Dutton, "YTS—Training for the Future," *Public Administration* 62 (Winter 1984): 483–94.
33. London *Sunday Times,* 12 September 1982, 2.
34. *Times Educational Supplement,* 30 March 1984, 17; 21 December 1984, 1. Anthony Lawson indicated his preference for withholding benefits the following year (*Economist,* 23 March 1985, 56).
35. Moon, *Policy Change,* 307; London *Times,* 22 November 1980, 11; *Employment Gazette* 89.3 (March 1981): 94; London *Times,* 2 December 1981, 1.
36. *Manpower Services Commission Annual Report, 1984–85* (London: MSC, 1985), 12.
37. *Employment Gazette* 90 (March 1982): 89; London *Times,* 3 May 1982, 5; London *Times,* 14 September 1982, 2.
38. Confidential MSC document quoted in London *Times,* 31 January 1983, 2.
39. *Employment Gazette* 92: 1 (January 1984): 31.
40. London *Times,* 30 July 1981, 19; 30 March 1985, 1. The 1986 budget included a "Restart" scheme subsidizing workers £20 for accepting a job paying less than £80 a week, and it revived the Young Workers Scheme for 18–20 year olds in a "New Workers Scheme"; London *Times,* 19 March 1986, 22.
41. S. Winyard, "Low Pay," in David S. Bell, ed., *The Conservative Government, 1979–1984; An Interim Report* (London: Croom Helm, 1985); Stephen Bazen, "Goodbye to Wages Councils?" *New Society* 71 (March 1985): pp. 485–86; London *Times,* 19 March 1986, 22.
42. London *Times,* 16 March 1983, 1, 8; London *Sunday Times,* 13 May 1984, 57.

43. *Economist*, 23 March 1985, 66.
44. *Employment Gazette* 92 (February 1984): 43; *Times Higher Education Supplement*, 27 July 1984, 3; *Times Educational Supplement*, 21 September 1984, 22.
45. Jeremy Moon and J.J. Richardson, "Policy-Making with a Difference? The Technical and Vocational Education Initiative," *Public Administration* 62:1 (Spring 1984): 23–33; *Times Educational Supplement*, 16 December 1984, 3; London *Times*, 3 July 1986, 5.
46. Jeremy Moon and J.J. Richardson, *Unemployment in the U.K.: Politics and Policies* (London: Gower, 1985), 56–57.
47. Riddell, *The Thatcher Government*, 75.
48. "Inspectors highlight flaws in YTS," *Times Educational Supplement*, 13 July 1984, 10; *Economist* 12 December 1984, 72; London *Times*, 15 April 1986, 2.
49. "President Reagan's Address on the Economy," *1981 Congressional Quarterly Almanac*, (28 April 1981), 20-E.
50. George Gilder, *Wealth and Poverty* (New York: Basic Books, 1981), 203–24, 304–15; William Greider, "The Education of David Stockman," *Atlantic Monthly*, December 1981, 27–54; "Acceptance Speech," *1980 Congressional Quarterly Almanac*, 17 July 1980, 37-B.
51. Donald C. Baumer and Carl E. Van Horn, *The Politics of Unemployment* (Washington: CQ Press, 1984), 160–61.
52. Gilder, *Wealth and Poverty*, 194. Minimum wages do tend to deprive ghetto business of cheap labor, in Gilder's view.
53. Congressional Quarterly, *Reagan's First Year* (Washington: Congressional Quarterly, 1982), 29, 62–3; "Reagan's State of the Union Address," *1982 Congressional Quarterly Almanac*, 5–E.
54. Richard P. Nathan, *The Administrative Presidency* (New York: John Wiley, 1983), 74–8; "Labor Department: It's in Business' Hands Now," *National Journal*, 25 April 1981, 726.
55. There is no evidence that the states have done much to cushion these cuts through funds of their own. The termination of CETA public service jobs coincided with an economic downturn that made financing of such efforts impossible for most financially strapped governments (Minnesota did launch a public jobs program during the recession). At most, one in four local CETA employees found permanent full-time jobs after the program ended (Baumer and Van Horn, *Politics of Unemployment*, 163–4). One test of state effort is Title III of the Job Training Partnership Act, which requires states to match Federal grants for assisting permanently "dislocated" workers. Only three of twenty states in a 1985 study actually appropriated additional funds to match the federal grant. Half claimed that the wages that employers paid to trainees constituted the match, and the rest used the value of ongoing related activities as the match; cf. Robert E. Cook et. al., *Implementing the Job Training Partnership Act: An Interim Report* (Rockville, MD: Westat, 1986), 9–18. During the recession, four states undertook new training initiatives with unemployment insurance trust funds, but none raised net employer tax rates to fund these programs; cf. U.S. Department of Labor, Employment and Training Administration, "Alternative Uses of Unemployment Insurance," unpublished mimeo, 17 March 1986.
56. Nathan, *Administrative Presidency*, 79; *Wall Street Journal*, 31 January 1983, 4. The most thorough study of the cutbacks in the Employment and Training

96   *David B. Robertson*

Administration is provided in Irene Rubin, *Shrinking the Federal Government* (New York: Longman, 1985), 77–100.

57. Information in the following four paragraphs was collected by the author in a series of interviews in the spring of 1982.
58. *Washington Post,* 11 March 1982, A27.
59. *Wall Street Journal,* 11 March 1982, 16.
60. Baumer and Van Horn, *Politics of Unemployment,* 177– 80.
61. "Job Training Partnership Act Preliminary Policy Guidance," U.S. Department of Labor, Employment, and Training Administration, 12 October 1982 (mimeograph).
62. *Employment and Training Reporter*, (22 June 1983): 1411–12.
63. Baumer and Van Horn, *Politics of Unemployment,* 167–8; *Employment and Training Reporter* 14 (24 August 1983): 1700.
64. *Wall Street Journal,* 11 February 1983, 3.
65. Baumer and Van Horn, *Politics of Unemployment,* 171; U.S. House of Representatives, Committee on Appropriations, Subcommittee on HUD-Independent Agencies, Hearings on *HUD—Independent Agencies Appropriations for 1985* (Washington, GPO, 1984), 341; Neal Peirce and Robert Guskind, "Reagan Budget Cutters Eye Community Development Block Grant Program on its 10th Birthday," *National Journal* 17 (5 January 1985): 12.
66. *Washington Post,* 25 March 1981, 17; *Employment and Training Reporter* 14 (24 November 1982): 301–2.
67. *National Journal* 15 (12 March 1983): 552–3; Bill Brock, "A Subminimum Wage is Worth Trying," *New York Times,* 2 June 1985, 2F.
68. "Labor Budget Seeks Trimmed Employment Aid," *Congressional Quarterly,* 9 February 1985, 258.
69. U.S. Senate, Committee on Labor and Human Resources, Subcommittee on Aging, Hearings on "Reauthorization of the Older Americans Act, 1984" (Washington: GPO, 1984), pp. 769–995.
70. *New York Times,* 31 October, 1984, 1.
71. Baumer and Van Horn, *Politics of Unemployment,* 168; "Disturbing Poll Data Prompting White House to Woo Alienated Voting Blocs," *National Journal* 15:10 (5 March 1983): 488–92.
72. U.S. Congress, Joint Economic Committee, Hearings on *Examination of the Economic Situation and Outlook* (Washington: GPO, 1974), 260–6.
73. Sorrentino, "Unemployment in International Perspective," 196.
74. *Employment Gazette* 92 (May 1984): 221.
75. Robert A. Goldwin and William A. Schambra, eds., *How Capitalistic is the Constitution?* (Washington: American Enterprise Institute, 1982), especially 49–74, 106–26.
76. On the dual economy, see the discussion by John H. Goldthorpe, "The End of Convergence: Corporatist and Dualist Tendencies in Modern Western Societies," in Goldthorpe, ed., *Order and Conflict in Contemporary Capitalism* (Oxford: Clarendon Press, 1984), 313–43.
77. Sar A. Levitan, Peter A. Carlson, and Isaac Shapiro, *Protecting American Workers: An Assessment of Government Programs* (Washington: Bureau of National Affairs, 1986).

78. Cathleen Steinbach, "Europeans Are Giving Unemployed an Opportunity to Become Entrepreneurs," *National Journal* 17 (9 March 1985): 527–9; *Employment and Training Reporter* 17 (21 May 1986): 914–6.

Changing the Course of Tax Policy: Convergence in Intent, Divergence in Practice

Jerold L. Waltman

Nowhere were the changes engineered by the Thatcher and Reagan administrations more significant than in tax policy. Committed to an economic ideology which rejected Keynesian demand management and embraced an emphasis on using taxes to increase productivity, within months of inauguration both had secured major cuts in income taxes. Initially, therefore, there was convergence in American and British tax policies, a congruence buttressed by frank admiration and acceptance of the same supply-side dogma as applied to taxes.[1]

Yet tax policy involves more than merely juggling a rate table and has ramifications reaching some distance beyond macroeconomic policy. Taxes have a direct impact on the government's budgetary situation as well as the distribution of wealth in society. To what degree did convergence also arise in these areas?

Before the question can be addressed fully we need to stake out some general information. First, a brief survey of the American and British tax systems is in order. Then a more detailed presentation can be given of the major tax policy changes wrought by the Conservatives and the Republicans. After that, we will be in a position to look more explicitly at the comparative outcomes.

AN OUTLINE OF TAX STRUCTURES

Comparing the American and British tax systems presents some difficulties, chiefly because of the former's federal structure.[2] Since state and local governments levy both consumption and income taxes, levies reserved to the central government in the United Kingdom, the use of aggregate data can be misleading. As for local government, the tax intake in both is about the same as a percentage of total taxes—in 1982 11.2 percent in the United States, 11.3 percent in the United Kingdom.[3] However, 100 percent of that was composed of property taxes in Britain, compared to 76.0 percent in the United States. Nonetheless, these problems are minor, and it is the state governments, absent in Britain, which introduce the greater problem. In 1982, they collected 17.7 percent of all American taxes, nearly half of which was from consumption taxes (48.6 percent) and over another third (36.6 percent) from income taxes. This means states collected 8.6 percent of all consumption taxes and 6.5 percent of all income taxes.

In spite of these difficulties, though, the central government is dominant in both countries and its economic strategy of greater consequence. For example, the United States central government collected 71.1 percent of all taxes while the British figure stood at 87.4 percent, a difference to be sure, but not one that negates any possibility of meaningful comparative analysis.

In 1982, all United States governments took in $923.1 billion compared to only $189 billion for Britain. Yet, on a per capita basis, Americans pay more. The numbers add up to $3,375 per British citizen and $3,978 for Americans. Nonetheless, the average American still pays a lower percentage of his income in taxes since incomes are higher in the United States.[4] If we examine taxes as a percentage of Gross Domestic Product (GDP), though, we can see that the British government extracts a rather larger percentage, 39.6 percent in 1982 compared to 30.5 percent for the United States. The composition of the tax structure of central governments and the revenue derived from the major taxes is remarkably similar in the aggregate. Income and consumption taxes, along with social security/social insurance levies or "contributions," make up 84 percent and 90 percent of British and American intake, respectively. Within these categories, however, there is marked variance. Income taxes (personal and corporate) account for 44.8 percent of America's taxes but only 38.0 percent of Britain's. The British derive 17.0 percent from social insurance levies and another 29.0 percent from consumption taxes. The comparable American figures are 27.8 percent and 17.5 percent. If, though, we analyze each tax type as a percentage of the GDP that it extracts the differences in income and social insurance taxes disappear. In Britain income taxes claim 15.0 percent of GDP, compared to 13.6 percent in the

U.S., and social insurance comes in at 6.7% for the U.K. and 8.4% for the U.S. It is in the area of consumption taxes that the differences are pronounced—Britain taxes more than twice the GDP for this category than the United States (11.5 percent to 5.3 percent). Thus, the major difference between the two nations is the much heavier reliance the British place on consumption taxes, a difference even more pronounced at the national level since these data include state and local levies.[5]

Both nations have a corporate income tax whose receipts are included above, but the personal income tax is the larger generator of revenue, over three times greater in Britain and six times greater in the United States. The structures of the two personal income taxes are not greatly different.[6] Income is defined in roughly analogous ways and a progressive rate schedule is employed above a certain base level. Britain has a system of personal allowances for single people and married men.[7] In 1984 these stood at £2,005 and £3,155 and since the Finance Act of 1977 have been automatically indexed to the inflation rate. There are no additional allowances for children as in the past, unless one is a single parent; however, the government provides cash child benefit allowances (which were restructured when the income tax allowance was abolished) to all families. The American law grants a $1,000 (now $1,040) exemption to each filer and each dependent claimed on the return.[8] In addition, an Earned Income Credit is available to those with a dependent child and a taxable income under $11,000. The purpose of all these provisions in both countries is to allow a subsistence income before taxation starts. Above these bases a series of progressive rates climbs through the various income levels. Earlier, both Britain and the United States taxed earned income at a lower rate than unearned, but the United States eliminated the distinction in 1981 and Britain followed suit in 1984.

Likewise, the social insurance taxes are quite similar, employees and employers both being subjected to a tax based on the employee's earnings. The levies are roughly equal, although both countries have occasionally made the employer pay more. This was accomplished in Britain by having a National Insurance Surcharge (now eliminated) and in the United States by the ingenious mechanism (now also abandoned) of raising both employee and employer rates but giving the employee an automatic credit when he earned his wages. In essence, whatever the name and whatever the rate, there are two taxes being levied: an income tax on the employee and a payroll tax on the employer.

It is in the levying of consumption taxes that the two nations diverge most clearly. While both levy a host of taxes on specific products—gasoline, alcohol, and tobacco being the favorites—Britain levies a Value Added Tax

(VAT).[9] In theory, this tax is levied at each stage of the production process for whatever value is added; in practice it can be viewed as a national sales tax. Its current rate is 15 percent, up from the two-tiered system of 8 percent and 12 percent, depending on the good or service, that prevailed before 1979. A variety of goods, primarily food not prepared on the premises, is exempt. The VAT accounts for most of the difference in the percentage of taxes collected from consumption. For example, in 1982 taxes on specific goods, excise taxes, accounted for 11.2 percent of the United States national government's revenue and 17.2 percent of Britain's; the VAT, though, provided 18.3 percent of the British total, with nothing comparable in the United States.[10]

TAX POLICIES OF THE THATCHER AND REAGAN ADMINISTRATIONS

Taxes affect aggregate demand by their total level and by their rates at various income levels. Manipulating these two factors has thus been a consistent theme of postwar demand management schemes on both sides of the Atlantic.[11] Fiscal policy designed to dampen inflation or stimulate spending, in short to "smooth out the business cycle," carried a set of maxims regarding the proper approach to tax policy.[12] Inasmuch as the income tax responded more readily to economic swings and was the most important tax, it was usually the one which was the focus of attention.

Supply-side economics alters this perspective, instead viewing tax policy as a penetration into microeconomic decision-making, decision-making which in turn affects the macroeconomy. "Supply-side economics stresses marginal tax rates, because supply-siders believe that taxation affects the economy by changing the incentives to work, save, invest, and take risks."[13] Though listed as equals, in practice the last two verbs seem dominant over the other two since supply-siders stress hardest the idea that if marginal rates are lowered investors will channel more funds into the capital pool, encouraging consequent innovation and growth. In time, they say, the increased productivity will lower prices and raise real wages.[14]

Whether or not this theory will work in the long run is not pertinent to our concerns here. What is important is the degree to which these ideas held sway among those responsible for tax policy and the manner in which all other considerations were relegated to secondary status. Prime Minister Thatcher's chancellor, Geoffrey Howe, pursued the approach almost like a zealot through all his budgets. Even when, during the deep recession with mounting unemployment, others deserted the fold and called for a return to demand stimulation, he steadfastly refused to move. In the United States, meanwhile,

Ronald Reagan put much of his political capital into securing massive reductions in income taxes. When faced with recession and unemployment, he, too, stuck to his guns and rejected the advice to change course.

The tenor of Howe's approach to public finance was set in his first budget, presented in June 1979. He opened by scoring the demand management policies of the past and held them responsible for most of the country's ills.

> Are we not driven to the conclusion that the notions of demand management, expanding public spending and "fine tuning" of the economy have now been tested almost to destruction? . . . (T)he poor performance of the British economy in recent years has not been due to a shortage of demand. We are suffering from a growing series of failures on the supply side of the economy. [15]

He left little doubt about what he intended to do about the condition. "Excessive rates of income tax bear a heavy responsibility for the lack-lustre performance of the British economy. We need, therefore, to cut income tax at all levels." [16]

Indeed, the budget's central thrust was designed to accomplish just that. For starters, the required increases in personal allowances were doubled, the effect of which was to exempt some taxpayers altogether and lower effective rates for everyone. In addition, the whole rate schedule was altered to make it less progressive. On top of that, the threshold over which the investment income surcharge began was also raised. [17] Finally, the basic rate, paid by all taxpayers, was reduced from 33 percent to 30 percent (although a small 25 percent band was left at the very bottom). In addition, Howe wanted it understood that this was merely "a first installment."

While lauding these income tax cuts as the "keystone" of Conservative policy, the chancellor made other important moves. First, the VAT was unified and raised to 15 percent, but certain goods remained exempt—food (not consumed on the premises), children's clothes, heating and light, public transport, and housing. Only gasoline saw a rise in excises; the others were exempted because of the new VAT rates. Public expenditure was slated to be slashed drastically, with reductions coming in most categories except health (although a rise in prescription and dental charges was included). Only defense and pensions were slated for increases. In addition, the size of the state was to be shrunk by the expedient of selling off government assets, £1 billion worth alone in the coming year. Thus, even though income taxes were reduced substantially, these other changes actually lowered the deficit or Public Sector Borrowing Requirement (PSBR). It had been slated to reach £10 billion but was now targeted for £8.25 billion, a full 1 percent reduction in its relation to GDP, making it 4.5 percent. Moreover, Howe stressed that the target was to reduce this still further in coming years.

Subsequent budgets were largely a replay of the 1979 measure, consolidating these policies still further. In 1980, new expenditure cuts were announced for all areas except defense, law and order, and health, where increases were granted (although again there were new charges for prescriptions, now totaling £1).[18] This time around there were also additions to excise taxes—primarily alcohol, tobacco, and gasoline—mostly, it should be noted, to keep them in line with inflation. On the income tax front, personal allowances were upped by the required 18 percent, a small attack was launched on fringe benefits,[19] especially for the higher-paid, and the 25 percent rate band was eliminated. Although last year's PSBR had exceeded the estimate, the new target was £8.5 billion, 4 percent of GDP.

By the spring of 1981, Britain was headed for its grimmest economic year since the end of rationing. Total output was down 2.5 percent, spreading unemployment and malaise in any number of directions. 1981 was the year that would witness the shocking riots in Brixton and Toxteth by the summer. The budget was affected by the recession in that increasing public expenditures and decreasing taxes sent the projected PSBR from £8.5 to £13.5 billion.[20] Political pressures mounted in Conservative ranks to reflate the economy but Howe remained adamant. Expenditure must be slashed even further, he held, but with the spectre of a growing PSBR he had to resort to higher taxes. Raises were concentrated, though, in the consumption area, the only concession to income tax hikes being freezing the scheduled raises in personal allowances. Alcohol and tobacco levies were increased, along with a host of minor taxes. The largest increases were saved for gasoline, though, upping its excise by 20p. This touched off a backbench rebellion and, in spite of a three-day arm-twisting session by Thatcher and a three-line whip (the most severe), thirty (of 336) Conservative MPs deserted on the key vote.[21]

When the next budget speech was delivered the following March, things were much rosier.[22] A recovery was underway, easing the strain on the PSBR. The goal of a £10.5 billion PSBR for the year just ended had been met, and £9.5 billion was the aim for 1983. Small increases in expenditures were allowed, especially in the area of capital projects. Excise taxes were raised as usual, although the politically sensitive gasoline by only 9p, which with falling pump prices kept the retail price about the same. The National Insurance Surcharge on employers instituted by Labour was cut and personal allowances were raised by 14 percent instead of the required 12 percent. Last, the rate band at which the investment income surcharge began was raised by the same percentage.

Howe's final budget was yet another rerun.[23] With the recovery proceeding, the PSBR had fallen to £7.5 billion (2.75 percent of GDP) and it was hoped to keep that percentage for the next year which, because of growth, would amount to £8 billion. Self-congratulatory statements expounded on the virtues of expenditure cuts, but no new ones were proposed. Excises on alcohol and tobacco were again brought in line with inflation, but only 4p was added to gasoline. A new and more serious assault was begun on taxing fringe benefits. Allowances, the level at which all bands began, and the threshold for the investment income surcharge were all raised 14 percent, whereas only 5.5 percent was required.

The chancellor for Thatcher's second term, Nigel Lawson, left no doubt about his policies when he presented the 1984 budget. "There will be no letting up in our determination to defeat inflation. We shall continue the policies that we have followed consistently since 1979."[24] The PSBR had risen to £10 billion for FY 1983–84; however, the economic forecasts were bright and a requirement of only £7.25 billion was anticipated for the next year. Excise taxes were, as usual, adjusted for inflation; the VAT was broadened slightly to include building alterations and take-away food.[25] The National Insurance Surcharge was abolished altogether. Since the revenue picture was so encouraging, Lawson took a leaf from the 1979 budget and doubled the increase in personal allowances, 10.6 percent rather than 5.3 percent. In addition, all brackets of the income tax were moved up 5.3 percent. This clearly helped all taxpayers, but especially those at the bottom. To help those at the top, at the same time the 15 percent investment income surcharge was also eliminated.

American tax laws are not necessarily, and in fact usually are not, considered at the same time as the general budget. Moreover, the complex legislative process in the United States makes the outcomes appear less coherent. Yet Ronald Reagan chose economic policy to be the major policy thrust of his administration and the cornerstone of that was tax policy.

Within a few months he had proposed and obtained a number of major spending cuts, giving rise almost immediately to a campaign for an across-the-board 30 percent tax cut spread over three years. Additionally, he proposed several other changes in the tax code designed to spur investment. Following intense administration pressure and a national television appearance, Congress adopted most of his recommendations under the title of the Economic Recovery Tax Act of 1981 (ERTA).[26]

First, the rate cuts were trimmed only to 10 percent–10 percent–5 percent despite Democratic opposition. Beginning in 1985 the rates were also all to be indexed to inflation. The earned/unearned dichotomy was swept away, lowering the highest marginal rate from 70 percent to 50 percent. A few minor tax cutting items were also included, minor that is for their economic effects. A new deduction softened the "marriage penalty," child care credits became more generous, and charitable contributions were made easier to

take. Equally important was the argument for changing business depreciation and expanding the investment credit.

Since it was such a central part of the Reagan program, and had no
counterpart in Britain, a brief note is perhaps in order.[27] Depreciation for tax
purposes is the allocation of cost, not physical wear and tear or market
replacement value. In essence, if the depreciation period is shortened and/or
the rates allowed in earlier years increased, the effective cost of plant and
equipment goes down. This cost decrease is covered by an interest-free loan
from the government, since the tax will eventually be paid, just later.

As preparations began on the budget message due in early 1982, a
noticeable split developed within the administration. One faction argued that
the deficit brought about by the tax cuts was threatening economic health and
recovery. Either expenditures had to be cut, meaning a dimunition of Reagan's cherished defense buildup, or tax increases had to be sought. Since the
defense budget appeared sacrosanct and the income tax cuts had been
acquired by the use of so much political prestige, excises were the focus of
the proposed hikes. Another faction pressed for no tax increase whatever,
seeing such a move as a negation of the supply-side policy.[28] After months of
infighting, the president sided with the latter group, saying simply in his state
of the union address on 26 January 1982, "I have no intention of retreating
from our basic program of tax relief."[29]

Nonetheless, by the summer pressures were building to put more cash into
federal coffers. Skillfully, Reagan allowed members of Congress to shape the
bill, expressing only his desire that the income tax cuts not be rescinded. In
the end, what emerged—the Tax Equity and Fiscal Responsibility Act of
1982—had his blessing but had to be passed over the objections of many still
staunchly opposed to any tax increase.[30] Since the legislation had been
developed with no executive guidance, it was even more of a hodgepodge
than most American tax laws.[31] The cigarette excise was doubled, the
telephone excise was tripled (to 3 percent),[32] and a variety of air traffic
excises were hiked. The Federal Unemployment Tax, a payroll tax, was
raised. The major income tax alterations were ones making the medical
deduction harder to take and jettisoning the even more generous depreciation
provisions scheduled to take effect in 1985 and 1986.[33] Otherwise, the act
merely closed loopholes here and there and changed technical provisions.

In 1984 another tax act, this time labeled simply the Tax Reform Act of
1984, passed Congress with little direct guidance from the administration.[34]
It raised excises on distilled spirits and other assorted goods such as fishing
equipment and crossbow arrows. It also extended the telephone excise to
1987. As for the income tax, there were only a few minor changes. There
was, for the first time in a long while, a serious attempt to crack down on

fringe benefits; the ceiling for the Earned Income Credit was raised from $10,000 to $11,000; and some complex tax breaks scheduled to go into effect in 1984 were frozen. From the standpoint of policy this act did nothing to overturn ERTA.

The only other tax changes to occur during Reagan's first four years of tenure were the Highway Revenue Act of 1982 and the Social Security Amendments of 1983.[35] The former raised gasoline taxes from four cents to nine cents per gallon, the first hike in twenty-three years, with proceeds pledged to highway construction and maintenance. The latter upped the social security levy on both employees and employers in several steps and made one-half of the payments received by individuals with incomes over $20,000 subject to income tax.

Both nations converged therefore in their cutting of personal income tax rates substantially. Both also increased excise and consumption taxes, although the British did much more in this area. It is there that the analogy ends, though, as can be seen when the governmental budgetary picture is analyzed.

THE IMPACTS OF POLICY CHANGES: DEFICITS AND WEALTH DISTRIBUTION

The basic purpose of taxation was at one time the meeting of revenue needs, and this is still an important function of all levies. If we compare 1983 figures, it is evident that the British system is performing much better on this score. A total of £125.9 billion was taken in by all British governments to fund expenditures of £134.1 billion, a shortfall of only $8.2 billion or 6.1 percent of the total. In the United States, on the other hand, federal revenues provided $600.6 billion of an expenditure total of $796.0 billion, leaving $195.4 billion to be met by borrowing, which was a full 24.5 percent.[36] In short, Great Britain met 93.9 percent of its expenditures through taxes while the United States met only 75.5 percent. Three-year averages might yield better measures, but the picture is much the same: 92.2 percent furnished in Britain and 79.6 percent in the United States. Moreover, as one can clearly see, the trend line for the debt is down in Britain and up in the United States.

Deficits are a concern in and of themselves, but of equal importance is their relation to Gross Domestic Product (Table 1). Again, the American shortfall is noticeably bigger, and growing. In FY 1983 the British figure is about 3.3 percent of GDP while the American deficit goes to a staggering 10.2 percent, although it has since dropped. Furthermore, when the time dimension is introduced, using 1979 as a base for both, the results or the tendencies are in the opposite direction.

TABLE 1:   *Comparison of Deficits, 1979–84, (in billions of £s and $s)*

	U.K.[1]		U.S.[2]	
	Deficit	*% of GDP*	*Deficit*	*% of GDP*
1979	10	5.5	27.7	2
1980	13.5	6	59.6	3.8
1981	10.5	3.5	57.9	3.3
1982	7.5	2.8	110.6	6.2
1983	10	3.3	195.4	10.2
1984	10.5	3.3	185.3	4.8
				(est.)

Note: Does not include state and local borrowing in U.S., about $10 billion annually.

[1] From yearly Budget Statements.

[2] Compiled from *Economic Report of the President*, 1986. Deficit is for fiscal years and GDP for calendar years, but that is not a major problem (three months off).

The reasons for these differences are three. First, the defense expenditures the United States has made dwarfed the increases in Britain, even with the Falkland Islands campaign. In FY 1984, for example, the British budget called for £16.0 billion for defense while the United States was to spend $272.0 billion. Using a $1.50 exchange rate, the difference is monumental: the British still spend less than 10 percent of the American total. A comparison of the percentages of total government expenditures is equally one-sided. Britain's £16.0 billion translates into 11.9 percent of its total, whereas the United States figure is 29.4 percent. On a per capita basis the British spend £286 per citizen (about $429) while the United States spends $1,172. This alone accounts for most of the variance. In fact, if the British tripled their defense spending and did not raise taxes, the deficit figures would converge. The PSBR would come in at 24.2 percent of expenditures and 13.4 percent of GDP.[37]

The second factor has already been stressed: while Howe's first budget cut income taxes as much as Reagan's ERTA, at the same time he sharply raised the VAT. The result was that receipts from the VAT climbed from £6,697 billion in 1979 to £14,480 by 1982. Some of this, of course, was due to inflation, but by comparison excises, which ordinarily reflect inflation as noted, went from £8,042 to £12,911 billion in the same period. Applying the same percentage growth to the VAT (62.3 percent) gives a "normal" increase of £4,172 billion to £10,869. Thus, nearly £3 billion extra went into the Treasury.

TABLE 2:   *Tax Composition 1983 and 1984 (in Billions of National Currency).*

| | U.K. | | | | U.S. | | | |
	FY 1983	%	FY 1984	%	FY 1983	%	FY 1984	%
Income								
Tax	30.2	30.0	31.4	29.5	278.5[1]	46.4	282.7[1]	42.2
Social								
Insurance	18.5	15.5	21.2	19.9	209.0	34.8	239.5	35.7
Excises	11.7	11.6	13.3	12.5	24.1	4.0	23.1	3.4
VAT	13.9	13.8	15.5	14.5	—	—	—	—
Other	26.4	26.2	25.2	26.6	89.0	14.8	124.8	18.6
	100.8	100.0	106.6	100.0	600.6	100.0	670.1	100.0

SOURCE: *Financial Statement and Budget Report,* 1983–84 (U.K.); *The Budget for Fiscal Year 1985,* (U.S.).

[1] Since capital gains are not excluded from income tax in U.S. budgets, the same percent as OECD subtracted for 1982 was subtracted from the reported totals to make the figures comparable.

A final item, not as big as the other two but exercising some influence, has been the sale of government assets by the British. Both the Conservatives and the Republicans, of course, came into power vowing to reduce the size of the state. It was simply that the Conservatives had more national assets to sell as the federal government operates few services.

Tax composition is another element of revenue pictures and can be calculated for these two nations in two different ways. One is to include all taxes, as most OECD data do; or a comparison can be drawn between central governments, using only national budgets. Actually, though, both comparisons yield the same general results and tendencies. Table 2 presents the figures from the 1983 and 1984 budgets for the major taxes. Since, though, OECD data are more easily comparable, even if they deal with total taxes and are a little less current, they are used in the following analyses.

Personal income taxes account for 37.8 percent of all American taxes but only 28.4 percent of Britain's (Table 3).[38] Social security taxes yield 27.7 percent of the United States' total and 16.9 percent of the United Kingdom's, while all taxes on consumption make up 15.1 percent and 27.3 percent respectively. Within this last category, general consumption taxes were 13.4 percent in Britain and 6.6 percent in the United States; excises were 13.9 percent in Britain and 8.5 percent in the United States. Thus it is easy to see that the United States relies more heavily on income and social security taxes and the United Kingdom much more on consumption taxes, both general and specific.

TABLE 3: *Major Taxes as % of Total Taxes*

TAX	1982	
	U.K.	*U.S.*
Personal Income	28.4	37.8
Social Security	16.9	27.7
General Consumption	13.4	6.6
Excises	13.9	8.5
Total of these taxes	72.6	80.6

SOURCE: OECD

When these figures are examined from the perspective of GDP, a slightly different picture emerges (Table 4). Personal income taxes are almost identical, 11.2 percent in Britain and 11.5 percent in the United States. Social security contributions take 6.7 percent in Britain and 8.4 percent in the United States. All consumption taxes total 10.8 percent in Britain and 4.6 percent in the U.S., broken down by 5.3 percent for the VAT versus 2 percent for state sales taxes and 5.5 percent to 2.6 percent favoring Britain on specific excises. Thus, income taxes in both countries claim almost the same percentage, but with the United States holding a lead in social security taxes; nonetheless, the most marked contrast is still the consumption taxes, with the British percentage more than doubling the American one in both categories.

A legitimate question is how much Reagan and Thatcher have changed the tax structures of their countries. Table 5 uses 1978 as a base for comparison. So far, Thatcher clearly wins any contest to see who has wrought the most change. The American figures show only a slight rise in social security taxes with other amounts reasonably stable. The percentage of British taxes derived from personal income taxes, however, has declined somewhat and the VAT increase is noticeable. In contrast, though, the percentage of GDP claimed has gone down in none of the categories. The interesting conclusion this suggests is borne out by the aggregate figures: The British state extracted 33.5 percent of the GDP in 1978 but claimed 39.6 percent in 1982. (American figures are 29.8 percent and 30.5 percent, an insignificant difference.) In short, in spite of the rhetoric, Prime Minister Thatcher and her cohorts control more of Britain's economy than their predecessors did. A ten-year comparison, by the way, leads to the same result: 33.8 percent is the 1972 figure (29.2 percent in the United States).[39]

Analyzing the question of distribution necessitates linking taxes with public expenditures. This can be especially tricky because the studies are

TABLE 4:   *Major Taxes As % Of Gross Domestic Product*
1982

Tax	U.K.	U.S.
Personal Income	11.2	11.5
Social Security	6.7	8.4
General Consumption	5.3	2.0
Excises	5.5	2.6

SOURCE: OECD

TABLE 5:   *Effects of Thatcher/Reagan Tax Policy Changes*

Tax	U.K. 1978	1982	Change	U.S. 1978	1982	Change
Personal Income Tax						
% of Taxes	31.3	28.4	−2.9	36.4	37.8	+1.8
% of GDP	11.0	11.2	+0.2	10.3	11.5	+1.2
Social Security						
% of Taxes	18.0	16.9	−1.10	25.0	27.7	+2.7
% of GDP	6.0	6.7	+0.7	7.4	8.4	+1.0
General Consumption						
% of Taxes	9.1	13.4	+4.3	6.7	6.6	−0.1
% of GDP	3.0	5.3	+2.3	2.0	2.0	—
Excises						
% of Taxes	15.6	13.9	−1.70	8.3	8.5	+0.2
% of GDP	5.2	5.5	+0.3	2.5	2.6	+0.1

SOURCE: OECD

sporadic and seldom report data in comparable fashion. Hence, much will rest on inference.

The Congressional Budget Office released a study in April 1984 purporting to detail the effects of all spending and tax cuts since 1981 (Table 6).[40] As can be seen, the net benefits rise steadily as one moves up the income scale, with the lowest group actually suffering a decline. Moreover, if one takes the amount by which each over-$10,000 group is better off as a percentage of its income, the skew is even more pronounced.

The reasons for this result are not hard to see. If one cuts progressive tax

TABLE 6: *Annual effect of combined spending and tax cuts on various income groups (U.S.)*

	Under 10,000	10,000 – 20,000	INCOME 20,000 – 40,000	40,000 – 80,000	Over 80,000
Tax Cuts	20.	330.	1,200.	3,080.	8,390.
Loss of Cash Benefits	– 250.	– 210.	– 130.	– 90.	– 90.
Loss on Non-Cash Benefits	– 160.	– 90.	– 60.	– 80.	– 40.
Net Gain/Loss	– 390.	30.	1,010.	2,900.	8,270.
Gain as % of Income[1]	X	0.2%	3.37%	4.83%	6.89%

SOURCE: Congressional Budget Office. *New York Times,* 4 April, 1984, 1.

[1] Midpoint used. $120,000 used for over-$80,000 bracket.

rates by a uniform percentage, as the ERTA did, then larger cuts will accrue to upper-level taxpayers in absolute and percentage terms. If taxpayer A—earning $20,000, say, and paying a 20 percent effective tax rate—and taxpayer B—earning $100,000 and paying 40 percent—are both given a 10 percent tax rate cut, they end up paying 18 percent and 36 percent respectively. A $4,000 tax bill becomes $3,600 and a $40,000 one becomes $36,000. Taxpayer A has saved $400 or 2 percent of his income, while the more fortunate B has saved $4,000 or 4 percent of his income. Thus ERTA's 10–10–5 cut (23 percent in net terms since each year's percentages were calculated on the new base) reinforced these effects each year. If, furthermore, at the same time, expenditure cuts are made in programs tilted toward those at the bottom, the effects are cumulative. Hence, the $8,600 spread (– $390 to + $8,270) is not surprising.

In Britain the results are similar in some respects but different in others. Examining the 1979 budget, Michael O'Higgins concluded:

> Overall, the likely position is that because those in the bottom 20 per cent. of the income distribution are mainly pensioners, this 20 per cent. will be slightly better off, in relative if not in real terms; the next 20–30 per cent.—the relatively low paid . . .—will probably be relatively worse off. . . . Those in the top half of the distribution should generally improve their positions. . . . Those at the very top will gain considerably.[41]

TABLE 7:   *Comparative progressivity of income tax and value added tax − U.K.*
(1977 data)

Quintile	Income Tax % of Gross Income	VAT % of Disposable Income
Lowest	1.	2.45
2nd	9.	3.0
3rd	14.	3.25
4th	16.	3.4
Highest	19.	3.2

SOURCE: O'Higgins, "Distributive Impact," 494. Drawn from Central Statistical Office, *Economic Trends,* nos. 292 and 303.

Given the character of the subsequent budgets, there is little reason to suppose that these conclusions would not hold up throughout the period.

Much of the reason for the differential impact on those above the bottom 20 percent can be understood by studying Table 7. It shows that the income tax was much more progressive on *income* than the VAT, and this, remember, was when there was a distinction between nonluxury and luxury goods with rates at 8 percent and 12 percent. (Also, recall that food and a few other items were zero-rated, which accounts for the slight progression through the fourth quintile.) With the new and higher unified rate, and the cut in income taxes, the progressivity of the entire tax structure naturally shifted.

For those at the bottom in Britain, the better fate accorded them than their American counterparts is attributable at least in part to the pension increases granted by the budget.[42] Moreover, one should keep in mind that these people have access to free medical care in Britain (and most were exempt from the new charges begun under the Conservatives).

Yet this type of analysis begs several vital questions. Most important, analyzing budgets to ascertain their *relative* impact assumes that there was some justification for the original distribution. More crucial is how everyone stands after the changes. On that score, it can safely be said, without judgment, that neither country's policy is designed to bring about equality.

It is here that the fundamental questions of political values enter. These policies were purposely implemented in an attempt to raise everyone's *absolute* wealth. If the policies work, which is of course uncertain at the moment, it is a question of value choice whether or not those at or near the bottom are better off. Both Thatcher and Howe and Reagan and Regan (then secretary of the treasury) stressed openly that the production of wealth, not its distribution, was their principal aim. But that is not a universally shared set of priorities. Put simply, suppose that a pie has 100 pieces, and A has 12 and B 20; the pie gets 40 percent bigger, with 140 pieces, and A gets 14 slices while B now has 35. Is A better off? "What amounts of absolute gains (at the bottom of the distribution as well as the top) compensate for greater inequality?"[43]

CONCLUSION

Conceptually, cross-national policy convergence could result from the presence of overridingly similar socioeconomic variables or from political systems being subjected to parallel international events. According to one school of thought, for example, modernization produces analogous public policies.[44] In the two cases here of Great Britain and the United States, there were certainly a number of similar economic variables when the two chief executives came to power. However, it is simply not the case that these conditions dictated in any kind of deterministic way what tax policies would be pursued. Alternatively, there may be and probably are instances in which convergent policies are produced by political accident. That is, decision-makers in two systems engage in bargaining and trade-offs, with the resulting policies taking on similar outlines. However, that was equally far from the truth here.

In this instance, the convergence in the policy of income tax cuts clearly came from the ideological predispositions of the people in power—and equally clearly, from the saliency they attached to accomplishing the cuts. While neither Margaret Thatcher nor Ronald Reagan is a professional economist, from all evidence both are strongly committed to tax cuts as a way to stimulate economic growth. Whatever the virtues of the theory, they seem to hold it with conviction.

Prime Minister Thatcher assured the tax cuts by securing Geoffrey Howe, more committed perhaps than the prime minister to the supply-side/monetarist creed, as her chancellor and point man. Even when others deserted the "dry"[45] ship, Howe refused to budge and Thatcher stood by him, at least to the extent of letting him have his way with the budgets.[46] When Howe moved over to become foreign secretary, his successor, Nigel Lawson, was quick to voice his commitment to staying the course. Reagan accomplished his tax cuts through a combination of commitment, skill, and luck. American presidents can usually get one particular thing from Congress if they want it badly enough. By staking his political capital on tax and budget cuts, and helped by the disarray of the opposition, Reagan pushed them through

Congress relatively unscathed. And, by stilling for the most part the discordant voices within the administration and threatening a veto, he kept the general rate cuts intact. Convergence, then, has resulted from conscious ideological design and political will.

The convergence in income tax cuts, as we have seen, was not matched by convergence in other areas of governmental finance. The most conspicuous differences were the British rise in consumption taxes and the American expansion of defense spending, the combination of which sent the borrowing requirement down in the former and spiralling rapidly upward in the latter. Too, the British cuts seem to have affected those on the very bottom less than American policies. Instead, the burden fell on the British working poor, largely because of the increases in the VAT; in the United States, on the other hand, those with incomes slightly above the poverty level emerged a little better off than before.

Obviously, in one facet of impact, though, the results of these policies converged dramatically: The wealthy and the nearly wealthy were helped immensely. Benefitting little from the types of programs reduced by the budget cuts, and having higher marginal rates of income tax than the VAT in Britain, the general income tax cuts, much less those regarding investment income, produced substantial gains in disposable income. Economists will no doubt debate for some time whether these funds were used for capital improvements, and if so, to what effect.

Politically, these patterns of convergence and divergence seem to stem from two quite traditional explanations. The first is that ideas and perceptions shape policy. Anthony King argued several years ago that political culture was the major determinant of public policy.[47] After examining a range of policies (but not including taxes), he concluded that American and British policy, for example, take their contours largely because the citizens of the respective countries want them that way. But I think it goes beyond that, especially in this case.[48] At any given time there is something we might label the "prevailing public philosophy." It may be a well-articulated, all-encompassing theory of politics or a more vague and general set of ideas, but its function is that it shapes the political debate, even for those who do not share it. Progressivism in the United States in the years before World War I and Social Democracy in Britain after the second world war are cogent examples of dominant public philosophies. In the late 1970s and early 1980s both countries witnessed the ascendancy of what might be called the "conservative economic theory of politics," especially among elites.[49] With the election of Margaret Thatcher and Ronald Reagan, this public philosophy moved from the pages of journals of opinion to the seats of power.

The second explanation stresses the role of institutions. The seeming coherence of British policy and the forthright dealing with the PSBR are hard not to attribute at least in part to the processes of tax and budget policymaking.[50] Certainly there were voices in both the Reagan administration and Congress which argued for following the British example, although in truth few said as openly as Howe did that the burden should be shifted from income to consumption taxes. Nonetheless, the internal squabbling within the executive branch, coupled with Reagan's fear of alienating ardent Congressional tax cutters such as Representative Jack Kemp, led to the only tax increases being sporadic and conceived on no general principle. The extreme institutional fragmentation of the American system thus leads to comparative policy fragmentation.[51]

In sum, Ronald Reagan and Margaret Thatcher listened to economic advisers who had more in common than the same language. By a combination of determination and, especially in Reagan's case, luck, they both got the tax policies they desired. At the same time, Howe's commitment to consumption taxes and PSBR control was made policy through his own political standing and the policy levers he had under his control. The American policy machine produced only marginal changes after 1981 and left the country facing gargantuan deficits. Clearly, there was a convergence in intent. It may or may not be that the sought-after long-term growth will occur and give us convergence in economic result; in the meantime, though, there is significant divergence in governmental finance.

NOTES

This chapter was originally written in late 1984, before President Reagan began his campaign for general tax overhaul. Since following that episode would require extensive space, I decided to omit it and confine the chapter to its original time span. Nothing that has happened through the late summer of 1986, though, seems to me to alter the basic conclusions.

1. There has been a good bit of discussion concerning the similarities and differences between the Thatcher and Reagan economic philosophies. The chief similarities involve the desires of both to restore competitive capitalism and stop inflation. The Thatcherites put more emphasis, however, on monetary factors as the major strategic weapon, hoping to control inflation by lowering the rate of growth in the money supply. Reaganites, on the other hand, have been dubbed "supply-siders" in that their solution was to focus primarily on tax incentives as a way to increase production. Thus, tax policy was somewhat less important to British macroeconomic planners than to their American counterparts. Within the area of tax policy, though, the ideas of supply-side economics took as strong a hold in Britain as they did in the United States—at least to the extent of cutting

income tax rates. In addition to the second chapter in this volume, see Steven Schier and Norman Vig, "Reviving Capitalism: Macroeconomic Policies in Britain and the United States," in Norman Vig and Steven Schier, eds., *Political Economy in Advanced Industrial Societies* (New York: Holmes and Meier, 1985), chap. 8.

 2. Good general treatments of each nation's tax system are J.A. Kay and M.A. King, *The British Tax System,* 3rd ed. (Oxford: Oxford University Press, 1983) and Joseph Pechman, *Federal Tax Policy* 4th ed. (Washington: Brookings, 1984).

 3. These figures are from OECD, *Revenue Statistics of OECD Member Countries, 1965–1983* (Paris: OECD, 1984). To save countless footnotes, all data presented hereinafter are drawn from or calculated from this source unless otherwise indicated.

 4. Calculating median income figures is tricky at best. The latest close to comparable figures given in the *World Almanac* are U.S. (1984) $12,700, and U.K. (1983) $8,214.

 5. In the United States, 82.4 percent of all income taxes were collected by the federal government in 1982.

 6. This is not surprising inasmuch as the American law was drawn from the British act. See Jerold Waltman, *Copying Other Nations' Policies: Two American Case Studies* (Cambridge, Mass.: Schenkman, 1980), chap. 1.

 7. Under certain conditions married women may file separate returns if they have income attributable to them. This whole area of income taxation is vexing. On British difficulties, see Brian Abel-Smith, "Marriage, Parenthood, and Social Policy," *Policial Quarterly* 53 (July/September, 1982): 304–17.

 8. In the United States a joint return may be filed by a married couple, which in effect splits the income between them. In its early years, the American law was similar to the British, but people in community property states started filing two returns, getting double mileage out of the exemption and shifting income to lower rates. Congress, after several futile attempts to assign all the income to the husband, extended the benefit to everyone.

 9. See A.R. Prest, *Value Added Taxation: The Experience of the United Kingdom* (Washington: American Enterprise Institute for Public Policy Research, 1980).

10. The American figures would be a little lower in actuality. For some reason, the OECD did not include social security taxes in the American total; however, it would not alter the point (see table 137). A national VAT has been proposed several times in the United States. A national sales tax was debated seriously in 1921 and a VAT was proposed recently by former Senator Howard Baker. However, the most serious proposal was by President Nixon in the early seventies. See John Nolan, "Advantages of Value Added or Other Consumption Taxes at the Federal Level," *National Tax Journal* 25 (September 1972): 431–35.

11. See, among others, Michael Stewart, *The Jekyll and Hyde Years: Politics and Economic Policy Since 1964* (London: Dent, 1977) and Herbert Stein, *The Fiscal Revolution in America* (Chicago: University of Chicago Press, 1969).

12. For a general treatment, consult Robert Lekachman, *The Age of Keynes* (New York: Random House, 1966). For a view of the political ramifications, see James M. Buchanan and Richard Wagner, *Democracy in Deficit: The Political Legacy of Lord Keynes* (New York: Academic Press, 1977).

13. Paul Craig Roberts, *The Supply-Side Revolution: An Insider's Account of Policymaking in Washington* (Cambridge: Harvard University Press, 1984), 5.

Actually, this theory is not particularly novel. See Andrew Mellon, *Taxation: The People's Business* (New York: Macmillan, 1924).

14. Although this is not the place to enter the debate on the effects of supply-side economics, note should be made that John Schwarz has produced evidence from the late forties and fifties which demonstrates that there is no guarantee private sector growth will raise even the absolute incomes of those at or near the bottom. John Schwarz, *America's Hidden Success* (New York: Norton, 1983).

15. House of Commons (H.C.) *Debates,* 12 June 1979, cols. 239 and 240.

16. Ibid., col. 258.

17. The new threshold was to be £5,000.

18. H. C. *Debates,* 26 March 1980, cols. 1439–90.

19. The biggest fringe benefit is the provision of a company car. There is a "scale" which adds a certain amount to one's income depending on the value of the car. However, everyone agrees that the scales vastly understate the actual value of the benefit, especially for the more expensive cars. Further, as one climbs the income ladder, the progressive rate structure makes the benefit more valuable. As a result, 40 percent of new car sales are to companies for employee use; and it is estimated that 75 percent of all cars on British highways are subsidized to some extent. *Economist,* 29 March 1980, 32–34.

20. H. C. *Debates,* 10 March 1981, cols. 757–83. Note should also be made that the Clegg Commission, set up to study civil service pay, had recommended increases, which sent public spending beyond targeted amounts.

21. See *The Economist,* 21 March 1981, 33. This left the Government with only a fourteen vote majority.

22. H. C. *Debates,* 9 March 1982, cols. 726–58.

23. Ibid., 15 March 1983, cols. 134–57.

24. London *Times,* March 1984, 8.

25. When the VAT was introduced, prepared take-away food, such as the perennial favorite fish and chips, was left untaxed.

26. A thorough analysis of ERTA from a lawyer's and accountant's perspective is *Concise Explanation of the Economic Recovery Tax Act of 1981* (Englewood Cliffs, N.J.: Prentice Hall, 1981), report bulletin no. 16.

27. Until 1984 Britain allowed 100 percent write-off in the year of acquisition. A gradual phasing in of a straight line, four-year depreciation schedule was then put in place. This was coupled, though, with another round of corporate and small company rate reductions.

28. See, for example, *New York Times,* 30 December 1981, 1.

29. Ibid., 27 January 1982, 16.

30. See Ibid., 16 August 1982, 1.

31. See *Concise Explanation,* Extra Issue.

32. The telephone excise was to be "temporary," and to expire in 1985. But then it was put on in World War I as a "temporary" tax and suspended only briefly once thereafter.

33. The medical deduction had required taxpayers to subtract 3 percent of adjusted gross income from medical expenses. The new law upped that to 5 percent.

34. See *Explanation of the Tax Reform Act of 1984* (Englewood Cliffs, N. J.: Prentice-Hall, 1984), bulletin no. 13.

35. Technically, there was another law, the Interest and Dividend Compliance Act of 1983, a most interesting study in tax politics. The TEFRA of 1982 had required

withholding on interest and dividend payments and this law repealed that provision, over strong presidential objection and veto threats.

36. These numbers are based on actual budget figures for the United States and forecasts for the United Kingdom. The British Budget Speech is accompanied by the *Financial Statement and Budget Report* (popularly known as the Redbook). In the United States the executive recommendations to Congress, along with a summary of the previous year's budget is published as *Budget of the United States Government*. [After this essay was completed the final figures became available for the U.K. Since they made no difference for the point, I did not alter the text.]

37. Total estimated expenditures were £134.1 billion with a PSBR of £8.2 billion. (Redbook, 1983–84, Table 5.5) If one tripled defense to £48.0 billion it would add $32 billion to both expenditures and the PSBR, making them £166.1 billion and £40.2 billion respectively. The OECD estimates the British GDP at £299.7 billion. Thus: 40.2/166.1 = 24.2% and 40.2/299.7 = 13.4%.

38. These are 1982 figures unless noted otherwise.

39. The OECD estimate for 1983 is 38.3 percent.

40. New York *Times,* 4 April 1984, 1.

41. Michael O'Higgins, "The Distributive Impact of the Budget," *Political Quarterly* 50 (October-December 1979): 497.

42. Three cautions must be kept in mind when dealing with data such as these. First, the American data are only for income *groups.* They do *not* represent equal percentages of the population. Second, the age demographics of poverty may be so different that comparisons are meaningless. That is, the elderly in the U.S. may not be the bulk of the bottom 20 percent. Third, this says nothing about comparative absolute standing.

43. O'Higgins, "Distributive Impact," 498.

44. See, for example, Philips Cutright, "Political Structures, Economic Development and National Social Security Programs," *American Journal of Sociology* 70 (July 1965): 537–50.

45. The terms "wets" and "drys" reportedly developed when Thatcher referred to her critics as "all wet."

46. See *The Economist,* 14 March 1981, 21–35.

47. Anthony King, "Ideas, Institutions and the Policies of Governments: A Comparative Analysis," *British Journal of Political Science* 3 (July and October 1973): 291–313 and 409–423.

48. I have argued this point more extensively elsewhere, in "The Origins of the Federal Income Tax," *Mid-America* 62 (October 1980): 147–58.

49. By "public philosophy" I am referring to an elite phenomenon. Polls, for example, tend to show little shift in values by the general public in Britain or America. However, even a cursory reading of the elite journals of politics and opinion in either country will suffice to demonstrate a change in the framework of informed debate. See Samuel Beer, "In Search of a New Public Philosophy," in Anthony King, ed., *The New American Political System* (Washington: American Enterprise Institute, 1978).

This contrast between mass and elite opinion and change is not surprising inasmuch as virtually every study has shown that in the population at large there is a low level of political awareness and interest. For these attitudes to remain stable seems therefore likely. On the other hand, political elites read, think, and talk about politics and are more acutely aware of social and economic changes.

V. O. Key once argued that those who link the masses with their governors are the major instruments of democratic stability. Similarly, it does not seem unrealistic to contend that their ideas about the proper contours of public policy are also vital. V. O. Key, *Public Opinion and American Democracy* (New York: Knopf, 1961), 536–43.

50. On British tax policy making see Ann Robinson and Cedric Sandford, *Tax Policy-Making in the United Kingdom: A Study of Rationality, Ideology, and Politics* (London: Heinemann, 1983).

51. On the formation of U.S. tax policy, see Thomas Reese, *The Politics of Taxation* (Westport, Conn.: Quorum Books, 1980); Susan B. Hansen, *The Politics of Taxation: Revenue Without Representation* (New York: Praeger, 1983); and John Witte, *The Politics and Development of the Federal Income Tax* (Madison: University of Wisconsin Press, 1985).

Energy Policy in the United States and Britain

Joseph R. Rudolph, Jr.

No concern is more important to a country's economic life than energy. As historians and political scientists alike have observed, throughout history civilizations have rested on and reflected their energy bases. Thousands of years ago, and separated by nearly half of the world, the Aztecs and Egyptians erected their respective pyramids with slave labor. A hundred years ago, on opposite sides of the Atlantic, the United States and Britain enjoyed a significant edge over most of their competitors in the industrial revolution by virtue of their indigenous coal holdings.[1] In this century America left Britain economically behind, at least in part because only America of the two then possessed oil and gas reserves. These clean and more efficient energy sources not only fueled upward mobility in America when the industrialization process accelerated but, together with the internal combustion engine, provided Americans with enhanced geographical mobility as well. As America's energy base altered, so too did American politics. Old King Coal lost its political influence during the interwar period, and the country's large and often internationally prominent oil companies began to gain political influence and reap benefits from the political process.[2]

The discovery of oil and gas in Britain's North Sea during the late 1960s has had a similar effect on the United Kingdom's energy profile, political economy, and political process during the last decade. The budgets of the Thatcher government have depended heavily on full production of oil in the North Sea, and the manner in which the government has utilized the wealth generated by that oil has, not surprisingly, become an important subject of partisan debate in Great Britain. During the 1983 parliamentary elections, for example, the Liberal-SDP alliance repeatedly charged that three-fourths of the revenue from oil and gas sales had to go to support the growing number of unemployed workers resulting from Thatcher's economic policies.[3] The Labour Party contented itself with stressing that "Britain would be lost without oil."[4] Nor were such charges without foundation. The declining per barrel value of Britain's oil exports during the early 1980s had a profound impact on both the country's public debt and the international value of the pound sterling. The three-dollar-per-barrel drop in the price of oil between 1982 and 1984 alone cost the government over half a billion pounds in lost income, aggravating the country's balance of payments position in the bargain. It also accounted for a substantial amount of the 40 percent depreciation of the pound during this period, just as the prior period of high oil prices had contributed to an overvalued pound.[5] Indeed, by the mid-decade the British economy in general and the currency's value in particular had become so sensitive to the international price of oil that even the expectation of further sharp drops in the price of oil caused, in early 1985, a plunge in stock prices in London and pushed the pound to an all-time low against the American dollar.[6]

In short, for the United States and the United Kingdom, as well as for other advanced industrial countries, developing a sound energy policy has become a basic part of managing the political economy. Yet since 1980 there has been a pronounced decline in concern with energy policy as energy policy in both the United States and the United Kingdom. Neither in Britain's 1983 parliamentary election nor during America's 1984 presidential campaign did energy policy receive any explicit attention by the candidates. In part, this state of affairs reflected the fact that the American and British publics are much less concerned with energy as a political problem today than they were a decade ago. But from another vantage point the recent decline in the importance attached to energy policymaking in the United States and the United Kingdom represents only the most visible of a series of recent similarities linking these two countries in the area of energy and energy policymaking.

In this chapter we will explore why there has been this recent convergence of energy policy (and nonpolicy) and energy policymaking in America and the United Kingdom. Our major inquiry is the extent to which this convergence reflects basic similarities in the energy profiles and energy policymaking processes in the two countries or constitutes only a momentary instance of convergence basically at odds with the underlying differences in the environment, actors, and issues involved in the energy decision-making process in the United States and the United Kingdom.

ENERGY AND THE POLITICIZATION OF ENERGY IN THE U.S. AND U.K.

Peacetime concern with energy as an explicit area for policymaking is a recent development in the United States and the United Kingdom, dating essentially from the oil crisis of 1973. It was then that the Western world discovered not only that OPEC could exploit a tight energy market for economic gain (the price of oil quadrupled during the fall of 1973) but that oil could also be used for political blackmail.[7] Prior to that time, energy seemed so easily available, either at home or abroad, and the Vienna-based Organization of Petroleum Exporting Countries seemed so insignificant (the Swiss did not even deem it important enough to permit it to open its headquarters in Geneva) that neither the United States nor Britain found it necessary to develop anything remotely resembling a cohesive and comprehensive energy policy for the oil, gas, coal, and nuclear industries supplying the energy on which their respective economies depended. Nor did either state develop an integrative energy policy after this first "energy crisis." Given their broad domestic energy bases, their governments had the luxury of considering many options in responding to the events of 1973, while governments elsewhere usually faced the necessity of pushing the one or two domestic sources available to reduce dependency on imported energy. Yet this shared luxury could not alone produce a convergence of energy policy in the United States and the United Kingdom, for the development of an indigenous four-fuel system occurred much later in the United Kingdom than in the United States—indeed, it was still developing in Britain in 1973!—and in a quite different context.

By the 1950s the United States already possessed large gas, coal, and oil industries, each dominated by private sector actors and all playing major roles in the country's energy profile. Some of the energy sectors were, and still are, more regulated than others. Gas, for example, has been the most controlled of the fossil fuels because of its end use in public utilities, which are state-granted monopolies in the United States. However, only the country's nuclear power industry has ever been brought under tight public control, and then initially only within the framework of an agency, the Atomic Energy Commission, charged with promoting as well as regulating the peaceful use of nuclear power. Even today the public sector contracts with the private sector in order to develop nuclear power for electrification purposes, and although such plants are tightly supervised by state and federal agencies in America, they are not a part of the public sector itself.

In contrast to developments in America, the United Kingdom's government became actively involved, *as management,* in most of the energy sectors of post-World War II Britain. In 1945–47, the government acquired all private electrical firms and nationalized the coal industry. The creation of the United Kingdom Atomic Energy Authority (UKAEA) in 1954 brought nuclear energy thoroughly into the public realm, and when oil and gas were discovered in the North Sea in the following decade, the government entered these areas as well. The petroleum industry did not come under full state control until 1975, when the North Sea began producing oil and when the Petroleum and Submarine Pipelines Act was passed. This act created the British National Oil Corporation (BNOC), provided it with the right to purchase 51 percent of the oil produced in Britain's continental shelf, and allowed it to engage in its own exploration, development, and production ventures. Gas had been subjected to similar controls in 1972, when the British Gas Company (BGC) was incorporated to replace the system of area gas boards brought under public control in 1949.

Despite the state's far greater and more direct involvement in energy in Britain than in the United States, neither country entered the 1970s with an overall energy policy. Rather, both possessed a variety of "fuel policies" concerned with the relationship between government and the specific (private or public) industry in each of their respective fuel areas. Moreover, to the extent that either country had an energy policy at all, the policy tended to be the by-product of other concerns; for example, national security considerations (encouraging a security of supply policy, even at high energy costs), environmental goals (discouraging the development of environmentally threatening energy sources), and consumer demands (such as for cheap electricity). As long as it was possible to supplement domestic energy supplies with a modest amount of seemingly secure, inexpensive oil purchased abroad, there seemed to be little reason for either country to develop a comprehensive energy policy.

Unfortunately for the United Kingdom and the United States, the difficult policy choices involved in energy planning could not be postponed indefinitely. In America, postwar energy self-sufficiency was steadily giving way to increased energy dependency as energy demand accelerated with postwar economic growth, jumping substantially during the 1968–1973 economic boom in the Western world. In the process, imported oil, especially from Middle Eastern producers, was becoming an increasingly important source of the energy being utilized. In Britain, as in that part of the postwar industrial world where self-sufficiency *never* existed, energy dependency reached alarming proportions. On the eve of the 1973 oil crisis, Britain was using oil for over half of its total energy needs (52.1 percent), and—with the North Sea still not producing—importing all of it. The United States was using oil for nearly 45 percent of its total energy needs by the same point, though at the time only importing approximately a third of it. Had Britain accelerated the development of its North Sea, or the United States pushed harder the development of the Alaska pipline, the energy dependency of these two countries could have been reduced during this period; however, the era of energy abundance worldwide was ending. The chronic surplus of oil on the world market during the 1950–1970 period was gone, and the cartel of Western oil companies which had so long dominated the international petroleum market was rapidly losing its ability to control oil production in individual countries or the price of oil. An oil-producing state could now find other petroleum companies eager to produce and sell its oil for it, and give it a larger share of the profits than the amount established by the cartel. By the early 1970s, it was a seller's market.

The October 1973 war in the Middle East brought these developments together when, in rapid succession, the United States supplied Israel with military equipment during the course of the war, the Arab oil producers declared an oil embargo on the United States and other countries sympathetic to Israel, Western oil purchasers panicked and jumped into the spot market to buy all available oil, and the Arab and non-Arab members of OPEC seized this moment of almost total Western disarray to establish their control over the production of oil and the price of oil on the world market. Quite literally overnight, OPEC quadrupled the cost of imported oil, from less than three dollars a barrel to nearly twelve dollars a barrel, and such was the panic in the energy-importing, policy-less Western countries that many exporters were able to get *double the new price* on the spot market. Yet even without the 1973 war, it is doubtful whether the West could have long avoided an oil crisis of significant proportions and similar consequences. Growing energy dependency by Western oil importers on OPEC producers represented a high degree of vulnerability because the consumers had nothing to offer the producers which OPEC states needed or wanted as much as the West needed the energy OPEC had to sell. In the international arena, vulnerability is usually exploited.

Whatever its origins, the oil crisis of 1973 represents a major point in the twentieth-century history of Western civilization. In undisputable form, it exposed the fragile nature of the oil-based, energy intensive Western industrial world—modern societies, perhaps for the first time in history, resting on energy sources beyond their control. Quality of life considerations, such as environmental cleanliness, were suddenly reduced in priority, if not dropped altogether, as high oil prices ushered in a period of stagflation throughout the oil-importing world. Foreign policy vis-a-vis the Arab-Israeli conflict was reassessed and modified by virtually every Western country. The United States adopted a more "even-handed" position in dealing with the conflict and assumed a broker role in it; other Western countries, with a far greater dependency on foreign oil, rather nakedly adopted the Arab position that Israel's occupation of the lands seized during the 1967 Arab-Israeli war constituted an illegal act and should be abandoned forthwith. Above all, in the United States and the United Kingdom, as elsewhere, energy became an issue of importance on both the public and governmental agendas. However, the initial policy moves in Britain and America differed substantially, and largely in accordance with the differing national perceptions of the meaning of the energy crisis.

In the United States, a global superpower with global obligations, the oil crisis was seen not just as marking the end of an era of cheap energy, but as an early warning of the dangers of too much energy dependency, including the unacceptable danger of political blackmail. Accordingly, the immediate reaction was to view the reduction of energy dependency as an absolutely essential national goal. The United Kingdom, on the other hand, could focus on the implications of the new, higher price of oil, which in the short term might be hard on Britain's economy but which in the long term would make the North Sea an attractive area for exploration and development. Eventually the oil crisis could mean an age of energy self- sufficiency which Britain had not known since oil became an important part of its energy profile during the first quarter of the twentieth century.

ENERGY IN THE POLICYMAKING PROCESS

Convergence and Divergence: An Overview of American and British Energy Decision-Making

A detailed discussion of the energy policy options which Britain and the United States have chosen since 1973 lies beyond the objectives or possibilities of this chapter. Nonetheless, the broad contours of energy policy in these two countries since 1973 can be easily summarized. In both, the critical events shaping energy policy and national approaches to energy policymaking have been similar, including the effects of partisan change, the growing strength of domestic opposition to nuclear power, and—above all—the consequences of the oil crisis of 1979. Furthermore, as Figure 1 indicates, similarities have also existed in the environment of energy policymaking, the process of policymaking, and the nature of energy policy.

In both countries, policymaking has been influenced—and complicated—by the regionalized nature of energy resources; that is, within each country new energy-producing regions fuel the economies of older, more densely populated industrial regions. As a result, regional rivalries have often complicated the already difficult problem of making energy choices. In the United States, federalism has recently begun to revolve around a sunbelt (the West and Southwest states) versus frostbelt (Midwest and east coast states) conflict—in place of the earlier North-South division in American federalism—with the federal government assuming the role of umpire in the dispute as part of its energy policymaking responsibilities. In the United Kingdom, the discovery of oil off Scotland's coast in the North Sea stimulated a significant nationalist movement for regional home rule in Scotland during the seventies.

The process of energy policymaking was also complicated by the fact that both states possessed indigenous coal, oil, and gas industries, as well as advanced, government-developed and subsidized nuclear power industries by the mid-seventies.[8] In this context, policy convergence grew out of something of an "Anglo-American model" of energy plentitude—as opposed to the "Continental model" of few energy options. Yet the impact of this plentitude was not always desirable. Given their advanced state of energy research and development, Britain and America could consider a variety of fossil fuel options, nuclear energy possibilities, conservation, such exotic options as tidal, geothermal, wave, and wind power, solar energy, and high-tech options of the synthetic fuels nature. In turn, the very availability of this rich option base meant that when the policy process did consider energy policymaking as a major national priority during the 1970s, the search for a future energy mix was often overwhelmed by a maze of possibilities. Compounding this problem was the fact that most of the indigenous energy industries possessed influential private spokesmen (the American oil lobby, the British miners' union) and/or public bodies (for example, the U.S. Atomic Energy Commission in America, the UKEAE and the National Coal Board in Britain), operating before and inside the political processes and each demanding governmental support and a share of the action. Often, the combination of many energy options and the unpleasantness of making the difficult trade-offs involved in energy development—including the societal costs of pushing risky or environmentally costly options over the loud protests of those industries not benefitting from the proposed policies—led to policymaking paralysis.

Most important, in both political processes external events and partisan political developments dovetailed at decade's end to produce a variety of parallels in the area of energy decision-making. For the United States and the United Kingdom alike, 1979 stands as a watershed year—the year when the doubling of the price of OPEC oil spurred the international petroleum industry to major exploration efforts throughout the world and to invest in expensive, alternative energy sources (for example, liquefied and gasified

FIGURE 1

Energy Decision Making in the United States and the United Kingdom

SIMILARITIES

DISSIMILARITIES

Background

By 1975 an indigenous, four-fuel energy system was available to supply energy in both countries.

Fuel systems in the United States are older and anchored in the private sector more than in Britain.

The energy supply is regionalized in both countries: coal in England and Wales in Britain, in the East and West in the United States; oil and gas in the North Sea in Britain and essentially in the Southwest in the United States; consumers principally in England and on the east coast and in the Midwest in America.

By 1980, Britain was self-sufficient in energy at home and a net oil exporter abroad, with a vested interest in high energy prices.

Government involvement in energy production is far more direct and extensive in Britain than in the United States. Public sector actors dominate energy policymaking in Britain; private sector actors dominate decision-making in America.

Energy policymaking very sensitive and reactive to external events, especially the 1973 and 1979 oil crises and the 1980s oil glut.

Process

Until 1973, energy policy is a function of other considerations in both states.

In the area of policymaking the British Department of Energy umpires an energy arena dominated by government corporations. In the United States, the task of umpiring the struggle for influence between numerous government and private sector actors concerned with energy falls to the Congress.

Until 1973, both states procrastinate in developing existing fuel options (e.g., building the Alaska pipeline, developing North Sea oil).

Partisan change operates as a significant and often destabilizing factor influencing the creation and implementation of a coherent national energy policy in both countries.

The British parliamentary system facilitates energy policymaking; the American system of checks and balances complicates policymaking.

The opportunities for citizen inputs in policymaking are much greater in America.

Policies

The emphasis in both countries is on the private sector's role in developing new energy sources; however, the government shares this role, 1977–80.

The inconsistent policies resulting from leadership change are much more apparent in the United States than in Britain.

The emphasis is on package deals and inter-fuel logrolling in policymaking.

The commitment to the free market system for energy development is much deeper in the United States.

In policy implementation, the emphasis is on the bureaucracies, with only slight legislative oversight.

coal) inside the oil-importing world, when the Three Mile Island accident virtually ended the development of nuclear power in the United States, and when Margaret Thatcher became prime minister and Ronald Reagan began his campaign for the presidency. Reagan's subsequent election assured that there would be a very similar approach to the development of energy in the United States and the United Kingdom, one in which the government would withdraw from the active role it assumed after the first oil crisis and rely on the market forces of today to develop the energy needed tomorrow. It was a dramatic policy shift, although the foundations for the move were put in place during the 1973–79 intercrisis years, when the evolving *mode* of energy research in both countries became public-private cooperation, with a stress on the development of commercially sound energy sources. Still, prior to Reagan and Thatcher, the governments in America and Britain had assumed active roles in encouraging research in costly unproven areas, and the energy options being explored did not have to have immediate potential for commercialization. With Reagan and Thatcher's emphasis on supply-side economics and economic issues, and de-emphasis of energy development as a major responsibility of government, commercial criteria became crucial to energy development in both states.

As Figure 1 also indicates, not all aspects of the setting, process, and nature of energy policymaking in the United States and the United Kingdom are similar. Substantial differences also exist in these areas. Most obvious is for the moment the United Kingdom is self-sufficient in energy at home and a net oil exporter. Hence, Britain—unlike the United States—has a vested interest in *high* oil prices.[9] Indeed, the recent decline in the price of oil, so cheered in the United States and elsewhere in the West, has constituted a "third oil crisis" for Britain, affecting the national economy much more seriously than either of the first two. Equally important, although both the United States and Britain currently have four fuel economies (plus electricity produced preponderantly from coal, gas, and nuclear power), these fuel systems have quite different histories in the two countries. Only the nuclear industry has been closely identified with the government in both, and coal— the first fossil fuel industry nationalized in Britain—remains the least regulated energy industry in America. Furthermore, although gas and oil are more regulated than coal in America, they are much less regulated than in Britain, where they are part of the public sector. Consequently, whereas the principal actors in the energy field in America remain private sector actors, in Britain their roles are assumed inside the political process by public sector actors concerned with producing and selling energy, as well as with regulating the oil, coal, and gas industries.

The institutional arena reveals still other, fundamental differences in

British and American energy policymaking. One of these is the role played by the Department of Energy in the two systems. In the United States, the DOE functions partially as a holding company of numerous public sector actors in the American energy field, which prior to the DOE's creation during the Carter presidency were scattered throughout the executive branch. Moreover, most of these are regulatory bodies. Only in the nuclear energy field has the United States DOE inherited a major, long-standing commitment to energy development. By contrast, the British DOE has operated more like an umpire of the empire-building struggles of Britain's public sector energy corporations: the National Coal Board, the British Gas Company, the British National Oil Corporation, and the United Kingdom Atomic Energy Agency.

There are also quite different relationships between the executive and legislative branches and major differences in the role of the legislature in energy policymaking in the two countries. Several recent works have noted that the complexities in governing modern democratic societies have taken a toll on the nature—if not the format—of Britain's majority rule-parliamentary democracy. Thus in many areas governments of the Conservative and Labour parties alike have departed from textbook models of disciplined party rule to engage in increased intraparty negotiations, more consultation with outside groups, and less doctrinaire approaches to problem-solving. Yet in the field of energy policymaking the traditional model has held up rather well, perhaps because it has fit so well into Thatcher's preference for a free market approach to the problems facing British society. Whatever the reason, the parliamentary nature of the political process, combined with the presence of party discipline and the solid majority which the Conservatives have enjoyed in the House of Commons since 1979, has prevented the legislature from being a major obstacle to energy policymaking in Britain. Conversely, Congress, with its decentralized and undisciplined party structure and central role in United States policymaking, has often paralyzed an American policymaking process already partially immobilized by the hard choices to be made and the multiplicity of interests to be reconciled. The truncation of Carter's comprehensive energy bill by over a hundred congressional subcommittees represents a case in point. So does the inability of Congress to act on the slurry pipeline proposal. Moreover, the American system of separation of powers builds interbranch tensions into the system. Thus, while Prime Minister Thatcher was able to prevent Labour from protecting British miners from her decision to close unprofitable pits, Democratic and Republican Congressmen have dueled Reagan repeatedly and often successfully in the energy field; for example, forcing the president to accept much smaller cuts in the nation's synthetic fuels program than he desired in 1984, persistently defending the country's conservation programs and the Environmental Protection Agency against administrative efforts to emasculate them through budget cuts, and blocking Reagan's plans to speed up the licensing of nuclear plants.

Nor should the effects of American federalism be ignored in this area. Energy bargaining in Britain, essentially intragovernmental bargaining even when the unions or international petroleum companies are considered, appears less complicated than the process in the United States. There, not only must the public actors of the central government compete against one another in policymaking, but at the same time they must harmonize the competing interests of the private sector and those of the state and local governments involved in energy politics either as investors in energy research and development schemes or through the administration of such matters as strip mining and atmospheric pollution laws. [10] Although Britain is not without its interests to be accommodated (the National Union of Miners, most conspicuously), they are less numerous, and bargaining is more focused.

Partisan change, too, has sometimes produced differences in energy policy in the two countries, chiefly by producing far more policy zigzags in the United States than in Britain. The British Labour party, which held office during the intracrises years, consistently pursued a multiple strategy, albeit one deferential to the miners and National Coal Board and therefore one in which coal and the government played major roles. The Conservative government which replaced it, with an emphasis on fuels paying their own way and a willingness to sell public holdings in the North Sea oil business, has been much less sympathetic to coal and much, much less interested in playing a leading role in the exploration for the development and deployment of fuel sources. One change in government; one shift in policy, essentially limited to these areas.

In the United States there has been a change of presidents on three separate occasions since 1973, producing several sharp effects on energy policy. In addition to Reagan's de-emphasis of the role of government in energy development, which separates his administration from the previous ones of Nixon, Ford, and Carter, major policy shifts are apparent in other areas, especially those involving coal and nuclear energy during the 1973–1980 period. Both Nixon and Ford, for example, strongly backed nuclear power for electrification. Carter de-emphasized nuclear power in general, and expressed strong doubts about breeder reactors in particular, fearing that the development of breeder reactors abroad, which Nixon had encouraged, would make nuclear proliferation more difficult to control. Enter Reagan, who has championed nuclear energy and made it the one exception to his general policy of the government staying out of energy development (on the grounds that if the government does not support the nuclear industry in the United States it will not be able to survive the combination of public opposition and extensive bureaucratic regulation confronting it).[11] At the same time, Reagan has virtually abandoned public support for the coal industry, which Carter pushed for electrification needs and as a feedstock for synthetic fuels.

Finally, it is much easier for citizens to influence energy policymaking at the grassroots level in the United States than in Britain. Not only has the American political process been more sensitive to opinion polls longer than the British system, but it contains opportunities for citizen initiative groups to intervene directly in the policymaking and implementation process via administrative hearings and legal action (for example, nuclear licensing proceedings and class action suits to block off-shore drilling). In contrast, British politicians have shown "considerable skill . . . in keeping opposition out of courts and out of politics."[12] The British leaders have been particularly adroit in using fact-finding, inquiry proceedings to defuse the nuclear power issue—most conspicuously, in the 1984 hearings on the proposed operation of an American-style reactor at Sizewell.[13] As Lucas has summarized, the value of public inquiry is that even though "the decision is [correctly] believed by the objectors to be predetermined . . . the inquiry does have the significant political effect of separating the hard core opposition, which is not recoverable anyway, from less committed objectors."[14] As a result of Britain's skillful use of such techniques, the steady increase in public opposition to nuclear power in post-1973 Britain has not had the crippling effect on the development of nuclear power that it has had on the nuclear industry in the United States.

To summarize, there are at least as many substantial elements working against policy convergence in the energy field in Britain and America as working in favor of it. Without the impact of the personal (Reagan- Thatcher) factor, the differences separating America's energy actors, needs, and policymaking process from Britain's would have led to considerable divergence in specific energy policies in the two countries, as indeed these variables did between 1973 and 1979.

United States Energy Policy: Nixon through Reagan

The principal characteristics of America's pre-1973 energy policymaking have already been identified: an absence of a specific concern with energy policy; energy policy as the by-product of other policies; the evolution of different relationships between the government and each of the country's fuel

industries; and a sense of energy abundance which discouraged conservation. Indeed, by the time of the oil crisis, America's appetite for energy
had become a recurrent source of foreign criticism of the United States and
perhaps the most conspicuous feature of the country's "energy system."
During the seventies the United States was consuming more oil than all the
developing world, and considerably more than America was producing, even
though it was producing more oil than was consumed by all the developing
world.[15]

America's consumption of oil had grown throughout the twentieth century,
giving rise in the economy and political process to the emergence of vast and
powerful petroleum companies with much greater influence inside Congress
than gas or coal ever achieved. Thus, within two decades of the early-century
application of antitrust laws to the industry, which produced a private-public
antagonism between industry and government that has never fully subsided,
the government began to enact a series of laws beneficial to the American oil
industry, including some which restricted competition and kept prices higher
than they would otherwise have been. Thus, between 1920 and 1970 the
industry was able to regulate itself, even to the extent of controlling domestic
production, lest intermittent gluts drive down the price of oil. Exploration
ventures were subsidized at home through the depletion allowance and
abroad by means of revised tax laws permitting the industry to count royalties
paid to foreign governments against its American tax bill. Even the numerous small (compared to the giants of the petroleum industry) but rich
(compared to most other American industries) oil firms received a share of
public benefits—in particular, a quota system to shield them from less
expensive foreign oil imports between 1958 and 1972.

By 1973, America's energy appetite had long since outstripped its ability
to produce energy domestically, and "energy abundance" in the United
States was primarily a state of mind, albeit one strongly felt and shared by the
American people and the American government. On the eve of the oil
embargo, President Nixon not only ignored but ridiculed the warnings of the
American oil companies in the Middle East that another Arab-Israeli war
would result in a serious Arab oil embargo against the United States and
other countries friendly to Israel. The warning was delivered against the
backdrop of a world oil shortage, but Nixon received it as though the world
was still living in the oil glut of the fifties, when he was vice-president and
when the prime minister of Iran could find no buyers for nationalized Iranian
oil. When the oil crisis and embargo did come in October 1973, the
American public's reaction was a combination of panic and shocked indigna-
tion that such a thing could happen to them.

Inside the government, the first oil crisis produced immediately a sense of peril and urgency, which was in part the result of public dissatisfaction with the inconvenience of having to wait in line for more expensive gasoline and in part the result of a sudden awareness of the country's vulnerability to the disruption of its economy and to political blackmail because of its growing dependency on foreign energy sources. Nevertheless, translating concern into policy proved to be a difficult task for a country with so many energy options, so many groups with access to the political process, and a system of democratic decision-making much more susceptible to minority checks on policymaking (by environmentalists, by the oil lobby, by the railroads opposing the slurry pipeline) than majority rule. Certainly the rhetoric of the time—"Project Independence" under Nixon, for example, or the Ford-Rockefeller proposal to create an $100 billion investment bank for energy development—varied considerably from the policies which emerged: an energy-saving 55 mile-per-hour national speed limit and thermostat control laws for public buildings under Nixon, a modestly funded Energy Research and Development Authority under Ford.

Analysts will be discussing for some time the effectiveness of energy policymaking in the United States from Nixon through Carter. Some adhere to the position that the United States never developed a true energy policy, pointing to Congress's dismemberment of Carter's energy bill—the one integrative and comprehensive energy proposal submitted to Congress during the intracrises years, but unfortunately one submitted after the air of crisis had declined and subjected to radical surgery before emerging as several bills totalling a poor shadow of the original proposal. Other commentators argue that the United States had too many energy policies during these years, citing the Nixon commitment to nuclear energy, the Carter commitment to coal, the congressional efforts to divest oil companies of their investments in other energy areas, the continuance of a "politics of fuels" approach rather than the passage of a comprehensive energy package, the general difficulty which all governmental actors had in making the hard choices involved in committing resources to the development of alternative energy sources, and the fact that it finally took a second oil crisis to direct the political process away from a series of minor moves to a major commitment in the energy field (the synthetic fuels investment program passed in the form of the National Energy Security Act in 1979).[16]

The most appropriate explanation of the 1973–1979 years is perhaps the Kash-Rycroft thesis that although the United States did not enact a comprehensive energy law it did develop, in a piecemeal and incremental fashion, a national energy policy embodied in both the numerous energy laws passed during this period and in the priority accorded to energy throughout the political process.[17] The traditional, if often only implicit, national energy goals of energy security, abundance, cleanliness, and cheapness were explicitly examined and redefined. Energy security came to mean a level of energy self-sufficiency capable of preventing economic distortions and political extortion resulting from foreign manipulations of the price and availability of oil. The term had previously been more limited in scope, referring essentially to enough energy to support the military in the event of war. Conversely, the meaning attached to energy abundance had to be narrowed to fit the new realities, to mean adequate energy for growth rather than a surplus of energy. In this context, conservation had to be also embraced as a major policy goal. Most important, to assure an adequate energy supply without sacrificing the commitment to environmentally safe energy systems, the goal of cheap energy had to be abandoned during the Carter administration.[18]

The deregulation of the price of gas and oil, which began under Carter, represented the principal means of encouraging conservation and increasing energy supplies by freeing the country's gas and oil industries from the controls on domestic production which had maintained American oil and gas at low levels during the 1970s, when the international price of oil increased tenfold but American gasoline prices grew by only 200 to 300 percent. Other steps in the incremental development of an energy plan during this period included the relatively easy legislative step of creating a Department of Energy and placing an emphasis on conservation, with the latter defined in terms of increasing the efficiency of energy use as well as dampening the nation's appetite for energy. Last, a variety of policies were pushed to reduce the amount of imported energy in the country's energy profile. The use of alternative, domestic energy sources was encouraged where substitution was possible; for example, the enhanced use of coal and nuclear power for electrification. The search for and development of domestic oil and gas was also encouraged, by policies such as those making available more onshore and offshore land for leasing and those removing the obstacles to the construction of the Alaskan pipeline. Even the pursuit of very costly and unproven technologies of the shale oil and liquefied coal variety was encouraged through the availability of generous federal subsidies justified on national security grounds.

Throughout most of the seventies, the artificially low price of gas and oil prevented the United States from making much progress in reducing energy dependency. So too did the unforeseen consequences of some of the programs pursued by the government. Policies enacted during the Carter administration, for example, made it more profitable for American refineries to import oil than to refine American crude, and hence led to still further oil imports. Following the second oil crisis, however, it appeared that the country would be able to respond to its energy problem on a short- and long-term basis. The controls on gas and oil began to be lifted, guaranteeing still higher marketplace costs of energy inside the United States than those already resulting from the second oil crisis and the doubled price of OPEC oil it produced, and promising to reduce the domestic demand for oil and to encourage domestic exploration for it. The National Energy Security Act, a product of crisis decision-making, was passed, making $20 billion immediately available to support the development of an American synthetic fuels industry, with an additional $68 billion to be made available if initial research and development efforts should justify the expenditure. Furthermore, in order to get their "hard path" energy option, the synfuels program, through Congress, advocates agreed to a package deal in which another $12 billion was appropriated to assist conservation, solar energy research, and other "soft path" options. The package also included tax breaks for Americans insulating their homes or purchasing solar energy units. Throughout, the federal government's central role in encouraging energy research and development and in fashioning an adequate national energy system was an implicit assumption behind the policy process. Frequently, it was an explicit part of the policy process.

The election of Ronald Reagan ruptured this developing approach to energy policymaking in the United States and eventually led to the dismantling of the country's emergent energy policy. The center piece of Reagan's "energy plan" (for want of a better phrase) is the philosophy that the government should not be involved in the development of energy. In his view, development should be limited to commercially sound energy ventures, and hence to the marketplace. The government's role should be as limited as possible—preferably to lending industry a hand by removing the obstacles to energy development (for example, by facilitating the leasing of public lands, removing the antitrust obstacles to intraindustry mergers, and decreasing the red tape restricting the nuclear power industry), accelerating the decontrol of gas and oil, and so forth.[19] Governmental subsidization of energy development is viewed as very undesirable. The encouragement of conservation efforts is not viewed much more favorably; to the Reagan administration conservation implies limiting economic growth and mandating personal sacrifices.[20] Conservation has hence been abandoned as a high priority national goal by an administration more inclined to achieve energy abundance by increasing energy supply than by decreasing the demand for energy—a strategy which works better when prices are increasing, thereby discouraging consumption and at the same time making investment in energy development an attractive financial proposition.[21]

The change in perspective which Reagan brought to the White House quickly led to changes in energy policies. During Reagan's first term in office, conservation programs in the federal budget were cut to approximately one-fourth their 1980 level.[22] Government support for the development of renewable energy sources also received substantial cutbacks; solar programs were especially hard hit. In general, all governmental research and development programs were significantly reduced, and a major assault was made on the newly created Synthetic Fuels Corporation (SFC) in particular. First, the administration selected to chair the SFC an Oklahoma oilman who had run for the Senate in 1980 on the promise to dismantle it; then the administration withdrew nearly two-thirds of the unspent portion of the SFC's initial five-year budget; finally the administration succeeded in closing the corporation altogether. Elsewhere, the $2 billion research and development budget of the Department of Energy was cut nearly in half during Reagan's first two years in office, and efforts were made to eliminate this department altogether, representing as it did to the administration the presence of the government in an area where it did not belong. Even federal transfer funds to states did not escape; funds earmarked for such purposes as the administration of clean air laws were also reduced. Perhaps most revealing of the changes in philosophy and policy underway was that the private sector was delegated a major role in providing the country with the strategic petroleum reserve, which all Western countries agreed to develop after the first oil crisis in order to minimize the impact of any future disruption in the supply of oil.

The type of laissez-faire free market system which Reagan envisioned developing energy for America has never fully existed in the American energy field, and certainly not since the 1960s, when the social and environmental costs of energy became major quality of life concerns of government. Nor has the administration been entirely successful in following its free market approach to energy development. Even before the end of Reagan's first term in office, the wall separating the administration from energy development had developed several cracks in it. In the 1983 tax reform, for example, the oil industry managed to extract a $12 billion tax break which the administration initially opposed; the industry justified its gains on the grounds it would contribute to the development of domestic sources of oil. The following year, the Synthetic Fuels Corporation managed to retain nearly $3 billion more of its initial appropriation than the administration wished, allegedly because SFC supporters agreed in return to support the administration's Latin America military aid bill, on which the administration put a high priority.[23] Still, the major exception to Reagan's "hands off" approach to energy development has been the nuclear power industry. There, the administration maintains that government support is essential for the industry to survive in the face of the high cost of constructing nuclear plants and the political uncertainty of their completion.[24] Administration support for the Clinch Valley Reactor project can also be seen in this light, though it may also be attributed to the fact that the project was located in Tennessee, home state of the Senate's Republican majority leader during Reagan's first term. In any event, by the mid-1980s the administration's pro-nuclear policy seemed to be paying dividends. For the first time since the Three Mile Island accident in 1979, nuclear plants began to receive licenses to initiate operations. Outside of the nuclear industry, however, the Reagan administration's rule of thumb seemed to be that the federal government should play no role in energy development, that the states should play at most only a small role in an area best left to the private sector, and that the channels for citizen participation in energy decision-making—chiefly through judicial and quasijudicial hearings—should be minimized as much as possible.

The United Kingdom: Energy Policy and Partisan Change

Following the 1979 election of Margaret Thatcher, with *her* emphasis on the free market as a cure for her country's chronically ailing economy, British energy policy began to move in the same direction that it would take in the United States under Reagan. Until 1979, however, energy policy in Britain differed substantially from American energy policy.

The first oil crisis produced far less panic and far fewer demands to "do something" in Britain than in the United States. To be sure, in 1973 Britain, like the United States, was a major energy importer. Yet unlike the United States, Britain did not have to look to conservation and technological fixes to solve its problem of energy dependency. It could look to its North Sea, where oil had recently been discovered in substantial quantities. Moreover, the sharp increase in the price of oil on the world market had suddenly made that oil commercially profitable.[25] Thus, the foundation of British energy policy during the next half decade became the development of North Sea oil, perceived by the Labour party which governed Britain from 1974 to 1979 as a means of making the country energy self-sufficient and hence as a resource in whose development government should play a major role. The exploration and production agreements which the government had negotiated prior to the oil crisis with the narrow band of multinational oil companies capable of drilling under the harsh conditions of the North Sea were quickly renegotiated in order to give the government a greater control over North Sea operations . . . and over North Sea oil! The device initially employed was to increase the government's stock holdings in British Petroleum (BP) from approximately 40 percent of all shares to nearly double that amount and to require that BP be a central partner in all North Sea operations. When the oil began to flow in 1975, the government created a 100 percent public agent, the British National Oil Company, to represent the Crown in North Sea operations in place of BP, which had historically functioned more like the other principal, multinational oil companies than a government flag carrier. After 1975, the BNOC was to be a majority partner in all North Sea ventures.

Coal was the second arm of British energy policy during this period—perhaps the one closest to Labour's heart and certainly the energy source closest to the Labour party's political base. It was also the energy sector which provided Britain with its nearest thing to a comprehensive energy proposal, an energy plan which emerged during the intracrises years in the form of a Green Paper based on the report of the Tripartite Commission appointed shortly after the 1973 crisis and composed of representatives from the government, the National Coal Board, and the miners' union.[26] Published in 1978, the report recommended (not surprisingly) heavy investment in the further modernization of the British coal industry, which for all of its unprofitable pits is perhaps the most technologically advanced mining industry in the world. The report also recommended using British coal as feedstock for developing synthetic gas and oil as national security hedges against the day when North Sea oil will begin to run out. Perversely, the investment which the coal industry did receive from the sympathetic Labour Government throughout the 1974–1979 period worked against the industry in the 1980s, when production and productivity in the coal industry sharply increased at the very moment when a major recession was cutting British demand and making the unprofitable pits appear even less justified to a Conservative government emphasizing the need for all public corporations to pay their own way. Nor did the Tories ease coal's situation any when they pushed nuclear power for the country's electrical needs. The electrical market accounts for over 70 percent of coal sales in Britain.

With North Sea gas already under a governmental monopoly by the seventies and entering Britain as a very competitive energy source (gas increased its share of the British energy market from 30 percent to 45 percent between 1973 and 1979,[27] the third area stressed by the 1974–1979 Labour government was not gas but nuclear energy. It was this industry which received the largest amount of research and development appropriations ($2.5 billion after 1973) and which even the Labour government pushed over coal for many electrification projects. Yet the momentum in plant construction was actually lost during the Labour years, as the result of a battle inside the British energy complex between the Electric Board, which wanted to adopt an American-designed reactor, and the UKAEA, whose "buy British" policy the government supported. The stalemate was not completely broken until the Thatcher years, when the government gave the Electric Board's plan the green light and construction commenced at Sizewell on the Suffolk coast on a nuclear plant utilizing the American technology.

Beyond nuclear power, energy research and development did not receive much public support in Britain. The country's prospects for energy self-sufficiency, at least during the immediate future, rendered unnecessary the pursuit of expensive, alternative energy options, and the government spending which did occur reflects pork-barrel politicking as much as energy policy. The funds tended to be funnelled through and spread out among the existing public actors in each fuel source area, with the funds devoted to the development of new technologies being very small by any standard. For example, the monies earmarked by the Labour government for synfuel research were not just small by American standards—the £27 million set aside by the National Coal Board in 1977 was dwarfed by the $20 billion capitalization of the American Synthetic Fuels Corporation in 1979; the funding was pathetic even in comparison to the funds being spent elsewhere on synthetic fuels development: £3 billion in West Germany in 1979 and £70 million by Royal Dutch Shell on only one project in Holland in the same year. The amount was also minor compared to the £5 billion which the NCB was then committing to a long-term program to increase the number, efficiency, and productivity of British mines.

The same research and development pattern prevailed throughout the British energy arena. The British Gas Company devoted only approximately £50 million annually to gas research and development while pursuing a £4.5 billion project to expand its production, storage, and transmission facilities. Furthermore, most of that £50 million was earmarked for developing *applied* technology, not new energy sources. Thus, even before the multibillion-dollar synthetic fuels bubble burst throughout the world in the 1980s as a result of the falling price of oil and growing cost of synfuel projects, the British Gas Company and the National Coal Board combined were spending only slightly more on their liquefaction and gasification projects than the amount being budgeted by the British Department of Energy for what one commentator has called the "fool's paradise of wind, wood, waste, and waves" as energy sources.[28] Even in the nuclear area, which persistently received the most research and development funding, the amounts were not large—£100–200 million per year—compared to the funding going to nuclear research in a dozen different Western countries, much less in comparison to the billions of dollars being spent by all sources to develop North Sea oil fields, where the British Government was appropriating only a frugal (not to say niggardly) £20 million per year to support research in offshore technology.

Conservation was not totally ignored by the Labour Government, but it was essentially the oil, coal, and nuclear strategies which combined to form Britain's energy policy during the intracrises years—a policy defined in terms of *the government seeking*, through its creatures, to increase oil production in order to provide national energy self-sufficiency, and to modernize and expand the coal and nuclear industries as enhanced sources of energy for the present and for those future years when the North Sea would no longer be able to provide for the United Kingdom's energy needs.

Some aspects of this policy survived the Labour party's defeat in Britain's 1979 parliamentary elections to emerge in Thatcher's "CO-CO-NUK" energy strategy, which emphasizes the role of coal, conservation, and nuclear power when North Sea production begins to decline.[29] On the other hand, the heart of Labour's approach to energy policy—its stress on the central role of government in energy development, ownership, and management—did not survive. For Labour's emphasis on the role of the public sector, Thatcher has substituted commitments to "privatisation" and "commercialisation," and has recast the operation of the country's fuel industries in this mode since 1979.

The most obvious reflections of this change in government policy can be found in the petroleum sector. Much of the government's North Sea holdings have been auctioned off to create private oil companies (for example, Enterprise Oil), and the BNOC has increasingly functioned as a state trading company, buying over half of the oil produced in Britain's North Sea, rather than a major producer in its own right. Even in this capacity BNOC has been a frequent target of governmental criticism on the grounds that it pays too much for the oil it buys.

At the same time that it has been criticizing its oil representative, the government has been offering tax incentives to private producers to develop North Sea fields, and until the mid-1980s production steadily increased. As a result, by 1985 Britain had become the world's fifth largest oil producer, pumping 2,650,000 barrels a day, 50 percent for net export, and a sufficiently aggressive competitor for the world's shrinking oil market that the country's 1983 and 1984 price cuts provoked crises in OPEC. Still, it is not clear whether the government's promotion of North Sea oil has been an "energy policy" or the by-product of essentially economic interests. The profits on the government's North Sea operations and the taxes on the private sector's profits have certainly helped the national budget, and petroleum exports have aided Britain's balance of payments profile, but the rapid development of the North Sea has also brought Britain closer to the day when the country will again become a net oil importer.

With respect to the country's nationalized coal industry, Prime Minister

Thatcher has made it clear that the government's commitment to coal is only to the economically profitable parts of the coal industry. Instead of keeping inefficient pits open for political purposes or to ease the country's unemployment problem, during Britain's recession in the 1980s the government took advantage of the resultant drop in energy consumption—below 1967 levels by 1982—to trim a substantial number of the National Coal Board's unprofitable coal mines. Elsewhere, the traditionally pro-union NCB itself was successfully pressured into adopting the government's "no compromise" approach to striking miners during the great 1984–85 miners' strike over the issue of job security, and research and development in the coal industry has been slashed, especially in the costly areas. Almost immediately on taking office, the Tory government withdrew from the NCB's proposal to build a 25,000-tons-per-day coal liquefaction plant; eventually, even the compromise proposal to build a 2,500-tons-per-day plant was tabled until such time as the plan seemed commercially sound enough to attract funding from both the European Communities and a major private partner.

The Thatcher government also cut research and development spending in most other noncommercial areas. In May 1982, the government announced that it was ending virtually all research projects involving renewable energy resources, although in 1984 approximately £10.5 million was made available by the DOE to create windmill-powered electricity for Orkney. Otherwise, where research funding has continued it has largely gone to the nuclear industry, which the Thatcher government, like the Reagan administration, has continued to push. Thus, by mid-decade, when only one coal-fired electrical station was in production, the Central Electricity Generating Board was committing £8.6 billion to the construction of seven nuclear plants using an American-designed reactor. However, by the mid-1980s opposition to nuclear power was becoming nearly as widespread and mobilized in Britain as in America, and the government was forced to conduct public hearings on the issue of licensing such a plant (the Sizewell inquiry). Indeed, most polls indicate that more opposition to the further building of nuclear power plants existed in Britain than in the United States by the early 1980s, and that an outright majority was against expanding the British nuclear power industry as early as 1981. This development has not been particularly deadly to Britain's nuclear plans because the channels open to opponents of nuclear power remain more restricted in that country than in the United States, but it did force the Thatcher government, well before the Chernobyl incident, to slow down its plans to expand nuclear power in Britain.[30]

In short, by the 1980s in both Britain and the United States, a more or less integrated energy policy had been replaced by a series of fuel policies, with only the nuclear industry still drawing the strong sponsorship of government.

In other sectors there was a movement away from government involvement in energy development, though the government necessarily remains more involved in this area in Britain than in the United States by virtue of Britain's public sector actors in coal, gas, and oil. Most important, in both countries there has been diminished interest in developing a comprehensive energy plan, as an energy plan. As Fell observed with respect to the United Kingdom, "There seems to be a marked reluctance to reach firm decisions for or against any particular energy option and a strong underlying belief that market forces will do most, if not all, of what is required. Such an approach . . . does little to provide a coherent strategy for the future."[31] Or the present! Yet it is this policy, or nonpolicy, which has been the convergent result of the similar free market philosophies of government shared by Thatcher's Britain and Reagan's America.

CONCLUDING REFLECTIONS: ENERGY POLICY IN THE UNITED STATES AND UNITED KINGDOM, TODAY AND TOMORROW

In 1980, when Margaret Thatcher was completing her first year in office and Ronald Reagan was winning the American presidency, the expectation that the price of energy would remain high influenced the approach to energy development of practically everyone. Oil industries invested heavily in such high-cost energy alternatives as synthetic fuels on the assumption that prices would continue to increase. Nuclear energy seemed to be an affordable energy option, despite the political obstacles to developing it, because the costs of all fossil fuels seemed to be moving upward with the price of oil. The United States and the United Kingdom based their hopes for a slackening of energy demand and/or an increase in energy supply on the assumption that the price of OPEC oil would increase above the $32-per-barrel rate to which the second oil crisis sent it.

In both countries, the market thus became the answer to energy needs. Government policymaking could be restricted to removing the obstacles to free market investment and profit-making. In the United States, the decontrol of gas and oil was accelerated and oil industry mergers were permitted which in earlier periods might have been threatened with antitrust action. In Britain, tax incentives were offered to make investment more financially attractive in some of the more marginal North Sea areas. In both countries, public subsidy of alternative energy projects was sharply reduced, except for those involving nuclear power. The Reagan administration also began to eliminate government support for conservation—lifting the controls on building temperatures, for example, and withdrawing the federal efficiency standards scheduled to be applied to home appliances. Even the government's role in emergencies was sharply downgraded, as reflected in Reagan's veto of a 1982 act giving the president stand-by rationing authority. His reasoning: the very presence of such authority might discourage the private sector from taking the necessary steps to cope with energy shortages.[32] Unfortunately, just as the 1980s plunge in the price of OPEC oil prompted energy developers to reconsider their expensive research and development projects in synfuels and the economics of nuclear power, the changing market price of energy has undercut the free market approach to energy development and conservation of the Thatcher and Reagan administrations.

Leaving the development of a country's future energy needs to the marketplace is a high-risk strategy which makes sense only in periods of increasing energy prices and profits, if it makes sense even then. High prices and profits have never guaranteed an enhanced or even a stable petroleum supply, primarily because there are many areas beyond additional oil exploration and development in which profits can be invested. Indeed, in the United States in 1984 alone nearly $100 billion was invested by major oil firms in increasing reserves, not by exploration for new oil but by the acquisition of oil companies with undervalued stock compared to their oil reserves. For the corporate giants, mergers represented a much less expensive and risky manner of increasing *their* holdings than drilling costly exploratory wells far into the ground or offshore; however, the addition of these "new reserves" to their corporate ledger sheets added nothing to America's domestic oil reserves. To expect these actors, and the marketplace, to be concerned with a nation's future energy needs at a time of falling oil prices and profits is hardly realistic. Indeed, the collapse of the price of oil to under $10 per barrel in the mid-1980s virtually halted additional private sector exploration of the unchartered North Sea areas, as well as the drilling of wells in the outer continental shelf and deep well areas of the United States. It also led to a significant shutdown of American refineries. Perhaps more than ever, future energy planning remains necessary to avoid future energy shortfalls, especially given the long lead times necessary to develop most energy sources.

Nor are such future energy shortages entirely problematic. There are already indications that the United States is "drifting slowly toward a shortage of electric power" as a result of a variety of financial factors. Similar warnings are also being heard in the area of natural gas, and a "power squeeze" is being predicted for the United States in the 1990s by numerous forecasters.[33] Similarly, most analysts believe that unless a major exploration effort begins soon, leading to substantial new finds in the North Sea, the United Kingdom will again become a net oil importer during the latter half of this decade,[34] and the foreseen market price of OPEC oil does not encourage that exploration. These forecasts involve crisis-free scenarios. Should there be a major disruption in the availability of international oil, the consequences could be even more serious if the United States and the United Kingdom continue to rely so heavily on market forces to solve their energy needs. Certainly the past is not encouraging. The market scarcely proved itself to be crisis-oriented during the 1973 and 1979 oil crises, when the "violent" overreaction of the marketplace intensified the shocks of these events.[35]

A similarly unhappy picture presents itself with respect to specific policies. The role of the private sector in maintaining supplemental inventories to support America's strategic petroleum reserve has already been mentioned. Yet in a period of falling oil prices the private sector is not likely to maintain the inventory of oil necessary to minimize the consequences of short-term disruptions. The inventory carrying costs on oil have been estimated to be approximately $9 per barrel, which probably explains why, during the months of 1984 and 1985 when the Iranian–Iraqui war was heating up in the Persian Gulf, American oil companies were drawing down their inventories on the assumption that, given the existing glut, they could replace them at lower costs in the future.[36] Their assumption was not universally shared. As one congressman surveying the situation warned his colleagues in a 1984 House of Representatives report, "[We] should not panic the American public at this point, but we cannot claim that we are prepared for any type of circumstance that might occur."[37]

Reliance on market forces for a nation's energy policy must also be rethought for a final reason: the inability of the marketplace approach to assimilate noneconomic goals and values, such as environmental protection and social equity. It is the absence of such thinking in Reagan's approach to energy which many believe most distinguishes it from the approach to energy policy and policymaking of his predecessors.[38] As Kash and Rycroft aptly phrased it, "By general agreement, market prices and costs, the essential figures used by private investors to evaluate return on investment, do not take broader social values into account."[39] Yet modern democratic societies need to find a way of building consideration of these values into their policymaking processes.

How long can the contemporary approach to energy policymaking endure and what will future energy policy be like in Britain and the United States? There are no easy or guaranteed answers to these questions, but some responses seem highly probable. In the short term, it is very unlikely that there will be substantial shifts in policy in either country because of the extent to which the current convergence of British and American energy policy is the product of the similarities of outlook of President Reagan and

Prime Minister Thatcher, both of whom will be in office until the late 1980s. In the middle to long term, though, national energy realities and necessities favor policy reassessment and policy change in the direction of greater direct government involvement in energy policy in both countries. At that time national differences in energy resources, energy use, the policymaking process, and policy needs should undercut the recent convergence of energy policy in the two states with respect to both specific fuel areas and overall policy implementation. Coal, for example, as a public corporation in the United Kingdom, should receive far greater emphasis in energy policymaking in Britain than in the United States, where the growing concern of environmentalists and government officials alike with acid rain may make coal a decreasingly attractive source for America's future electrical needs. Oil, too, will be treated differently in the two systems. In Britain, energy policies will have to reflect the importance of oil as a major export item at least for the rest of the century; in the United States, the challenge will be to hold imported oil to an economically and politically affordable level—one at which sudden international fluctuations in the price and availability of petroleum will not jeopardize America's domestic economic growth or tempt foreign suppliers to try political blackmail.

At the macrolevel, the broad contours of energy policy in the United Kingdom can be feasibly shaped around the goal of maintaining a self-sufficient energy system. It will not be easy but it can be managed by assuring the regular exploration of—and steady but not hasty drawing on—North Sea resources, by influencing the evolving patterns of energy use, and by adjusting public policies pertaining to indigenous energy resources to those evolving patterns. In the United States, on the other hand, energy self-sufficiency is still not a realistic goal, and the principal objectives of public policy must be avoiding serious shortages in specific areas (especially natural gas or electrification) and in minimizing dependency in those fuel areas where self-sufficiency is impossible (that is, oil). Similarly, in overall policy development and implementation the government can be expected to play a much more direct role in Britain than in the United States, due to the long tradition of active government involvement in managing the economy in general, and energy in particular, in the former and the always present bias in favor of the private sector in the latter. The Reagan administration may have carried this bias further than others in the energy field in the United States, but it did not invent this attitude.

The differences likely to separate future energy policy in the United States and the United Kingdom are thus important, but they are also essentially differences of emphasis (for example, on coal in Britain, gas in the United States) and degree (of government involvement in energy development and

coordination). Greater instances of divergence are precluded by the basic
similarities involving energy availability and energy policymaking in the two
countries. Just as a commitment to democracy as the form of government
limits the institutional options available to a polity, energy availability sets
real boundaries on energy policymaking in energy-intensive societies. In the
United States and Britain, as we have noted, energy sources are abundant, no
particular fuel source enjoys an overwhelming advantage over others, and
each has sufficiently important spokesmen before and/or inside the respective political processes to guarantee that it will not be neglected. Consequently, future British and American energy policy will certainly involve a
mix of four fuels (coal, oil, gas, and nuclear), with no single energy source
being groomed as *the* energy alternative of tomorrow, although in both states
oil will remain the central fuel source given its diverse applications in the
economy (transportation, industry, commerce), nonsubstitutability in much
of the transportation sector, and the substantial level at which it is being
currently consumed. Similarly, national approaches to energy research,
development, and deployment will remain alike, and will involve in both
countries private-public collaboration rather than exclusive reliance on either the private sector or the public sector. Specific policies will diverge
within these parameters—the policy mix is likely to remain more oriented
toward the free market in the United States, where private corporations
dominate gas, oil, and coal production, than in the United Kingdom—but
policy similarities should remain much higher between the United States and
Britain than between either and any state on the continent, where energy
options are far fewer.

A more specific estimate of future energy policy convergence and divergence in Britain and America would be imprudent. These two countries are
divided by similar four-fuel economies as well as by a single tongue, and
accents can change with surprising suddenness in both areas. Nor can one be
more specific in estimating when the policymaking process will again treat
energy as an important item in its own right, although the answer here is
probably sooner in the United States than in Britain. America's energy needs
are much greater than Britain's, and her energy shortfalls annual and
cumulative. Moreover, Reagan's term of office must expire in 1988 whereas
Margaret Thatcher and her free market philosophy have a genuine possibility
of a third term by grace of the divided nature of the Conservative party's
opposition and Britain's electoral system (which combined in 1983 to
provide Thatcher's party with nearly a 150-seat majority in the House of
Commons with only about 43 percent of the popular vote). Still, the most
difficult question of all to answer, and the most important, is whether
democratic political systems with several energy options can overcome the

pluralism of affected groups and the public–private dichotomy to develop coherent and comprehensive energy policies. It is a question which Britain and America may have to answer.

The recent extensive reliance on the free market system for energy development was a radical approach for both countries in the sense that it was an approach outside the mainstream of post-World War II energy policymaking in both the United States and Great Britain.[40] It has left both countries vulnerable to potential energy shortfalls, The good news is that both states possess energy sources which—albeit finite—can mitigate future energy problems. The bad news is that the lead times in developing these sources are long (nuclear power, marginal North Sea fields, outer continental shelf oil in the United States), and that if future energy shortfalls are to be hedged against, policy action must not be delayed too long. To do so is to risk serious consequences—perhaps a new round of energy shortages and high prices in America and potentially higher energy costs and less energy efficiency in Britain, whose economy is none too strong anyway. In the case of America in particular, the lessons of the past should be a guide to the future, but as the Arabs remind us with their word for human being—literally, "one who forgets"—errors of judgment are not the monopoly of any one state and constitute one problem for which no technological fix has yet been devised.

NOTES

1. See Carl Solberg, *Oil Power* (New York: Mason/Charter, 1976) for an excellent discussion of this theme in the context of American society and oil.
2. See David Howard Davis, *Energy Politics*, (3rd ed., New York: St. Martins, 1981), especially chapters 2 and 3.
3. "Oil millions 'squandered' on unemployment benefit," London *Times*, 3 June 1983.
4. "Britain would be bust without oil, says Labour," *The Guardian*, 18 May 1983.
5. See Roy Jenkins, "Oil: our chance to rebuild the world economy," London *Times*, 27 January 1983.
6. "Stocks Fall in London; Rates Rise," *New York Times*, 29 January 1985.
7. Concerning the 1973 Arab oil embargo and the resultant increase in the price of OPEC oil, see especially the special issue of *Daedalus* 104 (Fall 1975), entitled "The Oil Crisis in Perspective."
8. In 1970, coal still accounted for nearly 20 percent of U.S. energy consumed (down from 37.8 percent in 1950), whereas gas accounted for another third (32.7 percent, up from 18 percent twenty years before), oil nearly 44 percent (up slightly from approximately 40 percent in 1950), and nuclear power a substantial share of the remaining energy sources being utilized. In Britain, coal, as a protected and publicly owned indigenous energy source, still accounted for

approximately 40 percent of the energy being used in 1970 (though down from nearly 90 percent in 1950!). Figures taken from Joel Darmstadter and Hans H. Landsberg, "The Economic Background," *Daedalus* 104 (Fall 1975): 20, and Peter R. Odell, *Oil and World Power*, 7th ed. (Middlesex, England: Penguin, 1983), 118.

9. Technically, Britain cannot achieve energy self-sufficiency through North Sea oil. The petroleum on which British industry operates is much heavier than the grades produced in the North Sea, and as a consequence most North Sea oil is sold abroad to pay for the oil which Britain imports for its industries. On the other hand, by the mid-1980s, Britain had become a *net* oil exporter, selling at least a half million barrels per day more than the oil imported.

10. Additionally, Britain has supranational obligations which the United States does not face. These arise from Britain's membership in the European Communities and pertain primarily to coal and nuclear energy. In theory, these obligations should also set British policymaking apart from energy policymaking in America; however, in practice the European Community's impact on British energy policy has been slight, and basically limited to subsidizing coal, solar, and other energy research areas. Certainly the Community has never influenced British energy policy to the extent that the states (subnational units) have influenced energy planning and policy implementation in America.

11. James Everett Katz, "U.S. Energy Policy: Impact of the Reagan Administration," *Energy Policy* (June 1984): 135–56, esp. 139–40.

12. N.J.D. Lucas, "British Energy Policy," in Wilfrid L. Kohl, ed., *After the Second Oil Crisis* (Lexington: Mass.: D.C. Heath and Company, 1982), 105.

13. See G. Greenhalgh, "The Sizewell Inquiry—is there a better way?" *Energy Policy* (September 1984): 283.

14. Lucas, "British Energy Policy," 100.

15. Paul S. Basile, "U.S. Energy Policy," in Kohl, *After The Second Oil Crisis*, 197. At the time of the 1973 oil embargo, the United States was importing approximately 30 percent of its oil and 13 percent of its energy in the form of imported oil. By the second oil crisis, the figures had grown to 50 percent and 25 percent respectively, despite half a decade during which the country's avowed goal was to reduce oil imports.

16. See Basile, "U.S. Energy Policy," esp. 215f.

17. Don E. Kash and Robert W. Rycroft, "Energy Policy: How Failure was Snatched from the Jaws of Success," a paper presented at the meeting of the American Political Science Association, Chicago, 1983, and subsequently published with minor revisions in *Policy Studies Review* 4 (February 1985): 433–45. Between 1977 and 1980, Congress enacted two-and-a-half times as many laws involving energy as during the previous half century. See the charts in Basile, 210-11.

18. Kash and Rycroft, "U.S. Energy Policy," 7.

19. See especially James T. Bruce, "A Plan Not to Plan Is the Plan," *Environment*, 12 (June 1984): 135–45.

20. Katz, "U.S. Energy Policy," 142. Katz views Reagan's de-emphasis of conservation as his "most radical" departure from the country's prior energy policy. Much of Reagan's approach was radical, however, in the context of American history; for example, his efforts to curtail government involvement in the nation's fuel systems.

21. The administration attempted to cut away 90 percent of the existing budget for

conservation, and three times as much from solar energy as Congress eventually authorized.

22. Katz, "U.S. Energy Policy," 141–2.
23. Sabrina Willis, unpublished notes on interviews with Synthetic Fuels Corporation personnel and staff assistants to congressional subcommittees in the energy field, 26 November 1984, Washington, D.C.
24. The United States nuclear industry lost its competitive edge over coal-fired electrical plants during the seventies as a result of (1) the institutional options available to the opponents of nuclear power, (2) the cumbersome nature of the regulations governing the industry, and (3) the regional nature of the American electrical industry (in which state laws govern financial arrangements and development costs can be passed on to consumers only when new plants begin to operate). Licensing for the operation of new nuclear plants came to an almost complete halt following the Three Mile Island incident, with the result that no new stations are expected to be constructed in the United States until 1990, and the number of plants in operation has steadily decreased for nearly a decade despite the fact that public opinion samplings in the United States have regularly indicated plurality-to-majority support for the continued building of nuclear power plants. See Chaucy Starr and Chaim Braun, "U.S. Nuclear Power Performance," *Energy Policy* (September 1984): 253–56, concerning the "open-ended intervention process" available to Americans challenging nuclear power. Concerning the relationship between public opinion and the construction of nuclear power plants, see Joop van der Pligh, J. Richard Eiser, and Russell Spears, "Public Attitudes to Nuclear Energy," 302–5, in the same issue of *Energy Policy*, and S. David Aviel, *The Politics of Nuclear Energy* (Washington: University Press of America, 1981), chap. 4.
25. Calculated at the rate at which Britain was consuming oil in 1973, there was very nearly a 25-year supply of oil for the United Kingdom in the British sectors of the North Sea when production began in 1975, although it was not until 1981 that the United Kingdom became a net oil exporter.
26. The last energy White Paper published in Britain appeared in 1967!
27. Lucas, "British Energy Policy," 101. Much of the growth of gas in Britain's energy profile was directly at the expense of coal.
28. Davis, *Energy Politics*, 260, with reference to American energy options.
29. Derek J. Spooner, "Energy: 1973–1983—The Diversification Decade," *Geography* 69 (April 1984): 154.
30. van der Pligh, et al., "Public Attitudes," 302.
31. Ian Fells, "The World Nuclear Power Scene and United Kingdom Energy Policy in 1984," *Energy Policy* (September 1984): 308.
32. Kash and Rycroft, "Energy Policy," 19.
33. "Dissolve the Energy Department?" *Washington Post* editorial, 5 January 1985.
34. Lucas, "British Energy Policy," 104.
35. "Dissolve the Energy Department?"
36. Bruce, "A Plan Not to Plan," esp. 135–6.
37. Congressman Mike Synar, cited in "U.S. Readiness for An Energy Crisis Disputed," *Washington Post*, 21 May 1984, A17.
38. See Katz, "U.S. energy policy," for example.
39. Kash and Rycroft, "Energy Policy," 27.
40. Ibid., 14f.

Consumer Policy: Qualified Convergence

Richard S. Flickinger

Consumer policy. The term provokes quizzical expressions on the faces of the unsuspecting, even of some who are students of public policy. Although this field remains a relatively unfamiliar subject, a recent Organization for Economic Co-operation and Development report claims, "During the seventies consumer policy became an integral part of economic policy."[1]

As usually understood, consumer policy embraces three general concerns: (1) product safety; (2) the protection of consumers' economic interests; and (3) the provision of information to consumers.[2] The list indicates why this policy area is sometimes called consumer protection. While these substantive concerns help to identify consumer policy, equally important for defining the existence of a separate policy area are procedural concerns, particularly the development of institutional arrangements which recognize the existence of the policy area and provide for the representation of consumer voices in policymaking processes.

Compared to many areas of public policy, consumer policy is new. It is also new to both the United States and Great Britain. As such it offers an unusual opportunity to explore aspects of convergence theory. For example, were common stimuli involved in the emergence of consumer policy? If so, were the driving forces broadly based social and economic changes, or were they more specific factors such as the emergence of new interest groups or new ideas? Has the common recognition of a new policy area been followed by the adoption of substantively similar policy measures? Have the procedures through which the two governments make consumer policy also converged?

During the past quarter-century both British and American governments have taken many legislative and administrative actions which they recognized as consumer policy measures. Each also created new offices or agencies with consumer representation or protection mandates. Outside government, new consumer interest groups emerged and old ones became more prominent. Media attention grew, with print and electronic journalists on both sides of the Atlantic designated as consumer correspondents. "Consumer affairs specialists" appeared on the staffs of most large retail establishments. The 1980s have been marked so far by a notable cooling of the ardor of both national governments in the consumer policy field. No one familiar with the professed views of the Reagan and Thatcher administrations regarding the proper role of government in the economy will be surprised by the change.

According to the 1983 OECD report, consumer policy emerged as a distinct policy area in advanced industrial societies with market economies through a two-stage process. In the 1960s consumer concerns were recognized and consumer organizations developed in many countries. The second stage, in the 1970s, was marked by government actions establishing offices and enacting laws and regulations explicitly to deal with consumer concerns.[3] While the report's claim may be correct in general, it simplifies and distorts what has happened in Britain and the United States by overlooking earlier consumer policy developments, and by implying that widespread, organized popular concern for consumer issues preceded government action.

This chapter opens with a brief overview of each country's earlier experience with consumer policy, and then moves to a more detailed discussion of developments from the 1960s, with special attention to the policies of the Reagan and Thatcher administrations. Policymaking processes and participants are then comparatively analyzed. Through these steps it will become obvious that there are striking similarities in the British and American experiences. The preceding sketch of recent developments already suggests a prima facie case for substantive and procedural convergence. But important differences also will become evident. The final section offers an overall judgment of the degree of convergence in consumer policy.

ANTECEDENTS OF RECENT CONSUMER POLICY

Historians of the consumer movement in the United States like to trace the story of government involvement with consumer questions all the way back to the drafting of the United States Constitution and Article I, section 8, which empowers Congress to enact weights and measures standards.[4] From medieval times in England, courts and local governments had been concerned with weights and measures standards. As more and more people became urban dwellers with the development of the industrial society and as more processed foods appeared, the initial concerns with accurate measurements were followed by a growing concern about food purity. Food safety was the first consumer issue to be addressed by national legislation in both countries, with Britain's 1860 Act for Preventing the Adulteration of Articles of Food and Drink and the United States's Pure Food and Drug Act of 1906.

From these very basic beginnings the range of consumer issues expanded. By the end of the nineteenth century the British government had legislated a national system of weights and measures standards, inspection and enforcement (1878), and had recognized in the 1893 Sale of Goods Act that although the guiding principle in the marketplace may still be *caveat emptor*, sellers were obliged to provide goods of merchantable quality and suitable for the purpose intended.[5] Yet government attention to consumer issues was sporadic. Not until the New Deal would the United States government build upon the consumer actions of the Progressive era. The New Deal also saw the first serious attempts to build the representation of a consumer perspective into the federal excutive and its administrative processes.[6] None of these efforts was particularly successful. Most consumer representation schemes disappeared with the end of World War II. The first major provision for explicit consumer representation in public sector activity came when the 1945–1950 Labour government enacted its nationalization legislation. The laws creating this series of public monopolies included establishment of a consumer consultative council for each. These provisions were made not in response to public pressure but at the initiative of the government "as a demonstration to the public of its honorable intentions toward users of public services."[7] In this, the pattern was similar to the early attempts in America to provide consumer representation during the New Deal.[8] The 1950s were a quiet period for consumer policy developments in the United States. The only notable government actions occurred at the state level, as New York and then California created consumer councils. Once again, these efforts were initiated by key individuals on the inside; they did not come in response to outside pressure.[9]

No clear institutional focus for consumer concerns in government existed in either country, nor was there a large, well-organized supporting constituency for consumer policy initiatives. The consumer movement had a very low profile into the 1950s. The few consumer interest groups which existed were either in their infancy and little given to political action—for example, the Consumer's Union in the United States—or were primarily concerned with specialized interests not always obviously linked to consumer matters—for example, the Consumers' League in the United States and the

Women's Institutes in Britain. Britain's Consumer Co-operative Movement was in many ways the most impressive of consumer organizations in either country. Founded in 1844, it had gained members in half the country's households by early in this century. An elaborate organizational structure linked the retail societies and enabled them to create wholesaling and manufacturing affiliates and to form other units to pursue social and political purposes. Before World War I ended, the Co-operative Movement had both a parliamentary lobbying office and a political party.[10] Yet the efforts of these units were often devoted to the defense of the Movement's narrow interests and did not often reflect a general concern to improve the lot of all consumers through government action.

Before the 1960s in neither Britain nor the United States was there sustained, systematic attention by government to consumer matters. Laws were enacted to respond to particular episodes of threat to public health and safety or to especially abusive trading practices. Although it was not yet appropriate to speak of consumer policy in the sense of implying the existence of a body of substantive enactments, institutions, and distinctive policy processes, one does see in retrospect the gradual development of a consumer agenda. Initial concerns with accurate measurements and food purity broadened to include the safety of other products, and information to enable consumers to make better purchasing decisions. From the 1930s onward procedural concerns were added, especially the desire for consumers to be represented explicitly in the process of making policies which would affect them. The consumer agenda which appeared to burst forth in the 1960s actually had been building for decades.

EXPLOSIVE GROWTH: CONSUMER POLICY IN THE 1960S AND 1970S

The United States

The 1960s and 1970s were a period of unprecedented government involvement in consumer questions. New laws were passed, old ones amended and notable executive decisions were taken in the name of consumers and their interests. Several developments in Washington at the turn of the decade indicated that fundamental changes were under way. Senator Kefauver opened a highly publicized series of hearings on the drug industry in 1959. Truth in Lending and Truth in Packaging bills were introduced in 1959 and 1961, though neither proposal would reach the statute book for some years.[11] President Kennedy's declaration of consumer rights in 1962 followed soon

Table I: CONSUMER POLICY LEGISLATION*

Great Britain		United States	
1955	Food and Drugs	1951	Fur Products Labeling
1961	Consumer Protection	1953	Flammable Products
1963	Weights and Measures Act	1958	Textile Fiber Products
1964	Hire Purchase–Resale Prices		Food Additives Amendment
1965	Hire Purchase	1960	Hazardous Substances Labels
1967	Misrepresentation	1962	Drug Safety Tests
1968	Trade Descriptions	1965	Cigarette Labeling
1970	Administration of Justice	1966	Fair Packaging and Labeling
1971	Unsolicited Goods and Services		Traffic and Vehicle Safety
	Consumer Protection Act		Child Protection
1972	Criminal Justice–Legal Advice	1967	Commission on Product Safety
	and Assistance		Flammable Fabrics Amendment
	Trade Descriptions Act		Wholesome Meat
1973	Administration of Justice	1968	Consumer Credit Protection
	Insurance Companies Amendment		Wholesale Poultry Products
	Supply of Goods	1969	Toy Safety
	Hallmarking Act	1970	Fair Credit Reporting
	Fair Trading Act		Poison Prevention Packaging
1974	Consumer Credit	1971	Consumer Product Safety Act
1975	Air Travel Reserve Fund Act	1972	Consumer Product Safety Amnd
1977	Unfair Contract Terms	1975	Warranty/FTC Improvement Act
1978	Insurance Consumers Act	1980	Infant Formula Act
1979	Estate Agents Act		Household Goods Transport
	Sale of Goods Act	1981	Cash Discount Act
1980	Competition Act		
1982	Supply of Goods and Services		
1984	Restrictive Trade Practices		

*The lists are drawn from *Congress and the Nation* (Congressional Quarterly) 1965, 1969 and 1973; Lester Sobel, ed., *Consumer Protection* (Facts on File, 1976); Information Office of the Treasury, *Consumer Protection Legislation* (HMSO, 1973); the OECD's *Annual Reports on Consumer Policy;* and *Survey of Current Affairs* (HMSO, vols. 14 and 15, 1984 and 1985).

after his re-creation of a Consumer Advisory Council.[12] Rising congressional interest was suggested by the appointment in 1963 of a House subcommittee on consumer affairs, though the Senate did not take comparable action until 1966.

All the major areas of consumer policy eventually were addressed by the legislation of the 1960s and 1970s—protecting against threats to health and safety, safeguarding the economic interests of consumers, and providing more information about products and services. (See Table 1.) Although Table 1 suggests that substantial consumer legislation was passed in the 1950s, most of these measures—for example, the Fur Products Labeling Act, the Flammable Fabrics Act, and the Textile Fiber Products Act—were discounted by consumer activists as laws designed to protect domestic industries from either foreign competition or more stringent regulation.[13] The first major consumer legislation of the period was the 1962 Drug Safety Tests Act.[14] The banner year for congressional action on consumer policy was 1966. Examining the content and treatment of three major bills passed that year and one from 1965 offers important insight into the congressional consumer policy process.

The Cigarette Labeling and Advertising Act of 1965, the Child Protection Act, and the Traffic and Vehicle Safety Act, like the Drug Safety Tests Act, dealt with health and safety matters. Each also addressed a highly publicized issue; the last-mentioned marked the dramatic entrance of Ralph Nader as a consumer crusader.[15] As such, they enabled congresspersons to operate on familiar turf, on issues where they could expect public and media approval, and where affected industries would have difficulty mounting effective counter attacks.[16]

The Truth in Packaging Act broke new ground by addressing the information needs of consumers outside the relatively familiar health and safety arena. The greater delay between introduction and passage compared to the health and safety legislation suggests that packaging standards were a more politically controversial matter.[17] Indeed, industry representatives staunchly resisted proposals that the government mandate standard package sizes for consumer products, and the bill which finally emerged "required that household products generally sold in supermarkets and drug stores be labeled clearly and accurately as to contents, net quantity and manufacturer. . . . [But] it did not authorize mandatory standard package sizes."[18] Most of the other consumer legislation of the late 1960s and 1970s concerned health and safety issues. Actions outside this arena, like the packaging and labeling act, took longer to reach the statute books.[19]

The legislation of this period created new regulatory bodies, such as the Consumer Product Safety Commission in 1972, and it significantly strengthened others, such as the Federal Trade Commission in the Magnuson-Moss Act of 1975. Increased powers and growing budgets were followed soon after by increasing regulatory actions in consumer policy.[20] This and other growth in the regulatory activity of the federal government set the stage for the strong reaction against regulation which developed at the end of the 1970s.[21]

Congress ultimately refused to change the status quo in one area. No federal agency with overall responsibility for consumer concerns was created despite the fact that such a proposal became the consumer movement's number one priority for the 1970s.[22] Its high-water mark in Congress came in 1975 when both houses passed bills, but the conference committee did not press on in the face of President Ford's announced intention to veto the measure. Consumer advocates' hopes were raised again when Jimmy Carter reached the White House as a supporter of a consumer agency. However, by this time congressional support had waned in the face of powerful opposition from the Chamber of Commerce and others in the business community, as well as the impact of a changing political climate.[23]

Representation of consumer concerns was provided to a limited degree through presidential actions, beginning with Kennedy's appointment of an advisory council and Johnson's appointment of a special assistant for consumer affairs. President Nixon embellished this arrangement in 1971 with an executive order creating a United States Office of Consumer Affairs headed by his special assistant for consumer affairs. This basic and limited scheme underwent little change in succeeding administrations until President Carter's 1978 executive order requiring each executive department and federal agency to establish a consumer advocacy office to facilitate complaint handling, information provision, and citizen participation in agency decision-making.[24] Carter's action was an attempt to achieve some of the goals of the proposed agency for consumer protection which had just been defeated in Congress.

While major developments of the 1960s and 1970s were under way at the national level, parallel actions occurred in the states and localities.[25] Massachusetts was credited with being the first state to pass a comprehensive consumer protection law, in 1960. By 1977, each of the fifty states had at least one office or division dealing with consumer affairs; more than 90 percent of these were established after 1964, most after 1970. In January 1978, the *Christian Science Monitor* reported a total of more than 600 state, county, and local government consumer protection agencies in operation. However, austerity measures introduced in the aftermath of the recession have jeopardized the continued functioning of many local and state offices.

Britain

The British experience with consumer policy in the 1960s and 1970s was similar to that of the United States. This was a period of intense policy development. The legislative actions indicated in Table 1 were concentrated in this period. There was much institutional development—aimed chiefly at providing representation and redress for consumers.

A milestone in the development of British consumer policy was the Conservative government's decision to appoint the Molony Committee on Consumer Protection in 1959. In appointing the committee the government does not seem to have been responding to public pressure but rather anticipating an increase in public interest.[26] A number of recommendations in its

1962 report eventually found their way to the statute books, but the principal immediate response was the government's acceptance of Molony's recommendation that a consumer council be appointed to advise the government on all consumer matters. The council began its work in 1963, seemingly adding an important channel for consumer representation in British government.

The Consumer Protection Act of 1961 grew out of an interim report of the Molony Committee and granted the home secretary the power to make regulations about any goods in order to protect public health and safety.[27] The 1963 Weights and Measures Act modernized the 1878 statute and broadened the legal basis for taking action in cases of shortweighting. The following year, resale price maintenance was curtailed as the Conservative government adopted the principle from a private member bill introduced by John Stonehouse, a Co-op sponsored MP. Perhaps the most important piece of consumer policy legislation in the 1960s was the Trade Descriptions Act of 1968 which imposed significant new responsibilities on local authorities and introduced a period of rapid growth in their involvement with consumer protection.[28]

The most important legislative and administrative developments in Britain's consumer policy took place in the 1970s, especially in the first half of the decade. Legislative actions of the 1970s included a large-scale effort to regulate the provision of consumer credit, the Consumer Credit Act of 1974, and the Consumer Safety Act of 1978, a counterpart to the United States Consumer Product Safety Act of 1972. The most significant single piece of legislation was the Fair Trading Act of 1973. It consolidated much existing legislation relating to monopolies and restrictive practices, added new consumer protection provisions, and created a new organization to administer each of these areas—the Office of Fair Trading, headed by the Director General of Fair Trading.[29] The legislation also provided for a consumer advisory council to advise the director general.

The questions of whether and how to provide for consumer representation continued to receive attention from British governments in the 1960s and 1970s. Like the nationalized industry consumer councils, the Molony-inspired consumer council appointed in 1963 suffered from a number of limitations.[30] The Heath government put an end to the council in 1970, claiming that private consumer organizations had grown in strength and number to the point that the council was no longer needed. An irony of the government's position was that the principal consumers' organizations strongly advocated continuing and strengthening the council. The sharp media and consumer group opposition to the decision to drop the council appeared to surprise the government and prompted it to recognize consumer interests with a cabinet-level appointment just two years later. Harold

Wilson's first Labour government also gave some attention to the question of representing consumer concerns in government decision-making.[31]

Sir Geoffrey Howe's 1972 appointment as Minister for Trade and Consumer Affairs was the first time a consumer portfolio was represented in the Cabinet. Labour extended this development when it returned to power by appointing Shirley Williams head of a new department of Price and Consumer Protection, in 1974. Later that year the government took the additional step of creating the National Consumer Council. The council's charge was to represent the consumer voice to government and industry, to be available to be consulted by those who sought a consumer view on policy proposals, to represent the consumer on government bodies, to provide information to consumers, and to take special care to represent the interests of disadvantaged consumers.

The net effect of many of the actions described above—appointing cabinet-level consumer ministers, giving local authorities a greater consumer role, creating the National Consumer Council and the Office of Fair Trading—was to institutionalize consumer policy. Recent years have seen some reduction in the priority government attaches to consumer policy, but key structural elements remain as activity centers in their own right and as focuses for the attention of consumer interest groups.

The Reagan Approach

The Carter years coincided with a developing debate about the basic philosophy of consumer policy. Advocates and interest groups supporting the consumer cause and their allies in Congress tended to assume that government should be active in this field and that selective government intervention in the marketplace would benefit consumers. An opposing position which served well the interests of business groups and others concerned about the negative effects of regulation held that consumers were best served by a genuinely free and competitive economy. This position gained ground quickly in the last years of the Carter administration and is associated with its moves to deregulate the airline and trucking industries. Although in these two cases it was widely perceived that existing regulations benefitted the regulated industries more than the consumers of their services, opponents of regulation quickly translated the specific argument for deregulation into an attack on all government intervention. As many have pointed out, such a position dovetailed with growing public opposition to the large size of government. The Reagan campaign's skillful exploitation of these feelings in 1980 was followed by clear policy changes.

The contrast between the Carter and Reagan administrations' approaches to consumer policy is exemplified in the language of the United States sections of the OECD's reports on consumer policy for 1980 and 1983: "It is the fundamental policy of President Carter's Administration to ensure that each agency of the federal government adequately responds to consumer needs in the development of policies, and provides adequate opportunities for consumer participation in its decision making process."[32] While not a ringing endorsement of consumerism or government regulation, this statement contrasts sharply with the 1983 statement: "The most important development relating to consumers in 1981 was President Reagan's regulatory programme which seeks to increase productivity, employment and consumer choice by reducing burdensome government regulations and allowing increased competition in the marketplace."[33]

The Reagan administration used reorganization, appointments, and budgets to pursue its goal of reducing regulation of business. A presidential order gave the Office of Management and Budget superagency status over all regulatory authorities in an attempt to rein them in. Plans were announced to move the Consumer Product Safety Commission into the Commerce Department, but congressional opposition foiled the move.[34] Murray Weidenbaum's appointment as chairman of the Council of Economic Advisers was symbolic since Weidenbaum was a well-known opponent of government regulation. The consumer activists, many of them ex-Naderites, whom Carter had appointed to leadership posts in consumer protection agencies, were replaced as quickly as possible with persons more sympathetic to the Reagan administration's outlook. Funding for the principal consumer protective regulatory agencies—the Consumer Product Safety Commission, the Federal Trade Commission, and the Food and Drug Administration—was cut sharply.[35] Personnel reductions were a corollary of fewer funds; between 1982 and 1984 the CPSC and the FTC each experienced a 14 percent or more reduction in force.[36] Instead of the heavy hand of government, businesses were encouraged to develop a self-policing approach to their relationship with consumers.[37]

The Thatcher Approach

The Conservative government's orientation to consumer policy is reflected in several developments. The abolition of the Department of Prices and Consumer Protection was one of Prime Minister Thatcher's first acts.[38] Another early change was the termination of grant support for the development of local authority consumer advice centers, on the grounds that their work could be done "just as effectively and more cheaply by Local Authorities Trading Standards Departments or generalist advice services such as Cit-

izens Advice Bureaux."[39] The Competition Act of 1980 strengthened the
ability of the Director General of Fair Trading and the Monopolies and
Mergers Commission to deal with anticompetitive practices in the public as
well as the private sector. The Office of Fair Trading has been encouraged to
continue its sponsorship of industry efforts to develop voluntary codes of
practice, but the Director General of Fair Trading has noted that a changed
political climate now makes it more difficult to negotiate codes.[40] Perhaps
the most radical policy of the Thatcher administration is privatization.
Government spokesmen sometimes have cited consumers as the principal
beneficiaries of moves such as the British Telecom sale, claiming that
nationalized monopolies were simply not responsive to consumer needs, the
existence of consumer councils within them notwithstanding.[41] However,
most official statements about privatization do not mention this justification.
Taken together, these actions reflect a preference for competition and volun-
tarism rather than regulation in the Thatcher government's approach to
consumer policy. In this there is a clear similarity to the preferred approach of
the Reagan administration.

     Yet the changes since 1979 have not gone as far as many persons involved
with consumer policy had expected. The Office of Fair Trading has remained
a prominent institution for addressing consumer concerns despite its growing
focus on competition policy per se. Its activities continue to attract media
attention, and its publications provide a substantial amount of information to
consumers. The Director General of Fair Trading also has had some success
in providing consumers more information about professional services, by
ending some of the historic advertising restrictions.[42] Even though the
government cut funding to local authority consumer advice centers and
initially to Citizens Advice Bureaus, it later reversed its position on the CABS,
substantially increasing its grant to their national association.[43] The government also has undertaken an inquiry into improving the performance of
nationalized industry consumer consultative councils.[44] Most surprising is
the survival of the National Consumer Council. The council has relied
heavily upon research and reasoned appeals to influence the decisions of
government departments. It has encouraged the activities of local consumer
groups and the formation of a national consumer agenda through its sponsorship of an annual consumer congress, the counterpart of the Consumer
Federation of America's annual meeting.

     Other indicators suggest that the Thatcher government continues to recog-
nize consumer policy as a legitimate subject. A ministerial post responsible
for consumer affairs has been retained, although outside the cabinet. Four
persons have held the post since 1979. The enthusiasm and competence of
some of them have been questioned by consumer activists, but the key point

is the existence of a focus for consumer questions inside a line department, currently the Parliamentary Under-Secretary for Corporate and Consumer Affairs in the Department of Trade and Industry. Statements by the consumer ministers amplify the position of the Thatcher government:

> Most of the major measures of consumer protection legislation have been introduced under a Conservative Government, and it is certainly our policy to continue to provide cost effective protection for consumers in the public and private sectors.
> The essential framework of consumer protection legislation is already established. The most effective further action which can be taken in the interest of consumers is to continue to seek free and fair competition in the market place.[45]

The basic message seems to be that consumer policy is recognized, but is not an area where this government expects to be very active.

CONSUMER LOBBIES AND CONSUMER POLICYMAKING

One important facet of the development of consumer policy is the emergence of consumer lobbies in both countries. It is appropriate to review this set of participants before turning to an analysis of the consumer policy process.

The United States

No large consumer interest groups were present to advocate the cause of American consumers during the first half of this century. However, one reaction to excessive advertising claims was the formation of consumer product-testing organizations—Edward Schlink's Consumers Research in 1929 and, following a labor dispute within Schlink's staff, the breakaway, and ultimately much better known, Consumers Union in 1936. But neither of these organizations developed a mass membership or turned to lobbying in its early years. The only possible claimant to this role was the National Consumers League; founded in 1899, it had a number of local affiliates. But the League was more a part of the labor movement than a specifically consumer organization; until the late 1930s, and the passage of the Fair Labor Standards Act, its primary goal was to enlist consumers on behalf of improved conditions for workers.[46]

Only in the late 1960s did a large-scale consumer lobby emerge. In April 1966, the first nationwide meeting of organizations representing consumer interests was held in Washington.[47] The conference was institutionalized two years later when the Consumer Federation of America was formed; this umbrella organization had two membership classes, consumer organizations and supporting organizations—those claiming a consumer interest, especially organized labor.[48] The federation was to act as a lobby, assist state and local consumer groups, and to increase public and media awareness of consumer needs.[49] Ralph Nader developed a series of consumer advocacy organizations between 1968 and 1972.[50] In 1969, the Consumers Union, by then the best-known of the country's consumer organizations, opened a legislative affairs office in Washington following several years of the most explosive membership growth in its history.[51] The National Consumers League also moved into the consumer protection field in the 1960s.[52]

Recently, financial difficulties have troubled the Consumers Union, and Consumers Research has closed.[53] It is paradoxical that two nongovernmental organizations which specialize in producing comparative product information for consumers should experience problems at the very time when the government is telling consumers to rely less on it and more on the marketplace. The consumer organizations' problems may suggest diminishing public interest in consumer policy. Yet other indicators imply continued strong public interest. A Harris survey conducted in the fall of 1982 found that the public had grown more concerned about consumer issues in the seven years since Congress last enacted a major piece of consumer legislation.[54] Sixty-eight percent of respondents to a 1983 survey believed that government should be more involved in regulating product quality, although the higher the household income, the less likely this view was to be supported.[55] There is little prospect that consumer organizations concerned with influencing public policy will be reduced to their moribund pre-1960s state, but their influence has diminished since the mid-1970s.

Britain

Signs of a developing consumer movement became evident in the 1950s. The British Standards Institution created its own consumer advisory council in 1955, "to ensure that the consumer had a say in matters which had hitherto been regarded as the exclusive concern of traders and manufacturers."[56] The Consumers' Association, modelled after the Consumers Union in the United States, was formed in 1957. With its publication *Which?*, the Consumers' Association soon became Britain's best-known consumer group. The Cooperative Movement through its party, parliamentary committee and group of sponsored MPs began to articulate proposals for government action to address the needs of all consumers.[57] The formation of local consumers groups was encouraged by the Consumers' Association from 1961 on. Two years later these groups formed the National Federation of Consumer Groups. By 1973 some sixty groups claiming 10,000 members belonged to the federation.[58]

The consumer movement outside government has seemingly held its own during the past few years. The Consumers' Association, the largest specifically consumers organization, has survived some financial difficulties and has maintained its membership of over 600,000. Local groups have not fared as well. The poor performance of the Labour party in the June 1983 general election resulted in the reduction of the number of Co-op sponsored MPs to eight, fewer than half their number of the early 1970s, and well below the peak of twenty-three in 1945. In this an identifiable consumer voice in Parliament was diminished. On the other hand, the National Consumers Council has enjoyed some success in stimulating the development of specialized consumer interest groups, and in coordinating the efforts of many organizations with an interest in consumer issues.[59] In the media, consumer correspondents continue to serve on the staffs of many major newspapers, and local commercial radio stations have been receptive to broadcasting consumer information programs.

The concerns being expressed by the several consumer voices reflect an expansion of the public consumer agenda similar to what occurred during the Carter administration in the United States. One element of this is the growing demand for regulation in the provision of financial services—for instance, calls for government action to protect investors, and the National Consumer Council's major study of the banking industry.[60] The special needs of disadvantaged consumers have also received more attention, as has the desire to improve the consumer responsiveness of nationalized industries and other public services.[61]

No direct recent evidence is available to suggest how the general public now views consumer policy. There are indications that the public is becoming more acquainted with potential means of redress offered in existing policy arrangements—more and more persons are lodging complaints or seeking assistance from local authorities and voluntary consumer advice centers.[62] Yet the 1979–80 national consumer concerns survey commissioned by the National Consumers Council found that the vast majority of persons with a complaint about private or public goods or services did nothing about it.[63]

THE CONSUMER POLICY PROCESS

Consumer policy developed as an issue area in both Britain and the United States as a product of general social change and shorter-term political conditions. Among the former were (1) rising educational levels—presumably creating a larger body of more articulate consumers among the populations of both countries, and (2) the emergence of societies of high mass consumption where increased affluence and a wide variety of available consumer goods purveyed by large chain stores confronted consumers with a great many choices—choices involving both opportunities and risks. While societal changes created a readiness for many people to respond to and support consumer policy initiatives, public opinion did not compel action. There was no sustained period of agitation by groups and individuals outside government before consumer policy issues appeared on government agendas. This was particularly the case for the United States where government action on consumer policy, media attention to consumer concerns, and an active consumer movement arrived on the scene nearly simultaneously in the mid-1960s. Other factors, often linked to short-term political needs, play an essential role in explaining the emergence of consumer policy. As the foregoing analysis has demonstrated, much of the early action on consumer policy originated with individuals in Congress and the administration rather than with outside groups.

Consumer policy entered government agendas in both countries as a discretionary item. That is, it received attention at the discretion of political leaders. Why were politicians on both sides of the Atlantic prepared to give systematic attention to consumer policy by the 1960s if public pressure was not the driving force? Several considerations appear to have been involved.

The United States

For American politicians, positive experiences responding to public health and safety crises of the early 1960s fostered a willingness to entertain additional consumer policy measures. Politicians also were attracted to consumer policy as a part of their response to the problem of inflation; this was especially important in accounting for Lyndon Johnson's interest in consumer policy during his presidency.[64] They were aided and abetted by two other developments: public interest politics and entrepreneurial politics. Andrew McFarland's analysis of the rise of public interest politics attributes it to the development of "civic skepticism," questioning existing political arrangements and public administrative practices in terms of their utility for solving social problems.[65] A general reform mood was building.

One outgrowth of "civic skepticism" was the development of public interest groups committed to using public power to reform a disagreeable social reality. These groups, as Jeffrey Berry puts it, benefitted from the growing strength of the pluralist ideal; if pluralist democracy did not exist in fact, the way to put it right was to balance the influence of existing groups with new ones.[66] The public interest movement offered support to politicians who championed their issues or who offered proposals in line with the movement's program. The movement, however, did not itself spring from the grassroots. Rather it was in large part the handiwork of persons who came to be known as public interest entrepreneurs. Some of these persons were members of Congress or congressional staffers, but they were exemplified above all by the outsider Ralph Nader.[67] The entrepreneurs took particular issues and built constituencies for them by allying with concerned interest groups, but probably more importantly by their skillfully enlisting the media in behalf of the cause. The very heavy reliance on a few individuals implicit in this approach meant that the grassroots activism never developed very well, nor were the entrepreneurs able to build a national institutional focus for their efforts.[68]

Presidential leadership on consumer issues was sporadic. Kennedy and Johnson issued messages on consumer matters; Johnson's messages often outlined a consumer program and endorsed particular pieces of legislation. Nixon, too, was comparatively active in the consumer policy area. Subsequently, presidential attention to consumer policy waned. Jimmy Carter showed some enthusiasm for the subject as a candidate and was credited with appointing aggressive heads to the regulatory agencies, but his interest appeared to diminish in the face of increasing concern about the costs of regulation.

Individual members of Congress—such as Senator Kefauver initially and then-senators Magnuson and Philip Hart and Representative Moss—usually took the lead in bringing proposals to the legislative agenda.[69] In this they were supported and sometimes led by consumer interest entrepreneurs. But subsequent events demonstrated that the entrepreneurs could not sustain their agenda in a changing economic and political climate. For the past six years, consumer policymaking in Congress has been characterized by a role reversal among the participants. Partisan change in the control of the Senate and the White House means that many fewer persons sympathetic to the consumer movement's agenda are to be found in influential positions.[70] Defending the gains was further complicated when governments faced by continuing stagflation adopted deregulation and reduced government spending as prescriptions. Consumer advocates and interest groups now find their major challenge is to preserve existing arrangements rather than to press for additional legislation.

Business responses to consumerism may be grouped into actions of three types: (1) the development and expansion of customer relations programs by individual companies; (2) the development of self-regulation, usually in the form of industrywide voluntary codes of practice formulated by trade associations; and (3) the strengthening of lobbying efforts and institutional advertising aimed at heading off government action.[71] The second response pattern was especially evident when government regulation was a direct threat. For example, self-regulation was proposed—although unsuccessfully—as an alternative to government standards when the cigarette advertising, auto safety, and "truth in packaging" cases discussed above were before Congress. Business actions of the third type were quite successful in fostering the political popularity of deregulation at the end of the 1970s. The apparent failure of some consumer policy regulations assisted business efforts to undermine political support for further regulation.[72]

Explanations of the strength and success of the reaction must be sought in several areas. The broadened scope of the consumer movement's concerns generated a large number of potential adversaries, not just the retail merchants but providers of health services, public utilities, public transportation, auto manufacturers, and anyone else who disagreed with consumer groups' claims to a greater voice in public policymaking.[73] Alleged and admitted excesses of some consumer advocates, and the failure of some consumer policy actions to work well, also fed reaction. When consumer protection lost its political appeal, politicians moved on to other issues. Finally, as the logic of collective action suggests, consumers as individuals had fewer incentives to organize to press their claims than did business leaders who perceived government consumer policy actions as costly.[74]

The experience of the United States with consumer policy may be summarized as gradual, if sometimes isolated, developments both in and out of government, leading to a period of explosive growth in which consumer policy became one of the "hot items" on the government agenda. This "boom" was followed in the late 1970s by a period of intense reaction to government intervention which has carried into the 1980s. The results have been a changed consumer policy climate, a drastic reduction in the importance of consumer policy on governmental agendas, and an adverse impact on the health of some consumer interest groups. The consumer movement has been placed on the defensive at the federal level by an administration unsympathetic to regulation and eager to cut spending on civilian agencies. However, by no means have all of the policy initiatives of the growth period been reversed.

Britain

The British policy pattern does not differ radically. Yet there are variations in the process through which consumer policy emerged and in the relative importance of policy actors. Party programs gave more sustained attention to consumer policy questions before governments became very active in the field.[75] The British government also began to address consumer policy as a general issue earlier than the American government, through its appointment of the Molony Committee in 1959.

Perhaps there were special stimuli in the British case which account for this earlier attention. The growth of the welfare state and the post- World War II nationalization policies meant that the government itself had now become an important, often monopoly, supplier of goods and services. The amount and quality of goods and services delivered by government could be seen as consumer issues. Then, too, rationing had lasted longer after the war in Britain. When it finally ended there was a ready-made consumer backlash against retailers based upon accumulated grievances with rationing. For some, these constituted additional reasons to emphasize the need for consumer representation and participation in government decision-making beyond the recognition shared by consumer activists in both countries that producers and suppliers of goods already had access to relevant government decision centers.

The British experience with consumer policy also differs in that public interest and entrepreneurial politics never became a serious part of the policymaking process of the 1960s and 1970s. Party government, despite increased backbench restiveness in both parties, remained the policy paradigm. The occasional successes of private member bills addressing consumer policy issues notwithstanding, one must look to the needs and values of leading politicians and their links to interest groups to account for consumer policy development in Britain.

While in the United States consumer policy development is particularly associated with Democratic administrations or Democrat-controlled Congresses, in Britain both Labour and Conservative governments have introduced major consumer policy innovations, beginning with the Macmillan government's appointment of the Molony Committee. One key to understanding this is the relationship between consumer organizations and the political parties. In the United States most of the key consumer interest groups have been led by persons with ties to the Democratic party; the main allies of consumer groups have been the trade unions, most of which also have strong historic links to the Democrats. A similar situation appears to exist in Britain, especially if we consider only the case of the Co-operative Movement. But the early success of the Consumers' Association and its decision to try to influence government policy introduced a different element in the British situation. The founders of CA included persons with very close ties to both major parties, such as Roy Jenkins for Labour and James Douglas, a senior figure in the Conservative research department. This is not to say that such individuals exercised great personal influence on government agendas, but it suggests for CA a status and access to government seldom if ever enjoyed by the Consumer's Union or any other consumer organization in the United States. Even in the case of the Consumer's Union and the Democratic party, the CU board has not included national party leaders. When the Heath government abolished the original consumer council, the following outcry from consumer groups—including heavily middle-class local consumer groups—apparently prompted it to respond by creating the cabinet-level position of Minister for Trade and Consumer Affairs.

Like the public interest advocates in the United States, those who supported a strengthened consumer voice in Britain did so on the basis of appeals to pluralism. Before it created the National Consumer Council, the Labour government published a White Paper justifying the need for a national consumer agency on the grounds that

> there remains a lack of any independent national consumer body sufficiently representative and influential to ensure that those who take decisions which will affect the consumer can have a balanced and authoritative view before them. . . . Those concerned in the production of goods and services are extensively involved with government in the national councils through the TUC and the CBI. . . . The consumer ought . . . to have a similar opportunity to be heard.[76]

Group consultation alone is not enough to account for politicians in both parties being willing to introduce consumer policy measures. The long-time involvement of local authorities in consumer protection, and the bureaucratic channels of communication which exist between central and local government in Britain's unitary system, provided Whitehall with a nonpartisan source of information about consumer problems. The more decentralized American federal system and the dearth of consumer policy machinery in many states denied a comparable information source and impetus to Washington. In combination with the above-mentioned difference in party-interest group relations, this helps to compensate for the absence of public interest entrepreneurs in Britain.

The short-term political needs of particular administrations comprise another key to understanding the consumer policy process in Britain. As in the United States, the need to cope with inflation was a factor. The clearest example of this factor occurred when Harold Wilson's third Labour administration was attempting to sell the social contract to the unions. The creation of the Department of Prices and Consumer Protection in 1974, its "price check" program, and, less clearly, the creation of the National Consumer Council have been interpreted as responses to popular concern with inflation.[77]

To the extent that consumer policy measures may be understood as a response to inflation, one would expect them to decline in significance as inflation receded. The record of the past few years indicates some support for this reasoning, but in the United States it is less than compelling because enthusiasm for consumer policy measures seems to have declined before inflation did. Perhaps the business community's strong attack upon regulation took away any short-term incentives for American politicians to pursue consumer policy measures. This argument applies with particular force to consumer policy outside the health and safety area. On the other hand, there is little evidence of a concerted effort by British business groups to resist generally the development of consumer policy.[78] More recently, both the Reagan and Thatcher administrations eagerly sought programs to cut in pursuit of their goal of reducing both the size and the cost of government. While consumer programs were not big ticket items in either country's budget, they could appear to be tempting targets because most were relatively new and not defended by well-organized interest groups.

SIMILARITIES, DIFFERENCES AND CONVERGENCE

One conclusion which may be reached from the analysis of consumer policy in Britain and the United States is that the general concept of convergence needs to be refined and differentiated if it is to be very useful in the comparative study of public policies. The distinction between substantive and procedural convergence takes us part of the way. Reflection on consumer policy developments suggests several additional refinements where the question of convergence may be examined profitably. Under the rubric of substantive convergence one may distinguish between the declaratory policy (or doctrine) of a particular administration, the substantive actions it takes, and the impact of those actions. When we consider the processes and procedures used to make policy in a particular area, we may also consider convergence from the perspective of what led to the emergence of this policy area, what actors play key roles in the formulation and administration of the policy, and how alike and how well institutionalized are the policymaking processes in this field. Using this differentiated concept yields a second conclusion: there has been much convergence in the consumer policy field, but it is far stronger in some aspects of the policy area than others. The concept of qualified convergence is an appropriate way to capture these developments.

The earlier review of the substantive aspects of consumer policy makes it evident that the issues addressed in this policy area have been quite similar. Both governments have used legislative and administrative measures to deal with product safety concerns, packaging and labelling, consumer credit, and retail sales practices. Further similarities are evident in two recent developments: the tendency of governments to give less attention to consumer policy; and the emergence of a common new concern with financial service industries, such as banking, insurance, and investments, as potential subjects of future consumer policy actions.[79] Declaratory policies have undergone change in both countries during the transition from Labour to Conservative and Democratic to Republican governments, but the direction of change has been the same in both cases.

Among the more striking similarities in the countries' experiences with the policy process aspects of consumer policy is the nearly identical timing of the emergence of the policy area. This suggests the importance of social and economic background conditions as prerequisites to government action. Both also have been concerned with the representation of consumer interests in policymaking processes. Consumer advocates' use of pluralist theory-based justifications for improved consumer representation in government is another commonality. The flourishing of consumer interest groups and media attention to consumer affairs in the late 1960s and early 1970s also forms a common pattern. A similar claim could be made for the development of local authority and state and local government consumer activities in the 1960s. Consumer policymaking in both countries has been characterized by episodes of intense political struggle, but these generally have been limited in scope and duration, stopping well short of becoming "redistributive" conflicts.[80] The greatest controversy in either country was that generated during the protracted battle over the proposed agency for consumer protection in the United States.

The existence of so much commonality in the subjects addressed and remedies proposed leads one to wonder whether these developments occurred independently or whether direct borrowing took place. Answering this question ultimately requires detailed case studies of particular measures.[81] A shared language, frequent travel between the two countries by officials and other interested persons, and common membership in an organization (OECD) which facilitates sharing information about consumer policy all suggest a strong *prima facie* case for borrowing. Yet conversations with officials and the written record on both sides of the Atlantic, while revealing a general awareness of developments in the other country, provide little evidence of direct borrowing.

Differences between the two countries also are clear. The most important have to do with the policymaking process and the institutionalization of consumer representation. Executive leadership has been important in both cases, but more consistently so in Britain. For the United States, Congress has been an independent source of action and sometimes a source of firm resistance to executive initiatives. With the exceptional cases of a few private member bills, the executive has dominated the consumer policy process in Britain as students of British politics would predict. It also appears that groups sympathetic to the development of consumer policy have had more consistent access to the policy process in the United Kingdom.[82] In part this is a function of the previously discussed links between consumer groups and both major political parties. But one must also recall that British governments created and maintained an organization to focus and represent consumer interests, the National Consumer Council. Britain also has in the Office of Fair Trading a more centralized clearing house for consumer policy administration than one finds at the national level in the United States. The often proposed American office of consumer representation never materialized. The failure to establish a statutorily based agency with general responsibility for consumer representation left the United States without an important institutional support for preserving consumer policy achievements and supplying a locus of support for new initiatives. Administrative responsibility for consumer programs is highly fragmented in the United States. A very important but thus far unacknowledged institutional difference is the fact of federalism in the United States. Many areas of retail regulation and other issues of consumer policy are left to the states in the United States but dealt with by national government in Britain. To this extent, then, consumer policy is much more a patchwork quilt in the United States. Britain's central direction of local authority yielded both more uniform and more comprehensive approaches.

Although consumer protection emerged as a policy area in both countries almost simultaneously, the timing of legislative responses has differed. The most important United States consumer policy laws were made in the late 1960s and early 1970s; no wide-ranging measures have been taken by Congress since 1975. Legislative action peaked later in Britain. Despite supposedly common predilections, Margaret Thatcher's government has been more supportive of additional consumer legislation than has Ronald Reagan's.[83]

More importantly, Britain's preservation of more impressive consumer representation arrangements leads to the conclusion that a consumer policy process is better established there now than in the United States. Even after retrenchment, consumer policy institutions retain comparatively high visibility in the United Kingdom. Differences in executive-legislative relations in the two countries, as King suggests, created more opportunities in the United States for both initiative and resistance regarding consumer policy proposals.[84] Another institutional support for consumer policy in Britain is membership in the European Community. The Community has established a Directorate General for Consumer Affairs within its commission as well as numerous consultative groups, and has issued two consumer programs.[85] While the importance of this activity should not be overestimated, it does support the legitimacy of consumer policy.

Overall, the contents of the policy areas are quite similar. Yet the procedures of policymaking do differ in important ways. The most important consequences of this may be that British consumers have more opportunities to receive assistance from government with their consumer complaints— even if most of them do not use the available machinery, and that consumer interests are more likely to be taken into account on a continuing basis in Britain because of more developed consumer oriented institutions.[86] Aggrieved consumers in the United States are more often directed to the courts to pursue legal action while their British counterparts are encouraged to use advice centers and administrative remedies. United States citizens may now receive more information about products than Britons, and they are more likely to be encouraged to seek legal remedies to their individual consumer problems. Despite cutbacks and deregulation, American agencies continue to display impressive abilities to respond to threats to public health and safety in the food and drug area. A balance-sheet approach to the overall impact of consumer policy, including judgments about whose consumers are better served, is not easily rendered. Yet it seems clear that consumers in both countries have achieved much from government actions compared to their positions twenty-five years ago.

Having said these things, it is also necessary to emphasize that although one may speak of consumer policy as a distinct policy area, it exists on the periphery of governmental agendas compared to many areas of economic policy. Producers' interests as represented by business and labor continue to enjoy greater prominence than those of consumers in both political systems. The postindustrial society thesis—that more of us will work less and become more sophisticated and demanding consumers—holds the possibility that consumer policy will occupy a more central place on government agendas, but that day is not yet at hand.[87]

What, then, of convergence? From the vantage point of 1986 the case for policy convergence appears less compelling than it did a decade ago. At that time the emergence of societies of high mass consumption, the development of consumer interest groups, the prominence of similar consumer issues on government agendas, and the attention being devoted to providing consumer access to policymaking collectively made a strong case for convergence. Similar problems seemed to be generating common responses, as they did in the realm of welfare policy, for example.[88] Since then the consumer movement has been set back and consumer issues have declined in prominence on government agendas. Problems associated with economic decline rather than boom now occupy the attention of political leaders. Yet the new common problem has not produced a common result as far as consumer policy is concerned. The most striking facet of convergence between the Reagan and Thatcher administrations is doctrinal—their declaratory preference for market solutions and reduced government intervention. Beyond that, consumer policy legislative action, albeit limited, has continued in Britain. More important differences are the continued greater degree of institutionalization of consumer policy at the national level in Britain, and, perhaps not unrelated, the stronger initial deregulation thrust to United States economic policy. The developments of the past decade appear to offer some support for the hypothesis offered recently by Heidenheimer, et al., that the socioeconomic policies of capitalist democracies converge during periods of prosperity but diverge during periods of economic decline.[89] However, neither the Reagan nor the Thatcher government explicitly has disavowed consumer policy, and a stronger consumer infrastructure of groups and institutions continues to exist than in earlier periods when governmental attention to consumer matters was at low ebb. Does this mean that consumer policy will become more convergent with the next economic boom? Perhaps. For now, the most appropriate conclusion is that when common problems and issues are mediated through differing institutional arrangements and political traditions, complete convergence is unlikely.

NOTES

1. Organization for Economic Cooperation and Development, *Consumer Policy During the Past Ten Years.* Paris: 1983.
2. For definitions of consumer policy see: *Final Report of the Committee on Consumer Protection* (Molony Committee), Cmnd. 1781, (July 1962), 8; Thomas Krattenmaker, "The Federal Trade Commission and Consumer Protection" in Robert N. Katz, ed., *Protecting the Consumer Interest* (Cambridge, Mass.: Ballinger, 1976), 107–8; and Lester A. Sobel, ed., *Consumer Protection* (Facts on File, 1976), 5.
3. OECD, *Consumer Policy During the Past Ten Years,* 10.
4. Congress, however, never took up this power, apparently preferring to leave the matter to the states. See Leland Gordon, "Weights and Measures," in Erma Angevine, ed., *Consumer Activists: They Made a Difference* (National Consumers Committee for Research and Education, 1982), 121.
5. Gordon Borrie, *The Consumer, Society and the Law,* 3rd ed. (London: Penguin, 1973), 21–23.

Richard S. Flickinger

6. Implementation of the Agricultural Adjustment Act and the National Recovery Act included creation of a Consumer Council and a Consumer Advisory Board, respectively. As persons centrally involved recalled these developments, " . . . attention to the rights of consumers came on an intellectual level from those who designed New Deal agencies and not from an organized movement with public awareness and pressure." Caroline F. Ware, et al., "Consumer Participation at the Federal Level" in Angevine, ed., *Consumer Activists,* 171. This pattern also accounts for the creation of the Consumer Advisory Committee to the World War II Office of Price Administration and the Consumer Advisory Council to the Council of Economic Advisors. Awareness of growing abuses in the marketplace prompted passage of the New Deal's hallmark consumer legislation, the Food, Drug and Cosmetic Act of 1938.

7. John Martin and George W. Smith, *The Consumer Interest* (London: Pall Mall Press, 1968), 123–4.

8. Politicians affiliated with Britain's consumer co-ops soon pressed for improved public and consumer influence in the nationalized industries. See the Co-operative Party's 1951 election manifesto, *For All the People* (London: Co-operative Party, 1951). In 1955, the Co-operative parliamentary group consisting of 19 sponsored Labour-Co-op MPs drafted and the party's annual conference unanimously adopted a proposal for a ministry of consumer' welfare. [See Co-operative Party, *Proposals for a Ministry of Consumers' Welfare* (Manchester: 1963).] Although criticized at the time and dismissed later by a government commission as a "grandiose notion" (the Molony Committee), there are striking similarities between the contents of the Co-operative proposal and the arrangements created by British governments in the 1970s.

9. Governor Harriman of New York appointed a Consumer Counsel in 1955. See Persia Campbell, "Consumer Representation at the State Level: The Pioneer, New York" in Angevine, ed., *Consumer Activists,* 213–4. Harriman is said to have recognized the need for a consumer voice from his New Deal days in the NRA. His sister, Mary Harriman Rumsey, was chair of the NRA's Consumer Advisory Board. Harriman's creation disappeared with his defeat in the 1958 election. California Governor Pat Brown got his state's legislature to establish a state consumer counsel's office in 1959. Brown believed that legislative enactment would likely make the office more permanent. Brown's reasoning appears to have been correct for the California office has survived. Brown's consumer counsel claimed that he wanted the office because of his own commitment, not because of popular pressure; he was "ahead of the people" on this. Helen Ewing Nelson, "Consumer Representation at the State Level: California," in Angevine, ed., *Consumer Activists,* 229.

10. In 1880, the Co-operative Congress, the central governing body of the movement, voted to create a parliamentary committee to assist the movement in its relations with the government. In 1917, after many years of deliberation, the movement decided to create the Co-operative party as its own political arm committed to securing the election of co-operators to parliament and to local government bodies. By this time the Labour party had preempted the field of working class political organization. Thus it was not surprising that the Co-operative party entered into a working relationship with Labour which left it for practical purposes an adjunct of the Labour party.

11. Erma Angevine, "Lobbying and the CFA," in Angevine, ed., *Consumer Activists,* 336.

12. Esther Peterson, "Consumer Representation in the White House," in Angevine, ed., *Consumer Activists*, 198–212. The council is credited with convincing the president to appoint an advisor on consumer affairs in 1963, but the assassination delayed Esther Peterson's appointment until 1964. Neither the council nor the president's consumer advisor was notably effective in gaining media attention to consumer issues. Not until Ralph Nader had his famous encounter with General Motors in 1966 did consumer policy attract serious and sustained media coverage. ("The Consumer Movement, A Middle Class Movement," in the American Council on Consumer Interests, *Proceedings*, 1981, 163.) It is not clear just how far consumer consciousness had penetrated the public mind by the mid-1960s. For those who stress the role of socioeconomic conditions in the creation of consumerism, the society of high mass consumption was at hand. Yet there was not a popular outpouring of consumerist sentiment.

13. Michael Pertschuk, *The Revolt Against Regulation: The Rise and Pause of the Consumer Movement* (Berkeley: University of California Press, 1982), 8–9, 22.

14. Sobel, ed., *Consumer Protection*, 7. Although this legislation was partly a product of Senator Kefauver's earlier hearings, the catalyst was the international thalidomide tragedy.

15. The Cigarette Labeling Act required health warnings to be carried on cigarette packages and cartons from 1 January 1966. This act could be seen to be a direct consequence of the Surgeon General's 1964 report on the dangers of smoking to health, and to subsequent moves by the Federal Trade Commission to regulate cigarette advertising. (See Sobel, *Consumer Protection*, 74–77 and Sandra Stencel, "Anti-Smoking Campaign," in *Consumer Protection: Gains and Setbacks* [Congressional Quarterly, Editorial Research Reports, 1978], 61–80. The Traffic and Vehicle Safety Act is the classic example of Naderism. Speaker McCormack credited Ralph Nader with the critical role in securing the passage of this law enabling the federal government to establish vehicle safety standards. *Congressional Quarterly Almanac*, 1966, 268.

16. Even so, it might be noted that both the auto and tobacco industries were successful in securing Congressional compromises which prevented more vigorous regulatory proposals from reaching the statute books.

17. President Johnson had called for action on packaging standards in his first consumer message in 1964. Senator Philip Hart had pushed this idea two years earlier when his Senate Antitrust and Monopoly Subcommittee held hearings on deceptive packaging problems. (Sobel, *Consumer Protection*, 6.) A bill calling for improved packaging standards for consumer products had been introduced in 1961.

18. Ibid., 8. See also the 1966 *Congressional Quarterly Almanac*, 355ff.

19. Three examples are the "Truth in Lending" act of 1968, originally introduced in 1959; the Fair Credit Reporting Act of 1970, and the Product Warranty Act of 1975, introduced in 1967. Each took longer to become law than the health and safety proposals, and each encountered more effective opposition from the business community. See *Congressional Quarterly Almanac*, 1968, 205–11; *Ibid.*, 1970, p. 624; and *Congress and the Nation* Vol. 4, 435 for accounts of these measures.

20. See the United States chapters in the OECD's annual reports on consumer policy, especially 1976–1980, for summaries of these actions.

21. Consumers looked to these agencies for help; businesses often came to regard them as "the enemy," seizing on comments such as that by President Carter's

Federal Trade Commission chairman Michael Pertschuk: "Our role, as I see it, is to redistribute power to the people." Quoted in Susan J. and Martin Tolchin, *Dismantling America: The Rush to De-Regulate,* (Boston: Houghton Mifflin, 1983), 150. Pertschuk later acknowledged the difficulties his commission faced as a result of its sometimes playing a consumer advocacy role, "the role of the regulator, the unelected bureaucrat, as a public advocate to counterbalance the advocacy resources of business is inherently limited by the conflicting need for the regulator to maintain his own legitimacy as impartial decision-maker." (Pertschuk, *Revolt Against Regulation,* 126.)

22. The proposal for a consumer department or agency had been around for many years. It first seems to have surfaced among the "New Dealers" of the 1930s. Senator Kefauver introduced the idea in Congress in 1959 with a bill to create a Department of Consumers. The proposal was politically dormant until 1966 when it received some publicity from hearings held by the House Government Operations Committee and from the recommendation of its establishment in the year end report of the President's Consumer Advisory Council (*Congressional Quarterly Almanac,* 1966, 353–4). In 1968 Rep. Rosenthal introduced a revised proposal calling for the creation of an Agency for Consumer Protection rather than a department. This represented a compromise with those who saw the department as both too costly and too threatening. Karen Stein, "A Political History of the Proposal to Create a Federal Consumer Protection Agency," ACCI *Proceedings,* 1979, 126–31. The proposal remained on the congressional agenda for another decade.

23. A weakened proposal for what was then termed an Office of Consumer Representation lost badly on a floor vote in the House in 1978. This marked the end of active Congressional concern for the proposal, although it remains a priority item on the agendas of consumer groups (Consumer Federation of America, *Policy Resolutions,* 1984, 75).

24. OECD, *Annual Reports on Consumer Policy,* 1981, p. 157.

25. The information in this paragraph is found in *Consumer Protection in the States* (Lexington, Ky: Council of State Governments, 1970), 24; Editorial Research Reports, *Consumer Protection,* 4; and Office of Consumer Affairs, HEW, *State Consumer Action, Summary, 1974* (GPO, 1975).

26. Ronald Butt claims there was a growing sentiment among younger Tory MPs to pay more attention to consumer interests by the early 1960s. See his *The Power of Parliament* (London: Constable, 1968), 257.

27. This was designed to overcome the delays inherent in the existing practice whereby each needed change in product standards had to be dealt with by an act of Parliament. Borrie, *Consumer, Society, and Law,* 135.

28. This grew out of a promise in Labour's 1964 election manifesto to protect consumers against selling rackets, and represented the adoption of another Molony recommendation. Originally introduced in early 1966 and reintroduced following the 1966 general election as a Bill for Consumer Protection its title was changed in the Lords before final passage. See Thomas F. Carbery, *Consumers in Politics* (London: Augustus M. Kelley, 1969), 199–200. Its importance was affirmed in the present author's interviews with local authority trading standards officers. (Also see Borrie, *Consumers, Society, and Law,* 140). Local authorities had acquired over the years a number of responsibilities for weights and measures and food standards enforcement. Some also financially supported volunteer-

staffed Citizens Advice Bureaus which had been created during World War II. Molony recommended that local authorities throughout the country support CABs which could then act as a nationwide Consumer Council (Martin and Smith, *Consumer Interest*, 219–20). A few local authorities during the 1960s established their own consumer protection departments and directly administered advice centers. After the 1968 act most took the step of renaming their weights and measures offices trading standards departments. Trading standards officers, as they called themselves, developed their own professional identity including an association, the Institute for Trading Standards Administration.

29. The Fair Trading Act of 1973, Chap. 41, (HMSO, 1973).
30. "What Deal for Consumers?" *Economist* (28 October, 1972), 68. While charged with informing itself about consumer problems, taking action on them and providing advice to consumers, the Council was prohibited from engaging in comparative testing, handling individual consumer complaints or engaging in law enforcement. Although it made some attempts to coordinate consumer group policy stands and represent consumer concerns to government departments, its suggestions were brushed aside in Whitehall.
31. In 1964, Wilson appointed George Darling, a Co-op sponsored MP, Minister of State at the Board of Trade with special responsibility for consumer affairs. Darling was able to give only limited attention to this responsibility and his consumer portfolio was not widely recognized. Carbery, *Consumers in Politics*, 199.
32. OECD, *Consumer Policy in OECD Member Countries, 1980*, (Paris: 1981), 176.
33. OECD, *Consumer Policy in OECD Member Countries, 1983*, (Paris: 1984), 92.
34. Tolchin, *Dismantling America*, 35, 59.
35. See the figures reported for these agencies in the FY 1982–1985 federal budgets. All three agencies were cut sharply for FY 1982, the first real Reagan budget. FDA's budget recovered the next year, but CPSC and FTC budgets continue to remain below FY 1981 levels. See also "Regulation and the 1984 Budget," *Regulation* 7:2 (March-April 1983): 8–10.
36. "Regulation and the 1984 Budget," 9.
37. Virginia Knauer, President Reagan's special assistant for consumer affairs, stated that she favors allowing businesses to regulate themselves (*New York Times*, 21 August 1982, p. 9, col. 3). His appointee to the chairmanship of the Consumer Product Safety Commission has also supported the voluntary approach. "Interview with Terrence Scanlon," *US News and World Report*, 15 April, 1985, 74.
38. *OECD Annual Report on Consumer Policy, 1980*, 151.
39. *Survey of Current Affairs*, March 1984, 101, and April 1984, 137–8.
40. See the *10th Annual Report of the Director General of Fair Trading* (London: HMSO, 1984), 15–16; and comment entitled "A Duty to Trade Fairly" in the *Journal of Consumer Policy* 7 (1984): 197. Here he notes that "the present political climate is not particularly favorable towards legislation in the field of consumer protection" whose "hey-day" occurred in the period 1965–1975, and that without the threat of legislation voluntary action is more difficult to secure.
41. See the remarks of John Moore, Financial Secretary to the Treasury, quoted in *Survey of Current Affairs* (November 1983): 378.
42. *10th Annual Report of the Director General of Fair Trading*, 11. OECD reports suggest that the concern about services is a common trend among consumer

movements in its member countries. See OECD, *Consumer Policy During the Past Ten Years*, 7, 46. There also is evidence of tension between the Office of Fair Trading and the government, as in the Director General's 1984 report (p. 9) where he expresses disappointment with the government's decision to exempt the stock exchange from restrictive practices legislation.

43. *Survey of Current Affairs* 14:4 (April 1984): 137–8.
44. OECD, *Annual Report on Consumer Policy in OECD Member Countries*, 1983, 85.
45. The first statement is from Sally Oppenheim, MP, in *Hansard*, 20 July 1979, col. 869 (written answer); the second from Alex Fletcher, MP, in *Hansard*, 27 July 1983, col. 485 (written answer).
46. See Caroline Ware, "The Consumer Voice: Lobbying in the Consumer Interest," and Mary Dublin Keyserling, "The First National Consumers Organization: The National Consumers League," both in Angevine, ed., *Consumer Activists*.
47. *Congressional Quarterly Almanac*, 1966, 352. The purpose of the conference was to back consumer oriented legislation although it did not endorse any particular bills.
48. Erma Angevine, "Lobbying and the Consumer Federation of America," in Angevine, ed., *Consumer Activists*, 335.
49. *Consumer Federation of America*, information flyer (CFA, undated).
50. See, for example, ERR, *Consumer Protection*, 1978, 9–15.
51. Sobel ed., *Consumer Protection*, 149.
52. Keyserling in Angevine, ed., *Consumer Activists*, 362; Angevine with Newman, "NCL New Directions 1940–1980," in Ibid., 361.
53. *Consumer Reports*, January 1985, 5–6.
54. *New York Times*, 17 February 1983, p. 18, col. 1.
55. *The Whirlpool Report on Consumers in the 1980s* (Whirlpool Corporation, 1983).
56. Borrie, *Consumer, Society, and Law*, 33. For a few years it published *Shopper's Guide* which offered comparative product information and a complaint service. The consumer advisory council was replaced in 1963 by a newly appointed government body, the Consumer's Council.
57. See Carbery, *Consumers in Politics*, 197–9. In 1930 the Labour government's bill to establish a Consumers' Council was shepherded through the Commons under the leadership of a prominent Co-op sponsored MP, A.V. Alexander. The bill was lost in the crisis and break-up of this government, but the basic idea was one to which Co-operative politicians would return well before it became a popular item on the agendas of the consumer groups which developed in Britain during the 1950s. (See Ibid., 189.) Alfred Barnes, as long-time chairman of the Co-operative Party, began in the 1940s to articulate the idea of the party as a consumers' party, not just a pressure group for the trading interests of the movement operating inside the Labour party. Jack Bailey, who became party secretary in 1942, developed and extended this position. Both saw a need for consumer organizations to redress the producer-oriented character of economic policymaking. See Alfred Barnes, *Consumer Politics in Peace and War* (Cooperative Party, 1943), and Jack Bailey, *The British Cooperative Movement* (London: Hutchinson's University Library, 1955).
58. National Federation of Consumer Groups mimeo, dated 16 November 1973.
59. NCC, *Consumer Congress Directory*, 1984. One hundred sixty-nine organiza-

tions were accredited to this Congress; they ranged from the Campaign for Real Ale to Shelter to the Child Poverty Action Group.

60. NCC, *Annual Report 1981–1982*, 4.
61. See, for example, the 1984 Consumer Congress agenda in the *Congress Handbook* published by the NCC and the NCC's 1981 report on the findings of the consumer concerns survey which it commissioned in 1979.
62. See statistics reported in the annual report of the Director General of Fair Trading.
63. NCC, *An Introduction to the Findings of the Consumer Concerns Survey,* 1981, 5.
64. Laurence Feldman, *Consumer Protection: Problems and Prospects* (St. Paul: West, 1976). This appears to have come first in the United States, not figuring prominently in Britain until the actions of the 1974 Labour Government. See Richard Flickinger, "The Comparative Politics of Agenda Setting: The Emergence of Consumer Protection as a Public Policy Issue in Britain and the United States," *Policy Studies Review* 2:3 (February 1983): 437. Samuel Beer's analysis of British politics provides the additional suggestion that parties take consumer interests into account in the "collectivist age" by bidding for their support through popular welfare state programs. Beer, *British Politics in the Collectivist Age* (New York: Knopf, 1966), 318–9. Thus politicians might find it "good politics" to stress consumer concerns and appropriate policy prescriptions. Yet one does not find consumer policy as a high-profile item in any postwar election manifesto or party platform on either side of the Atlantic. One must turn elsewhere for a more complete answer. For Johnson's motivation see Mark Nadel, *The Politics of Consumer Protection* (Indianapolis: Bobbs-Merrill, 1971), 40.
65. Andrew S. McFarland, *Public Interest Lobbies* (Washington: American Enterprise Institute, 1976), 4.
66. Jeffrey Berry, *The Interest Group Society* (Boston: Little, Brown, 1984), 29–30.
67. Pertschuck, *Revolt Against Regulation,* 20–45; and James Q. Wilson, ed., *The Politics of Regulation* (New York: Basic Books, 1980), 370–71.
68. Ralph Nader has acknowledged the top-down nature of the consumer movement during this time. His recent work has aimed at building grassroots consumer organizations. See Jonathan Rowe, "Ralph Nader Reconsidered," *Washington Monthly* 17:2 (March, 1985), 12–21.
69. See Nadel, *Consumer Protection,* 242 and Jack L. Walker, "Setting the Agenda in the U.S. Senate: A Theory of Problem Selection," *British Journal of Political Science* 7:4 (October 1977): 423–45.
70. Barry R. Weingast and Mark J. Moran, in "The Myth of Runaway Bureaucracy: The Case of the FTC," *Regulation* 6:3 (May/June 1983):35–36, argue that changes in the makeup of Congressional committees after 1976 were very important in accounting for the more hostile congressional attitudes toward regulation which then developed.
71. See chapters 36 and 34 respectively of David A. Aaker and George S. Day, eds., *Consumerism*, 4th ed. (New York: Free Press, 1982).
72. See Editorial Research Reports, *Consumer Protection,* 7–8, for a discussion of the Consumer Product Safety Commission in this regard.
73. On the broadened scope of consumer concerns see Robert J. Kroll and Ronald W. Stampfl, "The New Consumerism," and Robert N. Mayer, "Consumerism in the 1970s: The Emergence of New Issues," in the 1981 *Proceedings of the American Conference on Consumer Interests,* 97–100 and 134–41, and the White House

National Goals Research Staff's 1970 report on the consumer protection movement reprinted in Sobel, ed., *Consumer Protection,* 139–53. This report ascribes
these new concerns to affluence: "Only an affluent society, where most people's
basic material needs are already met, would raise the issues . . . now discussed in
the consumerism movement" (140).
74. See Mancur Olson, Jr., *The Logic of Collective Action* (New York: Shocken
Books, 1968).
75. Flickinger, "Agenda Setting," 433.
76. Cmnd. 5726, 1974. Michael Young, the NCC's first chairman, spoke of making
it the consumer counterpart of the Confederation of British Industry and the
Trades Union Congress to redress the balance of consumer vs. producer bargaining power in national policymaking. *Guardian,* 1 June 1976.
77. Author's interviews with persons involved in British consumer policy formulation and administration.
78. Although they have supported Thatcher's moves to retrench in the consumer
policy area, business interests, especially the retail sector associations, have not
enjoyed particularly good access to or relations with the Thatcher administration.
See Wyn Grant, "The Business Lobby," in Hugh Berrington, ed., *Change in
British Politics* (London: Frank Cass, 1984), 163–82.
79. See 1984 *Consumer Congress Agenda, Consumer Federation of America Policy
Resolutions,* and recent articles in the *Financial Times* and *Wall Street Journal.*
80. See T. Alexander Smith, *The Comparative Policy Process* (Santa Barbara: ABC-
Clio, 1975), 5–8 and 63–65; and David Vogel and Mark Nadel, "The Consumer
Coalition: Dimensions of Conflict," in Robert N. Katz ed., *Protecting the
Consumer Interest* (Cambridge, Mass.: Ballinger, 1976), 25.
81. See, for example, Jerold Waltman, *Copying Other Nations' Policies* (Cambridge,
Mass.: Schenckman, 1980).
82. On the importance of consultation in British policymaking, see Grant Jordan and
Jeremy Richardson, "The British Policy Style or the Logic of Negotiation?," pp.
80–110 in J. Richardson (ed.), *Policy Styles in Western Europe* (London: George
Allen and Unwin, 1982).
83. However, the government was defeated in April 1986 on a measure to abolish
existing bans on Sunday trading. Although the outcome was shaped by other
factors (the interests of some traders in limiting hours, opposition from churches
and from trade unions) most consumer groups had favored ending the ban. This
case illustrates the difficulty of classifying some policy measures—it is doubtful
that most participants saw this as a consumer policy issue—as well as the
weakness of consumer interests when these are arrayed against traditionally
powerful groups. See *Survey of Current Affairs* 16 (May 1986): 156 for a brief
account of the defeat of the Shops Bill.
84. Anthony King, "Ideas, Institutions and the Policies of Government: a Comparative Analysis: Part III," *British Journal of Political Science* 3 (October
1973): 409–23.
85. See *The European Community and Consumers,* and *Consumer Representation in
the European Communities,* both published in 1983 by the EC Commission.
86. More than 650,000 consumer complaints were recorded by local enforcement
and advice agencies in 1985, according to the Director General of Fair Trading's
1985 report. See *Survey of Current Affairs,* 16 (July 1986): 237.

87. One recent bit of evidence that some persons continue to advocate political parties giving more attention to consumer claims is the publication of a Fabian society tract by Martin Smith entitled "The Consumer Case for Socialism." For a review see the *Guardian,* 25 July 1986, 21.
88. Hugh Heclo, *Modern Social Politics in Britain and Sweden* (New Haven: Yale University Press, 1974).
89. Arnold J. Heidenheimer, Hugh Heclo, and Carolyn Teich Adams, *Comparative Public Policy,* 2nd ed. (New York: St. Martin's Press, 1983), 315.

Do Policy Issues Determine Politics? State Pensions Policy

Gary P. Freeman

POLICY VERSUS POLITICS IN COMPARATIVE ANALYSIS

The question can be stated simply. Which is more important in the study of comparative public policy—the structure of politics in a particular country and the differences in such structures between countries, or the characteristics of the political issues with which public policy is attempting to deal? Will countries with dissimilar political systems produce significantly different responses to similar political issues, or will the imperatives of particular types of public problems compel more or less similar responses whatever the shape of the political system involved?

The analytical task of comparative policy analysis is to identify and explain the similarities and differences among nations in the way they define and deal with public problems. One school of analysts tends to be most impressed by the peculiariies of individual countries, advancing what I will call the "national styles" hypothesis. Proponents of this view tend to believe that the unique mix of political culture, institutions, and traditions in a country produces an identifiable method or procedure for defining and addressing public problems. These procedures tend to persist whatever the issue or material circumstances involved. The authors of the most elaborate statement of this view are well aware of tendencies toward what they call "sectorization," the propensity for a specialized kind of politics to develop around particular subsets of issues. They also recognize that changes in the composition of governing coalitions and in the economic fortunes of countries can produce new patterns of policy. Nevertheless, they contend that it is possible to describe overriding national decision-making styles.[1]

It is perfectly plausible that differences in the social, economic, and political characteristics of nations produce distinctive policy mixes. This is the dominant view of students of comparative politics who have generally assumed that differences in political structures (parliamentary vs. presidential, authoritarian vs. democratic), party and electoral systems (multi-party, two-party, or one-party; proportional vs. plurality), and political cultures (participatory vs. deferential) lead to systematic differences in policy outcomes. When scholars actually got around to testing this assumption, and initially found little support for it, their shock produced a great debate over the relevance of political variables.[2]

The "national styles" hypothesis emphasizes the causal significance of domestic political institutions and processes in the explanation of public policy. Such exogenous factors as international economic pressures or abstractions like industrialization or the laws of capitalist development tend to get short shrift. The unique mix of culture, tradition, and institutions ensures, in this view, that each country will both identify and deal with its problems in an idiosyncratic but more or less consistent fashion.

An alternative perspective holds that the differences among nations' political structures and processes may be less important than the similarities between them as their elites grapple with common challenges. Support for this view can be drawn from a variety of theoretical and empirical perspectives. Numerous scholars, among whom Lowi[3] is the best known, have tried to develop typologies of policy issues. Their premise is that there is a finite number of political issues, that the nature of these issues imposes important constraints on the options available to public officials, and, hence, that it generates a more or less predictable pattern of politics. If this approach is valid, then the characteristics of distributive politics in Britain, France, and Germany, for example, might be more similar than the characteristics of distributive and redistributive politics within any one of them.[4]

A more historically and geographically specific school of thought is that of convergence theory. It holds that all industrial societies, whatever their nominal ideological character, must deal with a common set of problems and, consequently, tend to move toward a common configuration.[5] Some intriguing empirical evidence does find surprising similarities in public expenditure patterns across ideologically diverse regimes, but students of comparative public policy have tended to be as much or more impressed with the differences than the similarities among even the advanced capitalist states.[6] Convergence theory, moreover, has been subjected to thorough-going critiques on conceptual grounds.[7]

I will call the notion that policy determines politics the "policy sector" hypothesis. The term *policy sector* is meant to refer to clusters of public issues and policies that share significant characteristics. I intend to dodge here the debate in the discipline over the most appropriate typologization of public policies. I take it to be an empirical question whether nominal, program,[8] or more analytically sophisticated categories are best employed in comparative analysis. Policy sector is a deliberately ambiguous term—it should be useful for describing either a cluster of related policies or, as in this chapter, a single program. The basic claim of the policy sector hypothesis is that the issue itself determines the politics of policy and that there are systematic patterns of policies associated with certain kinds of problems. This hypothesis would lead us to anticipate that, whatever the characteristics of domestic politics, all advanced capitalist countries will necessarily deal with a set of common issues and the similarities of both the decision processes and policy outcomes will be more impressive than the differences.

RESEARCH DESIGN

I propose to approach the competing claims of the policy sector and the national styles hypotheses through a comparison of one public policy in two countries. State pensions are a prominent aspect of the welfare state, nor-mally one of its most expensive items.[9] The state pension system is easily identified, its characteristics are readily described, and at least some of them are amenable to quantitative measurement. Moreover, pension systems seem especially affected by several trends that are common to advanced industrial nations. One of the most important is the aging of populations, which is everywhere raising the level of dependency and therefore the relative and absolute costs of state-run pension systems.[10] Like all social insurance systems, pension programs tend to go through a process of maturation as over time more workers and their families become eligible for benefits and as these are irresistibly raised in real terms. At least one explanation for this expansive tendency is that the bureaucracies set up to administer pension programs become themselves a source of pressure for the further elaboration of the system.[11]

If aging, program maturation, and bureaucratic expansionism all seem to suggest a convergence of pension policies across the advanced capitalist countries, there are also some good reasons for anticipating a peculiar politics of pensions in each country. Pension programs involve huge sums of money, affect practically the entire population in a direct way, and involve significant redistribution, if not between income classes then between generations. The stakes are large, the program visible and salient. It is reasonable to assume that such domestic political characteristics as the relative strength of parties representing business and labor would be strongly linked to the pattern of pensions development. The extent of state administrative centralization and, more generally, the strength of the state vis a vis the market should also affect pensions policy.[12]

Britain and the United States are especially interesting cases in the context of the present analysis. Britain is often cited as a pioneer welfare state and the range of services and benefits provided for British citizens is often contrasted, favorably or unfavorably depending on the views of the analyst, to the meager benefits available in the United States.[13] The United States is frequently described as a deviant case among the advanced capitalist states, the one country that has failed to develop a mature welfare system and that, consequently, disproves the convergence thesis.[14] At the very least the two cases provide a range of welfare state experience.

There is also considerable contrast between the politics of the two countries. Britain and America often appear in the traditional literature of comparative politics as polar political types. Britain, in the conventional view, is the model of a two-party competitive parliamentary democracy. The chief elements of this model involve programmatic, disciplined parties on the one hand, and a centralized political structure that translates electoral outcomes into public policies on the other. In contrast, the American model is dominated by fragmented interest groups rather than by the parties, which are disorganized, undisciplined, non-programmatic and incapable of ruling. Political institutions, for their part, are highly fragmented and decentralized. The combination of federalism and separation of powers—the Madisonian system—is seen as preventing coherent majorities from controlling the levers of power. Politics is an endless process of negotiation and compromise among a spate of roughly equal groups. Europeans, and critical American observers, are impressed by the capitalist bias of the system, the absence of an effective and institutionalized voice for the working class and dispossessed groups, and the pervasive antigovernment ideology. Both schools agree, nonetheless, on the fragmentation and weakness of central state power and the impediments to mobilizing popular movements.

Granting the large element of exaggeration in the foregoing models, and the growing irrelevance of the classic literature to contemporary British politics, it is still reasonable to expect that the two political systems will approach public problems differently. I have not, obviously, chosen the two cases with the greatest political contrasts. A comparison of Sweden with Switzerland, or France with the United States, would constitute a stronger test of the policy sector hypothesis. A confirmation of that hypothesis on the basis of an American-British comparison will, therefore, only increase its plausibility. If, on the other hand, the national differences view is sustained, the finding will be relatively compelling, indicating that the arena of retirement policy is open to a wide range of policy responses.

Two aspects of state pensions policy, the process by which policy is made and its content, require our attention. In what follows, process will be said to include the way in which public problems are defined, the manner in which policy is formulated, and the principal actors engaged at various stages in the process. I do not assume that each country will exhibit an identifiable policy process, nor that one process will be dominant in all policy arenas or over long periods of time. Nor do I make any *a priori* assumptions about the causal significance of process. The manner in which policy is made is a matter of inherent interest, but it may or may not have systematic consequences for policy content.

The content of policy appears on the surface to be much more straightfor-wardly susceptible to empirical investigation. Nonetheless, the bewildering-ly complex means by which old-age income assistance is provided in different countries makes the comparison of different pension systems a tricky proposition. At minimum we need to examine the structures of program benefits and finances, the extent of coverage, and costs. Such relatively hard indicators as replacement rates and pensions expenditures as a proportion of GDP can be indicative, but must be supplemented by more qualitative descriptions of program characteristics.

By dividing policy into two parts—process and content—I am able to test a weak and a strong version of the policy sector hypothesis. The weak version claims only that particular types of issues are systematically associated with a certain kind of political dynamics. Pensions policy ought to lead to the same kind of debates, conflicts, and decision-making processes in both countries if this hypothesis is to be confirmed. The stronger version of the hypothesis claims that pensions policy outcomes ought to be roughly similar. There are four possible findings, each implying a different conclusion with respect to the hypotheses (Figure 1).

Outcome 1 would support both the weak and the strong versions of the policy sector hypothesis, suggesting that an explanation of the convergence of process and content ought to be sought in variables other than those describing the national political system. Outcome 3 would also be consistent with the strong version, implying that even in the absence of a similar political process, both countries were producing similar outcomes. Outcome

FIGURE 1
Content

Process	*Both convergent* *1*	*Processes convergent, Content divergent* *2*
	Processes divergent, Content convergent *3*	*Both divergent* *4*

2 would be consistent with only the weak policy sector hypothesis, but would suggest that the national styles hypothesis was sustained with respect to content. Outcome 4 would be a strong confirmation of the national styles hypothesis.

To facilitate comparison, I begin by describing the content of the old-age pension systems in Britain and the United States. I move then to a consideration of the pensions policy process. The case studies will deal, for the most part, with the "normal" politics of pensions. In effect this means that I will treat extensively only the period after the founding of the modern state pension programs in the 1930s and '40s. There are good reasons to believe that the introduction of social insurance schemes presents a host of analytical questions that are separable from ordinary policymaking, at least in theory.[15] I will also treat the crisis period of state pension schemes separately. The conclusions about content and process drawn on the basis of the long development of state pensions after their founding will be used to interpret the responses of the two countries to the present international social security crisis.

STATE PENSIONS IN BRITAIN AND THE UNITED STATES

Both the British and American pensions programs are based on the principles of contributory social insurance. They assume that workers will make contributions during their working lives in return for receiving pensions when they retire. Apart from this underlying commonality, there are numerous differences between the two systems. This section is not concerned with determining whether or not British pensions are like American pensions in all or most particulars. Rather it asks if the two systems, in their own ways, seek to accomplish more or less the same things.

The American state pension system was adopted in 1935, began payment of benefits in 1940, and was expanded to include disability benefits in 1956. Medical benefits for the retired were added in 1965. The records of the debates during the 1930s leave no doubt that social security was meant to provide only a foundation of retirement income upon which individuals were expected to build through private annuities and savings.[16] Nevertheless, many social security advocates pushed for a state pension that would be sufficient for the needs of most Americans, and over the years benefits were gradually upgraded until they provided a reasonably adequate income for many aged couples.

From a comparative perspective, the principal characteristics of the American system are that it provides a single pension with graduated benefits based on previous income and work history (as well as marital status). The benefit schedule is tilted to give higher benefits to low-income workers than they would merit strictly on the basis of their contributions. These are in turn proportional, all workers paying the same percentage contribution on wages and salary up to a ceiling (now high enough to cover over 90 percent of payroll). The payroll tax is split evenly between employees and employers (in 1986–87 it was 7.15 percent for each). The program is totally self-financing, the state providing no monies out of its general funds. The program is organized on a pay-as-you-go basis. The social security trust funds (there are separate funds for old age, disability, and medical benefits) normally have less than one year's reserves.[17]

Britain has a two-tiered pension system. The 1946 National Insurance Act, which realized most but not all of the aims of the Beveridge Report,[18] created flat-rate pensions based on flat-*rate* contributions.[19] All workers, regardless of income, paid the same cash contributions (the term flat-rate is misleading and could better apply to the American system) and got the same amount in retirement benefits. The flat-rate structure imposed certain limits on pensions—contributions had to be very small so as to avoid creating a burden on low-income workers. Benefits, correspondingly, were also necessarily minimal. As in the original American plan, state pensions were seen as a base to be supplemented by private means. Apart from this fundamental structural difference, the most important distinctions between the American system and the one set up in Britain after the war were that coverage in the latter was much more extensive and the government routinely subsidized the costs of the program from the Treasury.

The flat-rate structure became too constraining early on. By the late fifties serious discussions of the feasibility of adding an earnings-related or graduated component to the basic benefit had begun. The history of pensions policy in postwar Britain is essentially the saga of how this reform finally came about. The opposition Labour party put forth the first proposal for graduated pensions in 1957. The Conservatives responded with a plan of their own, which was adopted in 1959. It differed considerably from the Labour proposal, primarily in promising very modest benefits to be earned after an extended contribution period. The principle of earnings-related pensions had been established, but adequate pensions would not be achieved under this act.[20]

When Labour returned to office in 1964, the party moved slowly on the pensions front. It was not until 1969 that it put out a new White Paper on retirement income. The plan would have replaced the flat-rate pension with an earnings-related benefit based on graduated contributions. The hope of the government was that the new state pensions would "normally be adequate, even for those whose earnings have been relatively low, to live on without other means."[21] There would be room for a private pension system, but occupational schemes could not substitute for the state scheme because, in the words of the White Paper, it was not permissible to have a "division of the population into two sectors of pensioners, State and occupational."[22]

Before Labour could pass its proposals into law, however, it was turned out of office. The Conservatives quickly responded with their own pension scheme proposal.[23] This program differed in important respects from that of the previous government, especially in its emphasis on private pensions. Though it called for the creation of a significant second tier of pension income, employers wishing to set up comparable plans for their employees could "contract out" of the state system. The effect of this plan would be to keep the flat-rate state pension at a modest level and encourage the development of private graduated pensions for most workers. Enacted in 1973, the program was not implemented before the electoral cycle intervened once more. Members of the Labour party, back in office first as a minority and then with only a slim majority, refused to carry out the Conservative program. Their own alternative, outlined in yet another White Paper,[24] retained most of the fundamental features of the Tory plan. It called for a system of earnings-related, contributory pensions which would supplement the basic flat-rate scheme rather than do away with it as Labour had intended in 1969. This time around the Labour government was also willing to live with the private pension industry—it accepted the Conservative proposal for "contracting out." Adopted as the Social Security Act of 1975, this plan went into effect in 1978.

Describing the structure of pension systems is one thing; assessing their effectiveness is something else. The enormous complexity of social insurance systems with their intricate tangle of eligibility and benefit criteria makes comparisons between countries exceedingly difficult. Any simple quantitative measure ought to be taken with a grain of salt. Still, it is necessary, and possible, to paint in the broad outlines of the performance of the British and American systems.

We may start with expenditure data. To those accustomed to contrasting the generosity of British welfare arrangements to the stinginess of the American system, these data ought to be a little surprising. Table 1 presents information on social security pensions expenditures as a proportion of gross national product. It shows that the United States went a considerable distance toward closing the gap on pensions spending by 1971, though this gap had widened again by 1974. Cameron has collected more recent figures that combine social security (pensions and other social insurance benefits) and social assistance spending. The average share of GDP spent on these purposes during the period 1977–78 was 12.1 percent in Britain and 10.7 percent in the United States. However, the rate of increase of spending between 1960–63 and 1977–78 was 5.1 percent in the United States, compared to 4.8 percent in Britain, indicating again that the United States was gaining ground.[25] Jurgen Kohl has traced trends in social transfer expenditures between 1950 and 1975. He finds that in Britain social transfers accounted for 5.7 percent of GDP in 1950 and 11.1 percent in 1975, an increase of 5.4 percent. In the United States, on the other hand, social transfers went up from 3.3 percent in 1950 to 11.5 percent in 1975, a change of 8.2 percent.[26] However social security expenditure is measured, and whatever years are included in the analysis, the differences between Britain and America are small and the growth of expenditure seems relatively faster in the latter.

TABLE 1: *Social Security Pensions as a Proportion of GDP*

	1968	1971	1974
Great Britain	3.8	3.5	4.5
United States	2.8	3.4	4.0

SOURCE: President's Commission on Pension Policy, 1980, 36.

There are a number of ways to assess the adequacy of pensions, but probably the two best indicators are the replacement rate and the proportion of pensioners in poverty if they have no other income. By either measure, the gap between Britain and the United States is not large and the United States is by no means the worse for the comparison. Replacement rates refer to the proportion of previous income provided by pension benefits. These are difficult to calculate (they have to be based on averages) and they can be misleading if they fail to take into account the availability of other income and support. Moreover, it is arguable that such rates should refer to previous take-home pay rather than to gross income.[27] Nevertheless, replacement rates are widely used as a rough indicator of the importance of state pensions and the role they play in the overall retirement system.

TABLE 2: *Replacement Rates for Men with Average Earnings in Manufacturing*

	Years Worked	Single		Aged Couples	
		1965	1980	1965	1980
Great Britain	Since 1961	23	31	36	47
United States	Since 1951	29	44	44	66

SOURCE: *Social Security Bulletin* (January 1978): 3–14; and ibid., (November 1982): 5.

Table 2 shows that in 1980 both a single American male and an aged American couple with average earnings would receive a significantly higher proportion of previous income through their state pensions than would their British counterparts. This picture will change as the new earnings-related scheme in effect since 1978 becomes fully mature. According to the government's projections when the plan was introduced, a fully qualified male earning average wages in manufacturing would receive pension benefits equal to about 44 percent of previous earnings, and couples about 59 percent.[28] In 1984 the actual rates were 33 and 49 percent, respectively.[29] The British system, then, is improving but not catching up with the American on this important dimension.

One of the most persistent and troubling issues in British pensions policy has been the problem of poverty among pensioners. This was an inevitable outcome of the Beveridge principle of subsistence flat-rate pensions. Even though, as I have noted, basic pensions were increased periodically to keep pace with prices, they did not suffice to pull many recipients above the government's poverty line. Hence, many retired persons found it necessary to apply for supplementary benefits. In 1974 the government estimated that of the eight million pensioners, about two million, or 25 percent, were also receiving supplementary benefits. Another million, it was believed, were eligible for some additional benefits but had not applied for them. This figure had apparently fallen to about 18 percent by 1985.[30]

In the United States since 1975 there has been a federally administered program of means-tested benefits for persons over sixty-five, the blind, and the disabled whose total income from whatever sources is below a governmentally determined minimum (Supplemental Security Income, or SSI). One way of determining the adequacy of social security pensions is to ask what proportion of social security beneficiaries are also receiving SSI. In 1975, 8.6 percent of persons on social security received some SSI benefits as well. In 1980 this figure was 6.7 percent.[31] Another way to determine adequacy is to ask what percent of families are still poor after receiving social security, using the federal poverty level as a benchmark. In 1976, social security benefits reduced the size of the poor population by over one-half, but 21.5 percent of families were still poor after receiving benefits.[32]

One of the most important issues of pensions policy is how they are to be adjusted to correct for inflation. The British and American records here are similar. In both countries pensions were originally adjusted in an ad hoc manner. Though it was considered inadequate by pension advocates, largely because of routine lags between price rises and adjustments, this method nevertheless resulted in the long-term growth of benefits in excess of prices and wages.[33] Automatic adjustments of flat-rate pensions were legislated in Britain in 1973 (annual reviews were mandated and upratings were to be taken to keep pace with prices) and liberalized in 1974 (flat-rate pensions would go up with wages or prices, whichever was more beneficial to recipients). In 1980 the Thatcher government changed this back to price adjustments alone for flat-rate pensions. Earnings-related pensions have been indexed to prices since 1978. The government has had the option to use a retrospective method of adjustment (pensions are raised in line with increases in prices over the previous fiscal year) or a prospective method (they are fitted in March to anticipated changes from the previous November to the next November). The prospective method, first adopted by Labour in 1976 and maintained by all governments since, has resulted in lower pension adjustments than would have occurred had the retrospective method been retained.[34]

The indexing method employed in the United States has been the subject of sharp and continuing controversy.[35] Indexing was first legislated in the United States in 1972 and went into effect in 1975. Benefits are adjusted once a year in line with the Consumer Price Index if it has increased by 3 percent or more. Supported by conservatives who hoped to restrain an over-generous Congress, the automatic cost-of-living adjustments (Colas) turned out to be much higher than had been projected. For example, benefits went up 14 percent in 1980 rather than the 5 percent that had been projected, and 11 rather than 4 percent in 1981. The Reagan administration saved some money in 1984 when it delayed the adjustment from July to January (the date at which subsequent adjustments will be made). In addition, in future, when the trust fund reserves fall below a fixed percentage of estimated benefits payments (20 percent after 1988), Colas will be based on the increase in wages or prices, whichever is lower. But no serious attack against inflation proofing of the benefits of the currently retired has been launched. Indeed, during the 1984 presidential campaign, Reagan announced that benefits would be increased in January 1985 despite the fact that inflation was projected below the minimum 3 percent. He has subsequently supported legislation to make this standard practice.

Even this sketchy overview of the British and American state pensions programs indicates that the American plan is large and relatively generous. Pensions enjoy a privileged place among public programs in the United States. Why is this so? And why has the British pension system developed so slowly? A possible answer to these questions may be found in an examination of the politics of pensions.

THE PENSIONS POLICY PROCESS

The politics and style of social security policymaking in the United States have been extensively documented.[36] One may identify two chief characteristics of the process: (1) subsystem autonomy with bureaucratic dominance, and (2) incremental expansionism in the context of economic growth and consensual politics.

American social security policy has normally been made within a small circle of policymakers, including congressmen on key committees, the bureaucrats at the Social Security Administration, and a few select interest-group representatives. For most of its life, the program bureaucrats have dominated social security policy, controlling the congressional agenda, providing the technical analysis, and managing public relations. What is surprising about the social security policymaking system is who is not a part of it. The president has not normally been personally involved either in the formulation of policy or in choosing among options developed elsewhere. Other than in the exceptional founding period, when Roosevelt ultimately played a decisive role, and in periods when major additions to the program have been proposed or adopted, presidents have limited themselves to reiterating their unswerving support for the program. This has meant, among other things, that decisions on social security finances and benefits that could involve millions of beneficiaries and billions of dollars have often been taken with only the passing involvement of the executive officials in the

Treasury and the budget office. Social security has been out of the normal budget process for most of its history because it is self-financing and revenues from the payroll tax go into special trust funds. In the 1960s President Johnson put the program in the unified budget so that its surpluses could offset deficits being incurred in the prosecution of the Vietnam war. After social security surpluses evaporated in the mid-seventies, it was taken out of the budget once again. Congressional jurisdiction over the program fell to the revenue committees, and such was their prestige and influence that the Congress as a whole had little impact on policy.

From time to time critics of the program tried to raise questions about agency proposals, but they almost always failed. The bureaucrats had a monopoly over technical expertise. Their data and projections were the basis for congressional decisions, and until recently the Treasury lacked the capacity to do independent analysis. The ideology of the Social Security Administration held that social insurance programs were not like other government endeavors. Once they had been set in motion they could not be tampered with. Tax increases could be deferred if unanticipated surpluses appeared, and benefits could be boosted, but it was impossible to propose any basic reordering of the system without being accused of breaking a trust with America's elderly. Consistent with this state of affairs, the ostensible mode of policymaking for social security was highly technical. The agency developed state-of-the-art actuarial techniques for social insurance and engaged in long-range (seventy-five years) projections of program costs and revenues.

Despite this patina of technical planning, the underlying impetus for social security expansion was political—not in the sense that sharp conflicts and mobilized interests pushed the program forward, but in the sense that the public officials who voted for program expansions knew they were popular with the voters and knew their costs could be deferred far into the future. Although there had been fundamental party disagreement during the founding and start-up years of social security, this gradually dissipated. By the time the first Republican administration took control of the program in 1952 there was an interparty consensus on the existing system, the only argument remaining being over how and how fast it should be expanded.

Bipartisan consensus did not take social security out of politics, it simply removed any possibility of a fundamental reassessment of its assumptions. Both parties played politics with pensions, creating a modest but discernible electoral cycle that affected the timing of benefit improvements and tax increases.[37] More seriously, the incremental expansion of coverage and benefits was an integral part of the Keynesian-style economic management that dominated American politics in the postwar period. Economic growth made the enhancement of social security benefits easy; the widespread distribution of benefits helped to prime the economic pump. Both parties took credit for America's most popular social program.

American social security politics have been distinctive, therefore, in several respects. A confluence of unusual circumstances served to insulate the program from criticism and promote its growth. In a country where the state is widely distrusted and social welfare is viewed with considerable distaste, the state-run old age pension system nevertheless enjoyed wide popularity and experienced rapid expansion. The importance of the special and temporary characteristics of the program—its low start-up costs in particular—in fostering its noncontentious politics can be seen in the reaction triggered by the emergence of potential trust-fund deficits in the mid-seventies. It is not too much to say that the politics of social security were thoroughly transformed. Satisfaction was replaced by fear and anger; consensus by conflict. Subsystem autonomy gave way to broad discussion and increased participation by the president, the Treasury, and other central executive agencies, and a host of extra-governmental actors.[38] What all this has meant for social security policy will be discussed in the next section. The implications of this change for an interpretation of the American pensions policy process are that the politics of incremental expansion and subsystem autonomy were a temporary though extended phase associated with the maturation of the program in the context of a growing economy. Now that the program is fully mature, the politics of pensions promise to remain much more conflictual.

Does the process by which British pensions policy is made differ in significant ways from the American case? The British policy style in general has been characterized by Jordan and Richardson as "bureaucratic accommodation," as a process that displays a "predeliction for consultation, avoidance of radical policy change and a strong desire to avoid actions which might challenge well-entrenched interests."[39] To the American reader such a description will sound both familiar and banal: familiar because it could easily be borrowed to describe American politics; banal because it is too general to provide much analytical insight. As a broad characterization of the way politics is organized it might well apply to most Western democracies with a modest qualification here or there. Our concern is not with national policy styles per se, but with the mode of decision-making in the social security arena. Because Jordan and Richardson claim that sectorization and clientelism are two of the primary features of British policy, it is necessary to consider whether a more focused analysis will confirm or disconfirm the surface similarities between the British and American cases.

The place to launch a comparison of how pensions policy is made in

Britain and the United States is with an analysis of the relevance to Britain of the two chief aspects of American policy: incremental expansionism, and subsystem autonomy with bureaucratic dominance. With some important qualifications, it is possible to apply these descriptive characteristics to the British pensions policy process.

Incremental expansionism is the easiest point to dispense with. British pensions began relatively early (1908) and developed gradually (major legislation passed in 1911, 1946, 1959, and 1975). Policy development was incremental in two meanings of the term. After the initial whirlwind of activity during the postwar Labour government, the pension system grew at a modest but steady rate. Benefits and contributions were raised periodically, the additional risk of long-term disability was grafted onto the original structure, and expenditures rose without cease.[40] Second, change was incremental in the sense that there was never any radical shift from the underlying principles of the pension system. Program structures were not overturned by successive governments, though this claim needs to be specified precisely when the subject is earnings-related pensions. Party differences combined with the accident of electoral outcomes to delay the development of a graduated scheme, as I have shown. With respect to the tendency of pension systems to grow in terms of benefits, coverage, taxes, and relative expenditures, the British and American systems look much the same, following the general pattern of all Western welfare states.

The process produces incremental decisions in Britain, but who makes policy? Again, perhaps the best way to address this question is by way of contrast with the American case. The leading figures in United States policy development, as I noted, were program administrators and leaders of the relevant congressional committees. This produced a strong element of subsystem autonomy. British policy, I would argue, has been significantly less dominated by the permanent social security bureaucracy and appreciably less confined to a policymaking subsystem. Pensions have been a larger political issue in British elections over the years and have attracted a wider variety of participants. But it is not clear that this moderately distinctive policy process has made much difference for policy outcomes.

Several students of British social security have argued that policy has been more or less dominated by a combination of activist civil servants and policy analyst-intellectuals. They point to the historically significant role of reformers like Booth and Rowntree; the watershed contribution of the civil servant William Beveridge; and the continuing legacy of Titmuss and his disciples, notably Townsend and Abel-Smith. Heclo, for example, concludes his study of British and Swedish social policy by stating that "the place of civil servants in the development of modern social policy has been crucial," that "the bureaucracies . . . loom predominant," and that "the activist civil service role is a pervasive policy phenomenon rather than the exception."[41] His elaboration of this claim, however, makes it clear that his notion of the civil service is broad enough to encompass persons like Titmuss and Able-Smith, who were not public employees but belong to a more amorphous category he labels "policy middlemen." These individuals, according to Heclo, have guided social policy more or less free of interference from the political parties or pressure groups.[42] A collaboration of this view may be found in Banting's study of British social policy (excluding pensions, however) in the 1960s. He notes that "our most striking finding is the pervasive influence of intellectuals and professionals."[43]

This view of the civil service-policy activist role must be qualified in a number of respects. First, the social security bureaucracy, especially in its early years, did not exercise the kind of total monopoly over information and expertise that was enjoyed by its American counterpart. Heclo claims that the "British lag in administrative inputs to policy had been quickly eliminated during and after World War I,"[44] but Hall and her associates note that the social security bureaucracy was at a disadvantage vis a vis university-based intellectuals in its ability to analyze the system as late as the early sixties.[45] Second, ministers played a much more important and direct role in policymaking in Britain than they did in the United States. Crossman, Castles, and Joseph, to name just three, all put their mark on policy. Ministerial participation implies at least the indirect influence of the cabinet and party. In Crossman's case, especially, it meant that extra-departmental advisors like Titmuss and Abel-Smith had direct access to decision-making.[46]

In addition to these deviations of the British case from bureaucratic dominance, we need to consider the role of parties and elections. It is Heclo's chief contention that they were only minor factors in British policy development. A major theme in Ashford's study of British social security is, on the other hand, the effect of "adversary politics," with its frequent changes in governments, on the evolution of the social security system.[47] As we have seen, defeats of sitting governments at various general elections resulted in the delay of the implementation of earnings-related pensions for almost a generation. Banting observes that "party ideology and electoral considerations, when they were congruent, were decisive" for the social policies he studied.[48] Judge finds strong confirmation of the political sources of the timing of pension upratings in 1958 and 1974.[49] Even Heclo concedes that "one would . . . have to be particularly obtuse not to recognize the important differences—in content and orientation—between British Labour and Conservative superannuation proposals in the 1950s and again in the 1960s. . . ."[50]

There were, it seems clear, important differences between the parties on the issue of pensions throughout the postwar period. These involved such fundamental matters as the adequacy of benefits, the role of private annuities, and the preferred degree of income redistribution. As these ideological commitments were played out through the electoral process, they had one very significant effect—they retarded considerably the achievement of an earnings-related state pension system. Ultimately more striking, however, is the extent to which party differences were ultimately brokered into a cross-party consensus. The 1957 Social Security Act is the best evidence of this. Labour accepted the Tory argument that the state system must coexist with a strong private pensions industry. In his account of the process by which the policy became law, Harold Wilson stresses the cooperation of Conservative shadow minister, Sir Geoffrey Howe, and the "ready response" and "constructive help" from the opposition. He notes the "infinite dedication" of Labourite Barbara Castle "to produce legislation acceptable to both parties which would endure for a political generation."[51] The very real threat, in other words, that the ideological disagreements between the parties might continue to disrupt social security policy, and the evident unacceptability of such a situation when the retirement pensions of the nation's elderly were at stake, made it essential that normal party conflict be suspended and long-term agreement on fundamentals be secured.

One more aspect of the British process needs consideration. The Treasury intervened in social security decision-making in a much more regular and effective manner in Britain than in the United States.[52] Along with this, the costs of social security seem to have been, ironically perhaps, more of a constraint on policy in Britain, even before the reversal of economic fortunes set in during the late sixties. The Conservatives' modest earnings-related scheme of 1959 appears to have been primarily a way of raising revenues to keep the flat-rate plan solvent. The approval of the Exchequer was necessary for every general increase in the basic pension, and several observers have concluded that the critical delay in the passage of an earnings-related scheme by the 1964 and 1966 Labour governments was the result of Treasury fears over costs.[53] That the Treasury enjoyed a more prominent role in Britain than in America is not only a reflection of its much more pervasive institutional influence and power there, and the more centralized nature of the governmental machinery as a whole, but of the peculiarities of the old age pension system. The state had from the beginning made a contribution to the finances of British pensions and, hence, any changes in the program had immediate and unavoidable consequences for the government's budget. In the United States, on the other hand, because social security was self-financing and formally outside the state budget, the Treasury was consigned to the margins of policymaking.

There are strong similarities between the pensions policy processes in Britain and America. By the late seventies these similarities were on the wane as the social security crisis in the United States sparked a growing debate over the future of the program. Britain was not, of course, exempt from the world recession of the seventies. Indeed it struck there earlier, with more vengeance, and, arguably, with more lasting effects. The crisis of the pension system was slower to develop in Britain, however, because of the relative youth of the earnings-related scheme.

RESPONSES TO THE CRISIS

If Britain and America are similar with respect to their pension systems and the processes by which policy was made, they share one other characteristic as well. As both countries slipped into increasingly hard economic times at the end of the seventies and as pressures on income maintenance programs grew due to high inflation and unemployment, their electorates put militantly right-wing governments into office. Both Thatcher and Reagan were committed to broad cuts in public expenditures, to drawing in the reins on what they saw as the uncontrolled growth of the welfare state, and to re-emphasizing the private sector, self-reliance, and social discipline.[54] Their joint appearance on the political scene provides an opportunity to enquire into the fortunes of state pensions in hard times when governments hostile to state welfare schemes are in office.

Despite spirited efforts on the part of both the Reagan and Thatcher governments to slash the welfare state, and despite their recognition that not much progress toward this goal could be achieved without cutting income maintenance programs like pensions, neither government was able to control pension expenditure. Both Reagan and Thatcher seriously considered deep cuts in old-age pension benefits. Some of these proposals were deliberately made public, others were leaked. In both cases they provoked widespread public protest and in no case were they implemented in anything like their original shape.

President Reagan was forced to settle for a plan that "rescued" the social security system from its short-term financial problems by advancing the date of previously legislated payroll tax increases and by cutting costs in a variety of ways. Benefits were not slashed. Money was saved by tinkering (the date at which inflation adjustments are to be made was moved from July to January as previously noted) and by trimming certain marginal benefits (those for students, for example). The most substantial changes involved the taxation of one-half of pension benefits and the gradual extension of the retirement age (sixty-seven by 2022). The losses of benefits due to these changes are real and will become more so over the years, but they hardly represent a disavowal by the government of its commitment to the preservation of the old-age pension system.[55]

The Thatcher government has had, in certain respects, even less success. The indexing method was conservatively changed, as I have noted. Other than that the government has not made much headway against pensions costs. The state has cut its subsidy to the national insurance fund from 15 to 13.5 percent, but this has been achieved by raising contribution rates, especially for employers. The basic rate of pensions has been raised and the government has retained the £10 Christmas bonus for pensioners instituted by the previous Labour administration. The real value of pensions increased by about 7 percent between November 1978 and November 1982.[56] Social security expenditure went up by 20 percent in real terms during the first four years of Thatcher's rule and 28.4 percent by 1984–85. Spending on retirement pensions alone rose by over 14 percent from 1979 to 1984–85, primarily as a result of increased numbers of beneficiaries.[57] Like Reagan, Thatcher has had to console herself by squeezing economies out of the social services and other noncontributory programs.[58]

One caveat needs to be entered here. Frustrated by her inability to cut short-term pension expenditure and frightened by hair-raising estimates of the long-term price of the new state earnings-related pension system when it becomes fully mature in the twenty-first century, Thatcher called in 1983 for a major investigation into the pension system as a whole. A Green Paper (Cmnd. 9517) was duly issued in June 1985, calling for the gradual elimination of the earnings related scheme and its replacement by mandatory private or occupational provision. It is difficult to predict if this proposal will be approved but it is one of the ironies of pensions politics in Britain that elimination of these benefits is more likely to happen there than in the United States. The very late arrival of earnings-related pensions in Britain means that a government there potentially has considerably more flexibility in harnessing the long-term costs of such a program than in the United States where it is already fifty years old. From Thatcher's perspective, she arrived in office one year too late to prevent the implementation of a ruinously expensive plan, the financial consequences of which ought to have been evident to British policymakers given the social security crisis that was already full-blown in America and elsewhere by 1978.

CONCLUSION

This chapter has sought to assess the national styles and the policy sector hypotheses through a comparative case study of British and American pensions policy. The evidence has shown that both the content of pensions policies and the processes by which they are formulated are broadly similar in the two countries. Because the British and American domestic political systems and socioeconomic structures differ significantly, this convergence of pensions policy supports the policy sector hypothesis.

It is perhaps especially notable that anti-statist, anti-welfarist America possesses a state pension system that by many measures is equal to, or even superior to, that of the British with their long tradition of Fabian socialism, their periodic Labour governments, and their special version of Tory democracy. The convergence of policy content reflects the fact that the United States does rather more in the pensions field than one would predict and Britain rather less. The one glaring structural difference between British and American pensions—the flat-rate structure of the one and the graduated structure of the other—was eliminated when Britain adopted superannuation in 1975. Another important structural feature that has distinguished the two systems in the past—the British provision for a state subsidy to the national insurance fund—is diminishing and, if governments have their way, will eventually be reduced to an inconsequential amount.

The evidence on policy processes is a bit murkier. One needs to keep in mind that the pensions policy process changes in line with the phase of pension system development. A different process is associated with the initiation, expansion, and maturity of pension systems. The United States and Britain have not always been in sync, but in comparable stages their pensions policy processes have taken on the predicted shape. In the expansionist phase (which must be qualified for Britain to take account of the absence of a real graduated scheme from 1946 to 1978) there were some national peculiarities. British policy never exhibited the strong subsystem autonomy of the American case. Pensions policy was more thoroughly and obviously politicized in Britain. Moreover, perceptions of the key issues were different, largely, I would contend, because of the structures of the pension systems themselves—flat-rate versus graduated. In Britain poverty was the overriding issue in the pensions arena and arguments over the system tended to be dominated by questions of how poverty would or would not be affected by proposed changes. Poverty, or adequacy, was also important in the United States, but the ostensible pensions debate in that country was always much more technical, hinging on individual equity issues arising out of the social insurance model and entailing the use of the principles of actuarial science.

With the introduction of an earnings-related system in Britain, we would normally predict that British policy would take on even more of the characteristics the American process exhibited as its program slowly matured. There is some evidence of this already. Economists, producing computer-simulated projections of program costs, individual rates of return on contributions, etc., are emerging as a major new force in British pensions politics.[59] But there is an odd twist to this story. Much has been made by economic historians of the disadvantages of being first, by which they mean that Britain, as the world's first industrial economy, has found it hard as the years pass to compete with late industrializers who can copy her successes and avoid her mistakes and who have the advantage of newer industrial infrastructures. In the social security arena, oddly enough, the position of Britain may be reversed. Because the country was so slow in developing an earnings-related pension scheme, she may be able to learn from the problems of her neighbors whose systems are fully mature and already exhibiting the symptoms of fiscal crisis. The late development of Britain means that the full implications of the maturation of the earnings-related scheme will come home to roost much earlier than they did in other countries. The administrators of the American system had forty years of peace and goodwill before serious criticisms were heard. The British scheme was under bitter attack before it began operations. Such is the ineluctable logic of pensions system development that it will be extremely difficult for a British government actually to dismantle the infant program and go back to a flat-rate plan. But governments will undoubtedly move much more cautiously in broadening their commitments to future generations of retirees. The presence of a large and powerful private pensions industry makes privatization a real option. The American system, by this account, seems much more secure from attack.

The evidence in this essay supports the policy sector hypothesis in its strong version. Both process and content seem fundamentally affected by the characteristics of the pensions issue. Of course, political institutional structures of the two countries have an impact, but there is a broad, undeniable pattern of convergence. It seems best to account for this, not with variables describing domestic political structures, but by a recognition of the imperatives and constraints of pensions systems themselves.

NOTES

1. See Jeremy Richardson, ed., *Policy Styles in Western Europe* (London: George Allen & Unwin, 1985), 9–10. The concept of national styles, as developed by Richardson, involves "the main characteristics of the ways in which a given society formulates and implements its public policies" (3). This is not perfectly congruent with the more general view that characteristics of nations lead to dissimilar policies. Styles might be seen as one dimension of a larger set of national differences. Nevertheless, because styles is an easily understood and broad concept that has received considerable attention recently, I will employ that

term. For an extensive critique of many of the conceptual and empirical issues raised in this essay, see Gary P. Freeman, "National Styles and Policy Sectors: Explaining Structured Variation," *Journal of Public Policy* 5 (1986): 467–96.

2. Thomas R. Dye, *Politics, Economics and the Public* (Skokie, IL: Rand McNally, 1966); Francis G. Castles, "How Does Politics Matter? Structure and Agency in the Determination of Public Policy Outcomes?" *European Journal of Political Research* 9 (1981): 119–32.

3. Theodore J. Lowi, "American Business, Public Policy, Case Studies, and Political Theory," *World Politics* 16 (1964): 677–715.

4. T. Alexander Smith, *The Comparative Policy Process* (Santa Barbara: ABC-Clio Books, 1975).

5. See Clark Kerr, *Industrialism and Industrial Man* (London: Heinemann, 1962); *The Future of Industrial Societies* (Cambridge: Harvard University Press, 1983); John K. Galbraith, *The New Industrial State* (New York: New American Library, 1967).

6. For evidence that can be interpreted as supporting the convergence thesis, see Frederick Pryor, *Public Expenditure in Capitalist and Communist Nations* (Homewood, IL: Irwin, 1968); Harold L. Wilensky, *The Welfare State and Equality* (Berkeley: University of California Press, 1975). For opposing views, consult Arnold J. Heidenheimer, Hugh Heclo, and Carolyn Teich Adams, *Comparative Public Policy*, 2nd ed. (New York: St. Martin's Press, 1983); Charles W. Anderson, "System and Strategy in Comparative Policy Analysis: A Plea for Contextual and Experiential Knowledge," in William B. Gwyn and George C. Edwards, III, eds., *Perspectives on Public Policymaking* (New Orleans: Tulane University, 1975); and Charles Lockhart, "Explaining Social Policy Differences Among Advanced Societies," *Comparative Politics* 16 (1984): 335, 350.

7. John Goldthorpe, "The Development of Social Policy in England, 1800–1914," *Transactions of the Fifth World Congress of Sociology* 4 (1964); Dorothy Wedderburn, "Facts and Theories of the Welfare State," *Socialist Register* (London: Merlin Press, 1965); Zbigniew Brzezinski and Samuel P. Huntington, *Political Power: USA/USSR* (New York: Viking, 1963); and Daniel N. Nelson, "Political Convergence: An Empirical Assessment," *World Politics* 30 (1978): 411–31.

8. Richard Rose, "The Programme Approach to the Growth of Government," *British Journal of Political Science* 15 (1985): 23–50.

9. See *Social Expenditure 1960–1990: Problems of Growth and Control* (Paris: OECD, 1985).

10. *Old Age Pension Schemes* (Paris: OECD, 1977), 14–21.

11. Harold L. Wilensky and Charles Lebeaux, *Industrial Society and Social Welfare* (New York: Free Press, 1958), 233–334; Carolyn Weaver, *The Crisis in Social Security: Economic and Political Origins* (Durham, NC: Duke Press Policy Studies, 1982); Hugh Heclo, *Modern Social Politics in Britain and Sweden* (New Haven: Yale University Press, 1974); and Martha Derthick, *Policymaking for Social Security* (Washington, D.C.: The Brookings Institution, 1979).

12. See Wilensky, *Welfare State and Equality; The "New Corporatism," Centralization and the Welfare State* (Beverly Hills: Sage Publications, 1976); and "Leftism, Catholicism, and Democratic Corporatism: The Role of Political Parties in Welfare State Development," in Peter Flora and Arnold J. Heidenheimer, eds., *The Development of Welfare States in Europe and America* (New Brunswick: Transaction Books, 1981).

13. Norman Furniss and Timothy Tilton, *The Case for the Welfare State* (Bloom-

204 *Gary P. Freeman*

ington: Indiana University Press, 1978); Joan Higgens, *States of Welfare* (London: Basil Blackwell and Martin Robertson, 1981); Leslie Lenkowsky, "The Welfare State," in R. Emmett Tyrrell, Jr., ed., *The Future that Doesn't Work* (Garden City, NY: Doubleday, 1977).

14. See Goldthorpe, "Development of Social Policy"; Wedderburn, "Facts and Theories"; and Higgens, *States of Welfare*.
15. See Lockhart, "Explaining Social Policy Differences."
16. E. E. Witte, *The Development of the Social Security Act* (Madison: University of Wisconsin Press, 1963); A. J. Altmeyer, *The Formative Years of Social Security* (Madison: University of Wisconsin Press, 1968).
17. For overviews, see Alicia H. Munnell, *The Future of Social Security* (Washington, D.C.: The Brookings Institution, 1977); Robert Ball, *Social Security: Today and Tomorrow* (New York: Columbia University Press, 1978); *Social Security and Retirement* (Washington, D.C.: Congressional Quarterly, Inc., 1983).
18. William Beveridge, *Social Insurance and Allied Services* (New York: Macmillan, 1942).
19. For general historical accounts, see Karl de Schweinitz, *England's Road to Social Security* (New York: A. S. Barnes & Co., 1943); Richard Titmuss, *Essays on the Welfare State* (Boston: Beacon Press, 1958); Bentley B. Gilbert, *The Evolution of National Insurance in Great Britain* (London: Michael Joseph, 1966); Bentley B. Gilbert, *British Social Policy, 1914–1939* (Ithaca: Cornell University Press, 1970); Heclo, *Modern Social Politics*. For a contemporary overview, see *Reform of Social Security*, vol. 3, Cmnd. 9519 (London: HMSO, 1985), 99–138.
20. Tony Lynes, *Pension Rights and Wrongs* (London: Fabian Society, 1963), 11–12; J. C. Kincaid, *Poverty and Equality in Britain: A Study of Social Security and Taxation* (Harmondsworth: Penguin, 1975), 82–87.
21. *National Superannuation and Social Insurance: Proposals for Earnings-Related Social Security*, Cmnd. 3883 (London: HMSO, 1969), 5.
22. Ibid., 17.
23. *Strategy for Pensions*, Cmnd. 4755 (London: HMSO, 1971).
24. *Better Pensions*, Cmnd. 5713 (London: HMSO, 1974).
25. David Cameron, "On the Limits of the Public Economy," Paper delivered at the Annual Meeting of the American Political Science Association, New York, 1981.
26. Jurgen Kohl, "Trends and Problems in Postwar Public Expenditure Development in Western Europe and North America," in Flora and Heidenheimer, eds., *Development of Welfare States*, 317.
27. See Ken Judge, "State Pensions and the Growth of Social Welfare Expenditure," *Journal of Social Policy* 10 (1981): 503–30.
28. *Better Pensions*, 3.
29. *Reform of Social Security*, vol. 3, Cmnd. 9519 (London: HMSO, 1985), 30.
30. *Better Pensions*, 13; Kincaid, *Poverty and Equality*, 12–16; *Reform of Social Security*, vol. 3, 107.
31. *Social Security Bulletin, Annual Statistical Supplement* (Washington, D.C.: GPO, 1980), p. 235.
32. Ball, *Social Security*, 89.
33. Martin B. Tracy, "Maintaining Value of Social Security Benefits During Inflation: The Foreign Experience," *Social Security Bulletin* (November 1976).
34. *Social Security Bulletin* (June 1983): 14.

35. See, for example, Colin Campbell, *Over-indexed Benefits: The Decoupling Proposals for Social Security* (1976); Rudolf G. Penner, *Social Security Financing Proposals* (1971); and Robert S. Kaplan, *Financial Crisis in the Social Security System* (1976), all published by the American Enterprise Institute, Washington, D.C.
36. Derthick, *Policymaking for Social Security*; Weaver, *Crisis in Social Security*; Gary P. Freeman and Paul Adams, "The Politics of Social Security: Expansion, Retrenchment, and Rationalization," in Alan Stone and Edward J. Harpham, eds., *The Political Economy of Public Policy* (Beverly Hills: Sage Publications, 1982); "Ideology and Analysis in American Social Security Policymaking," *Journal of Social Policy* 12 (1983): 75–95; and Gary P. Freeman, "Presidents, Pensions, and Fiscal Policy," in James Pfiffner, ed., *The President and Economic Policy* (Philadelphia: ISHI Press, 1986), 135–60; "Voters, Bureaucrats, and the State: On the Autonomy of Social Security Policymaking," in Richard F. Tomasson and Nelson Pugach, eds., *Social Security: The First Half-Century* (Albuquerque: University of New Mexico Press, forthcoming).
37. Edward Tufte, *Political Control of the Economy* (Princeton: Princeton University Press, 1978).
38. For a fuller discussion of events after 1972 see Freeman and Adams, "Politics of Social Security"; and Paul Light, *Artful Work: The Politics of Social Security Reform* (New York: Random House, 1985).
39. Grant Jordan and Jeremy Richardson, "The British Policy Style or the Logic of Negotiation?" in Richardson, *Policy Styles*, 81, 83.
40. Judge, "State Pensions," 510-25; Frank Gould and Barbara Roweth, "Public Spending and Social Policy: The United Kingdom 1950–57," *Journal of Social Policy* 9 (1980): 337–57.
41. Heclo, *Modern Social Politics*. The first two quotations are on 301, the third on 303.
42. Ibid., 293–301, 311.
43. Keith Banting, *Poverty, Politics and Policy: Britain in the 1960s* (London: Macmillan, 1980), 143.
44. Heclo, *Modern Social Politics*, 312.
45. Phoebe Hall, et al., *Change, Choice and Conflict in Social Policy* (London: Heinemann, 1975), 78–79.
46. Douglas E. Ashford, *Policy and Politics in Britain: The Limits of Consensus* (Philadelphia: Temple University Press, 1981), 209–10.
47. Ibid.
48. Banting, *Poverty, Politics and Policy*, 145.
49. Judge, "State Pensions," 525–7.
50. Heclo, *Modern Social Politics*, 297.
51. Harold Wilson, *Final Term: The Labour Government, 1974–1976* (London: Weidenfeld and Nicolson and Michael Joseph, 1979), 125–7.
52. Hall, et al., *Change*, 82–85.
53. Ashford, *Policy and Politics*, 214; Heclo, *Modern Social Politics*, 274; Richard H. Crossman, *The Diaries of a Cabinet Minister*, vol. 3 (London: Hamish Hamilton and Jonathan Cape, 1977), 258, 616, 714.
54. Paul Adams and Gary P. Freeman, "Social Services Under Reagan and Thatcher," in Norman and Susan Fainstein, eds., *Urban Policy Under Capitalism* (Beverly Hills: Sage Publications, 1982), 65–82.
55. Freeman, "Presidents, Pensions, and Fiscal Policy," 135–60.

56. Peter Riddell, *The Thatcher Government* (London: Martin Robertson, 1983), 140.
57. Michael O'Higgens, "Privatization and Social Security," *Political Quarterly* 55 (1984): 129; and Ray Robinson, "Restructuring the Welfare State: An Analysis of Public Expenditure, 1979/80–1984/85," *Journal of Social Policy* 15 (1986): 4, 17–18.
58. Sara Rosenberry, "Social Insurance, Distributive Criteria and the Welfare Backlash: A Comparative Analysis," *British Journal of Political Science* 12 (1982): 421–47.
59. See for example, Richard Hemming and J. A. Kay, "The Costs of the State Earnings-Related Pension Scheme," *Economic Journal* 92 (1982): 300–19.

Health Policy In A Period of Resource Limits and Conservative Politics

Beth C. Fuchs

Comparing the American and British systems reveals that both are troubled by many of the same pressures. In Britain's National Health Service (NHS), there are severe resource shortages in money, equipment, and certain categories of personnel. Labor disputes frequently cripple hospital service, and there is widespread discontent among NHS employees. The queue for hospital care is long and continuous, some people waiting years for elective surgery. Facilities are old and outdated; hospitals are considered young if they are less than a century old. Due to an aging clientele, wage and salary demands of personnel, and costly technological innovations in direct medical services, inflationary pressures within the NHS are severe. Prime Minister Thatcher's efforts to hold down NHS spending have exacerbated what was already a tightly rationed system of care, and forces in favor of privatization are jeopardizing the universality of the system.

In the United States, surveys show that a majority of Americans are becoming increasingly dissatisfied with their health care, with costs an almost universal concern.[1] More subtle are the widespread reservations about the access to and quality of care; indeed, the word "crisis" is commonly applied to America's health care system.

The parallels between the American and British cases suggest an interesting dilemma for policymakers and theorists alike. Here are two different health systems, experiencing similar pressures and responding in surprisingly similar ways. We find in both countries that medical personnel are restless, fearful of losing their clinical autonomy. Politicians, faced with what seems like an unlimited demand for health care and hemorrhaging national budgets, seek to place lids on health care spending. Free market forces and competition are heralded as the panacea for exploding costs by the conservative governments of the day, and pressures to privatize medicine are pervasive. Widespread rationing of care appears imminent and poses wrenching ethical and political questions about how to distribute scarce medical resources and equipment.

To what extent, though, are the systems converging? In the discussion that follows, I will show that while pressures for convergence are substantial, the two systems retain significant differences. These differences, however, could diminish if political and economic forces continue to erode the basic values underlying the NHS and hasten America's entry into a national cost containment program that affects all payers and providers of care (known as an "all-payers" system) or an explicitly rationed system of care.

THE NATIONAL HEALTH SERVICE UNDER THATCHER

The Thatcher government assumed office in 1979, replacing a Labour government whose main objectives for the NHS were to reduce the growth of the private sector, eliminate pay beds (private beds in NHS hospitals), and bolster access to care in the underserved areas. The policies of Labour were, in short, those sympathetic to the underlying socialist principles of the NHS. While Labour did not always follow through on its intentions, its health agenda was relatively straightforward and consistent with its historical support for the health service.

Thatcher entered office declaring inflation to be Britain's chief economic problem, and her first budget indicated the program with which she was going to respond. The primary objectives of this budget were "redistribution of the tax burden, lower government spending, and strict control of the money supply."[2] Strongly influenced by Milton Friedman, Thatcher committed herself to a stiff monetarism in which a tight money supply would reduce inflation and an adjusted tax burden would stimulate corporate investment. Unlike Reagan, Thatcher was acutely concerned that her policies not add to the government's budget deficit. As her government took power, the deficit was already equal to 5 percent of GNP,[3] a dangerous level in the view of the financial community.

The effects of Thatcher's economic policies were directly felt by Britain's welfare state. In a most sympathetic light, Thatcherism could be seen as government helping people to help themselves. Klein has aptly described the Conservative government's approach as it came to power:

The new approach not only marked a break with the preceding Labour government. Much more significantly, it also marked a break with the stance of previous post-war conservative governments. Thatcher Conservatism not only repudiated the paternalistic corporate policies of the Macmillan era, 1958–1964, with their emphasis on involving employers and trade unions in the planning of economic strategy. It also repudiated the managerialist policies of the Heath government, 1970–1974, with their emphasis on government intervention to make the economy more efficient. The Thatcher program was shaped by a deep distrust of government as such. The role of government, it was argued, was not to do things for people. It was to create an environment in which people could do things for themselves. Individual decisions in the market place, rather than collective decisions in the political market place, should shape the allocation of resources. So government spending would be cut, in order to allow people to choose for themselves as to how to spend their money. New policies would be shaped by a new ideology.[4]

Since the creation of the NHS in 1948, its basic principles and goals had been enveloped in consensus; partisan differences only whittled away at the margins. Conflicts had emerged over the classic tensions between the Conservative party's emphasis on efficiency and labour's desire to achieve a more equitable health system. Nevertheless, the NHS as a universal, comprehensive nationalized health system, organized to maximize the benefits of medical science, had been sacrosanct from the daily struggles of the Left and Right.[5] With the entry of Thatcher, however, this consensus appeared in jeopardy. Free market economics, fiscal austerity, and distrust of government were to decide the rules of the game. If this new philosophy was implemented, changes for the NHS, perhaps even its termination, were imminent. Of course, ideology and rhetoric are not always consistent with action, and the Conservatives were not dogmatic in their approach to the NHS. Their party manifesto in 1979 reflected a moderate course, their ideological puritanism tempered by political ambitions. Spending on the NHS would be maintained and resources would be used more efficiently by streamlining the bureaucracy. More consistent with the new Conservative ideology was the pronouncement that the government would end "Labour's vendetta against the private health sector" and that it would look toward possible changes in the way in which health care was financed.[6] In sum, the Thatcher health program would be shaped by the objectives of privatization, budgetary austerity, and decentralization of the health service through reorganization.

PRIVATIZATION, REORGANIZATION AND BUDGETARY AUSTERITY

When the creation of a nationalized health service was first being debated, numerous interests pressed for retaining as much health care as possible in the market sector. In order to win support for the NHS from these promarket interests, especially the British Medical Association, Aneurin Bevan (minister of health, 1946–1950) forged a compromise in which private medicine would coexist alongside the nationalized system. In addition, health-related industries, such as pharmaceutical manufacturers, would be left untouched. Since the creation of the NHS, this state of coexistence has continued with varying degrees of tension.

Private medicine in Britain consists of independent fee-for-service general practitioners and consultants, part-time NHS general practitioners and consultants who take private patients on a fee-for-service basis, "pay beds" in NHS hospitals, and private hospitals, nursing homes, laboratories, and other health-related facilities. Some of the ancillary facilities are run by charitable organizations and nonprofit concerns. Until Thatcher, private medicine only served a tiny share of the population.

The most visible and contested aspect of private health care is the system of pay beds in NHS hospitals. Some are located in regular NHS wards; others are located in separate wings or buildings. The NHS hospitals charge the patients for the beds, and the consultants bill the patients for their services directly.[7] In 1949, pay beds made up about 1.5 percent of the 453,000 beds in NHS hospitals. By 1963, the number had dropped to 1.2 percent of the 472,000 NHS beds.[8] And by 1978, the number had decreased to less than 1 percent of the approximately 376,000 NHS beds.[9] The number of patients served by these beds has fluctuated over the years, but it has always constituted a small share of the total patient load. Moreover, there has consistently been an excess number of pay beds to meet demand.

Pay beds have always been a sore spot for the Labour party, which views them as a means to jump the queue for hospital treatment and as a last stronghold of the perverse market forces in health care. This resentment was fueled by the increasing queues of the financially depressed NHS of the 1970s, and pressures mounted to abolish pay beds completely. For example, nurses in London went on strike in 1974 to protest the existence of pay beds. Objecting to the two-class system of care, "they were directly attacking the highest paid hospital employees, the physician consultants who were deriving the most benefit from the pay bed arrangement."[10] In the Health Services Act of 1976, a compromise was struck which "enjoined the secretary of state to reduce the number of pay beds by 1,000 within six months of the act becoming law. After that, the remaining pay beds were to be phased out by an independent board. . . ."[11]

With the elimination of so many pay beds, much of the private patient demand was channeled to for-profit hospitals. Klein reports that between 1975 and 1980 the number of private acute care hospitals increased from 105 to 153, boosting the number of private beds in these hospitals from 2279 to 3150.[12] Some of these hospitals were owned and operated by foreign (primarily American) concerns. But prior to Thatcher, the number of privates remained small and the government kept tight reins on the proliferation of new for-profit facilities.

The vast majority of the British public likes the NHS. Survey data reflect remarkably consistent and high support for the NHS and high levels of satisfaction with its services. Indeed, over 90 percent of the public declares satisfaction with the NHS,[13] although 80 percent believes that the government is spending too little on health and one recent poll revealed that 75 percent of the voters disapprove of present government policy regarding the NHS.[14] Many of Britain's doctors, however, still prefer a return to private medicine, and the British Medical Association has been particularly vocal in its support for "reprivatization" of health care. This is ironic, given the vast power and authority of the medical profession within the NHS. Nevertheless, private medicine, with the promise of less government red tape and higher remuneration, remains a popular alternative with much of the medical profession.

For obvious reasons, privatization is also favored by those groups with a vested interest in Britain's relatively small private health care market. These include Private Patients Limited and the British United Provident Association, two of the largest private insurers. But it is the support of Britain's Conservative party which has been most important in stimulating the privatization move. "The conservative ideologues surrounding the central organs of the Conservative party—including Arthur Seldon and others associated with the Centre for Policy Studies, which has close ties with Margaret Thatcher—seem particularly influential."[15]

The Conservatives believe that NHS costs are rising because there is no check on demand. Individuals overutilize health services, and thus contribute to endlessly increasing drains on resources.[16] Therefore, the major thrust of Britain's reprivatization under the Tories is the shifting away from government financing of personal health services and "back to individuals through private health insurance schemes."[17] Private purchasing schemes are viewed as competitive and thus more efficient financial arrangements, less likely to stimulate inflation in the health care sector. If patients are forced to bear the costs of care, they will be more prudent purchasers. The bias toward private purchasing schemes also reflects Conservative preferences for consumer choice and for physician autonomy in the control of which patients he or she shall serve. Private insurance schemes also fit into Thatcher's personal preference for a two-tiered system in which the NHS would "preserve access only to a basic level of health care."[18]

In 1979, Patrick Jenkin, secretary of state for social services (1979–1981), announced that it was the new government's policy to welcome the contribution that independent medicine could make to the health care of the nation.[19] Jenkin established a working party to respond to the more than 100 recommendations made by a Royal Commission's report, issued during the last year of Labour rule. The working party proposed that the government study how a system of insurance could be introduced in Britain. This proposal was loudly condemned by Labourites and more moderate Tories. Norman Fowler, who replaced Jenkin in 1981, indicated publicly that he would not act on the working party's recommendation.[20]

The new government would therefore have to make do with less radical measures and ones less likely to attract loud condemnation by the opposition. One possibility was to seek greater private involvement in the support services of the NHS, such as laundry, catering, and security. Concerted efforts were made to stimulate private vendors to bid for NHS services, but these efforts succeeded more or less, depending on the specific local health authority. As of 1985, the Tory government was heralding a savings of £19 million as a result of contracting out support services to private concerns.[21] Another, more direct, strategy was to encourage the British public to use private medical services by making them more attractive and affordable. Such a strategy could prove especially successful if NHS services became increasingly scarce.

The Thatcher government encouraged growth in private medical services through a number of legislative and administrative initiatives. One of the most important was the Health Services Act of 1980. The first section of this legislation was inspired by the Conservative party's consultative document, *Patients First,* which had recommended a streamlining of the NHS administrative apparatus and greater delegation of responsibility to those in the hospital and community services. *Patients First* was the first major contribution of the Conservative government to the debate on the NHS structure. Specifically, the act mandated the elimination of one of the three administrative tiers (the Area Health Authorities). This was not a privatization provision; rather, it was yet another effort to make the NHS more efficient in the delivery of services. In Jenkin's words, "The more economical it [the NHS] can be, the more resources there will be for patient care. On the quality of management will depend the effective planning and day-to-day operation of the National Health Service."[22]

In contrast, the second section of the 1980 Act, "Private Practice," was designed to "restore the political balance whch had been caused to swing in the other direction [left] by the Labour Government's Health Services Act 1976. . . ."[23] Under the 1976 law, the NHS had been given the legal power to limit the construction of any new private facilities ("controlled premises") over seventy-five beds (one hundred in London). At the time, this was viewed as a way to protect the NHS from a major loss of hospital staff to the private hospitals.[24] Under the 1980 act, the government amended the definition of "controlled premises" to raise the bed limit to 120 before authorization from the secretary was required. In effect, the act opened the door to the development of private facilities and lessened central planning by transferring authority over new developments to local health officials.[25]

The 1980 act also abolished the Health Services Board, which had been responsible for the gradual elimination of pay beds and for reviewing proposals for putting up new private hospitals. Power was also restored to the secretary to authorize the use of NHS facilities for the private treatment of patients.[26] Thus the Labour pay-bed policy was completely reversed and the principal government instrument for regulating private sector growth was eliminated.

To encourage workers to enroll in private health insurance schemes, the government restored a tax deduction for employer contributions to employee health insurance, which had been eliminated by a previous government. Under this provision, the employers' contributions were tax deductible for all workers earning up to £8,500 a year. In the first two years of the Thatcher administration, there was a significant increase in the number of persons enrolled in private health insurance plans. In 1980, there was a 28 percent increase over the previous year; in 1981, private subscriptions went up 12 percent, bringing the total number of enrollees to four million.[27]

Private health insurance in Britain, as in the United States, allows for health coverage through any one of about sixteen insurance companies.[28] Largest of these companies is the British United Provident Association (BUPA), first established in 1947.[29] BUPA and other insurance schemes act as a major stimulus for privatizing medicine because they actively solicit membership from people enlisted within the NHS. Their sales pitches stress the advantages of greater privacy for the patient, the economic security of receiving cash benefits while being hospitalized, the speed and convenience of private treatment, and the freedom of choice of specialists that patients can get through the private fee-for-service sector.[30]

BUPA also directs its sales in the form of group policies to companies, which are easy targets because of the tax break for the employers' contribution to employees' health insurance plans (thereby extending a substantial subsidy to private medicine). Not surprisingly, BUPA has been especially successful in this sector, acquiring a large business from companies, particularly as fringe benefits for employees on the professional and management levels for whom private medicine means avoiding the financial hardship and inconveniences of long queues.[31] It is ironic that, because of the success of Thatcher's government in achieving increased penetration of for-profit hospitals, BUPA and other insurers have experienced large hikes in their bills. In 1982, BUPA reported an underwriting loss of £1.9 million and "attributed this to the high charges in proprietary hospitals."[32]

The government also implemented several administrative changes to further the growth of the private sector. For example, it adjusted the contracts of consultants (specialists) so that they could serve more private patients. This reversed the policy of the previous Labour government, which had been seeking contracts designed to encourage consultants to work full-time with the NHS and thus drop whatever private patients they had. The new contracts now allowed all consultants to engage in part-time private practice.[33]

In addition, the government provided that local health authorities could raise extra revenue by means of local fundraising campaigns. This was consistent with the Tory emphasis on the doctrines of self-help and local autonomy. But it served another purpose as well. Given the increasingly strict limits on government spending for the NHS, local health authorities faced grim shortages of new equipment, especially some of the more expensive items such as CT scanners. Local fund-raising campaigns gave the authorities the possibility of reducing these shortages by seeking help from charitable groups and individuals.[34]

The government's intent to "reprivatize" health care climaxed in September 1982, when it was leaked to *The Economist* that the Central Policy Review Staff, the government's think tank, had prepared an analysis outlining alternatives for radical spending cuts, including the dismantlement of several parts of the welfare state. The report had been commissioned by Geoffrey Howe and was motivated by the government's objective to put a major dent in government social spending.[35] It explicitly recommended replacing the NHS with private health insurance, a move which was estimated to save £3 to £4 billion pounds a year from the 1982–1983 health budget of £10 billion.[36] Because lower-income persons might not purchase adequate coverage, the paper suggested a compulsory minimum of private health insurance for everyone.

The plan met with immediate resistance from ministers within Thatcher's cabinet. "Cabinet wets were so appalled at the think-tank's suggestions that they argued successfully that it would be wrong for the cabinet to give it serious and instant consideration. But that will not be the end of the matter."[37] Although the government took no action to implement the plan, it gave political ammunition to the labor unions and the opposition parties and forced the prime minister onto the defensive. At the Conservative party's 1982 annual conference, Thatcher responded to the outcries by promising that the NHS was "safe in our hands."[38]

The government's efforts to privatize health care never reached the extremes recommended by the Central Policy Review Staff. Nevertheless, the government's concerns about the appetite of the NHS for the public's money continued. Given the Conservative's ideological bias against the NHS, and the welfare state more generally, it was widely expected both within and outside of the Tory ranks that public expenditures on the health service would be reduced. But the Tory record of support for the NHS does not clearly fit these expectations.

The British Medical Association has estimated that to maintain current services, the NHS must experience 1.2 percent real annual spending growth.[39] Given this calculation, for the years 1979–1980 through 1983–1984, real growth should have been 6 percent. In fact, government expenditures on the NHS experienced about 5 percent real growth during that time period. This growth was less than under the previous Labour government, which in turn was less than under the previous Heath government.[40] However, the Tory government also raised the fees charged to NHS users. The proportion of NHS income derived from these charges, primarily from prescription, dental, and ophthalmic charges, increased from 2.4 percent of the total NHS income in 1978–1979 to 3.6 percent in the 1984 fiscal year.[41] Such actions signaled the Tory government's inclination to hold down NHS expenditures by shifting costs to patients.

This rather ambiguous record has been reflected further in the general debate between the Right and Left over the effects of the Thatcher government on the NHS. In April 1983, the government released a report, "Health Care and its Costs," which showed how the NHS spent its money during the period 1971–1981 and analyzed the extent to which spending had been efficient. The conclusions of the report proved controversial. While the Tory government sought to bolster its claim of adequate and increasing spending on the NHS, members of the opposition parties tried to show these claims to be bogus.[42] Of course, the problem with such analysis was that actual expenditures must be measured against actual needs. As opposition spokesmen argued, you need to account for the 1 percent annual real increase needed for health care of the old, 0.5 percent increase for new techniques and technology and 0.5 percent for "efficiency" savings that are required of health authorities. When these factors were considered, Tory claims of adequate spending on the NHS were subject to serious question.

This debate over the NHS budget extended into the 1983 general election. To Labour's charge that Thatcher was proceeding with her plans to dismantle the health service, however slowly, the Tories pointed to their spending record and claimed credit for the increased number of nurses and doctors employed in the NHS.[43] Critics countered that the greater numbers stemmed from the reduced working week for nurses and from a decision years ago to increase the number of medical schools.[44] Thatcher responded by reasserting her claim that "the NHS is safe in our hands." The government also pointed to data showing that more patients were being served by the NHS than ever before because of its success in making the service more efficient and its workers more productive.

In Thatcher's second term, government policy on the NHS has reflected broader concerns with overall spending and its priority on meeting very expensive defense commitments. A sign of things to come was given early in the new term when the government announced cuts of over 4,800 jobs in the work force of the NHS Regional Health Authorities.[45] In addition, Thatcher and Fowler (secretary of state for social services) continued to press for management reforms to squeeze greater efficiency out of the service.

In a move similar to Reagan's establishment of the President's Private Sector Survey on Cost Control (the Grace Commission), Fowler assembled a panel of four businessmen to look into ways to improve the efficiency of the NHS.[46] The assumption was that NHS administrators needed to learn the lessons of private business. The panel was chaired by Roy Griffiths of the Sainsbury's stores, and its findings were damning to all levels of NHS management. The Griffiths panel made several recommendations which Fowler endorsed and reported to Parliament. These included the creation of a Health Services Supervisory Board chaired by Fowler, to coordinate the functions of DHSS relating to various parts of the service. The panel also recommended changes at the regional, district, and hospital levels, to accomplish the "most effective use and management of all resources."[47] These recommendations have not been implemented. There are now managers at all levels of the NHS, who are responsible for making decisions but who must also report to the health authority and meet certain targets.[48]

The Griffiths report has raised questions about physician control over the demand for resources. Clinical autonomy is extensive under the NHS. There are few controls over the way physicians practice their trade and only minimal auditing procedures.[49] Because physicians are the key determinant of resource use, some DHSS officials are eager to develop measures of physician performance and productivity. There is even interest within the Department in adopting some measure akin to Diagnosis Related Groups (DRGs), used in the United States as a Medicare cost-containment measure. At the least, interest is developing to obtain records on costs generated by each medical specialty.[50]

Will private medicine continue to expand, however, especially if Labour returns to power? By 1985, about five million Britons had bought medical policies from private insurers.[51] The majority of these policies included coverage for inpatient elective surgical procedures, meaning an ability to choose one's own consultant. At this time there were 40,000 beds in private hospitals and resident nursing homes.[52] Between 1979 and 1985, the number of for-profit private hospitals increased 141 percent.[53] However, premiums were climbing and the fees for patients in for-profit hospitals were high. Between 1981 and 1983, the retail price index increased by 14 percent whereas the average health insurance premium rose by 61 percent.[54] Such economic realities appeared to be dampening corporate and individual enthusiasm for the private insurance option.

Nevertheless, the rise of private medicine places the NHS and its underlying principles of universal health care, free at the time of service, in jeopardy. One reason is that private medicine tends to "skim" the most healthy patients, those who require routine and more profitable acute care services. The chronically ill and the mentally and physically handicapped, considered by private insurers as bad risks and too expensive to insure, are left to the NHS.[55] Moreover, consultants who reduce their hours spent with the health service to earn fees from private patients do little to reduce the long waiting list of NHS patients requiring nonemergency care. Finally, because of the comingling of NHS resources with the private sector (for example, pay beds in NHS hospitals), NHS resources subsidize the private sector.

Ultimately, the future of private medicine in Britain rests on the financial deprivation of the NHS. Even if the Thatcher government continues to fund the service to maintain current levels of service, which is unlikely, the NHS will become increasingly desperate for funds. Rationing of certain types of medical technology is already practiced. While the decision rule for rationing may appear to the individual patient to be based on medical criteria and thus fair in its administration and effects, the origin of the decision is primarily political, based on how much the government has allocated to the service.[56] The length of the queue continues to grow, hospital facilities continue to age into obsolescence, and labor strife regularly interrupts the delivery of services.

In this environment, it would be surprising if the private health sector did not expand. When transplants are rationed within the NHS, desperate patients with an ability to pay are going to seek transplants outside the service. When waits for elective surgery for painful conditions extend into years rather than months, those who can afford private physicians and private beds will go that route. When there is an insurance policy to cover the costs of a shiny new hospital bed in a plush private hospital, the policy holder is going to exit the NHS. There is, in sum, a real danger that British health care will become inequitable, with access to care determined according to income instead of according to medical need.

The question is, how much can the British nation as a whole afford to spend for health care? The NHS is a relative bargain; few other industrial nations support a quality health system for so small an investment of GNP. If the private sector takes off in Britain, however, Britain may experience the kind of double-digit inflation in health care that the United States experienced in the 1970s, as government pressures to contain costs are circumvented. In the face of that inflation, the British government may have to take more extreme steps to curb health care costs. In this light, convergence between the American and British systems may take on more meaning, as we will see as we turn to analyze the American health system under the Reagan administration.

HEALTH CARE POLITICS AND POLICY UNDER REAGAN

Prior to Reagan's presidency, the national health agenda reflected a basic consensus that government had a responsibility to provide health care at the very least to those unable to pay or to those who would be bankrupted by a major medical emergency. The overriding goal of health reformers, though, was a system of comprehensive national health insurance, and most of the principal federal initiatives through the 1970s were incremental steps toward that end.

Reagan's election dramatically changed this agenda.[57] He entered office using much the same political rhetoric as Thatcher, although his economics reflected a more radical departure from the status quo, with much less deference to conservative economic tenets. Monetarists were clearly uneasy as Reagan outlined a plan for American economic recovery which drew its central inspiration from supply-side economics: reduce personal income taxes by 30 percent over three years; balance the budget by 1984; restore market efficiency to the economy by removing the "tentacles of excessive government regulation which are strangling our economy"; and control the growth of the money supply.[58] Simultaneously, however, President Reagan called for massive increases in military spending. More mainstream Republicans were skeptical of such an unorthodox approach. They were convinced that by doing all things at once, the new administration would achieve nothing at all, except unprecedented deficits.[59] But Reagan seemed unfettered by such long-range concerns.

In its approach to health care, the Reagan administration made cost control and competition the centerpiece. Inflation in health care was climbing even faster than the consumer price index, and eating up an increasing share of the federal budget. In 1980, spending on federal health programs exceeded $71 billion and made up almost 12 percent of the total federal budget. This was up from $3 billion in 1960 (3.2 percent of the federal budget). Another way of viewing the statistics is that in 1980, health care spending equaled 9.5 percent of GNP as compared with 3.2 percent of GNP in 1960.[60]

The basic strategy of the Reagan administration for reducing health costs was to stimulate competition among providers. This would be accomplished by paring federal regulation of the health industry, reducing government activity in health by cutting government expenditures; and encouraging marketplace operations by providing appropriate incentives. In pursuing this strategy, the administration expressed concern that these policy changes not endanger access to basic health services for the poor. Thus arose the concept of the "safety net," in which our nation's "truly needy" would not be harmed by the administration's shifting of spending priorities. In Reagan's words:

> While recognizing the need for bold action, we have ensured that the impact of spending reductions will be shared widely and fairly by different groups and the various regions of the country. Also, we have, as pledged, maintained this society's basic social safety net, protecting programs for the elderly and others who rely on government for their very existence.[61]

The safety net would prove more an effective political device for defending Reagan policies than a realistic instrument for protecting the poor against budget cuts and program changes—symbolic politics at its best.

Reagan shared with Thatcher similar perspectives on reducing the central government's role in the health arena by giving localities the opportunity to work things out for themselves. Accordingly, in his first budget request to Congress, Reagan outlined a plan to curb and decentralize government involvement in the health arena. For example, he proposed the consolidation of twenty-six federal categorical grants into block grants. This action was justified under the guise of returning the locus of power to the states and providing for a more efficient investment of government expenditures. But with this consolidation was proposed a 25 percent budget reduction from 1981 spending levels (or 32 percent below current services level), thus shifting the onus of cutbacks to state and local officials.[62] Reagan also proposed tightening of eligibility standards for Medicaid, a joint federal-state program which provides health services to low-income persons on an entitlement basis. In addition, Reagan asked for a cap on the federal contribution to Medicaid. Thus, decentralization of government control under Reaganomics would, in effect, produce new obligations on the states and localities to pick up costs no longer shouldered by Uncle Sam.

Reagan proposed several other changes in the discretionary spending arena, including the elimination of certain health programs with established constituencies. He asked for the closing of the eight public health service hospitals and twenty-nine clinics. These hospitals had originally been established to provide free medical care for merchant seamen, but had expanded their patient profile to include civilian charity care. Reagan also proposed a reduction in Indian Health Service facilities and restrained growth in the National Health Service Corps (originally created to encourage physicians to practice in medically underserved areas). Major regulatory instruments were targeted for termination, and federal support for biomedical research, occupational health and safety, and training for the health professions were included on the list of programs to be curtailed.[63]

The initial stages of the Reagan health program signaled a new and harsh reality for the millions of direct and indirect beneficiaries of federal aid. Although the Carter administration had taken its toll on federal health programs, this new administration was threatening a fundamental revamping of budget priorities. To many observers familiar with the budget game, it was hard to take such radical intentions seriously, for it was one thing to propose such measures and quite another to marshal them through Congress. The protracted budget battles between Congress and the president, and between the Republican Senate and the Democratic House stood in stark contrast to the British budgetary process where Parliament had little control over the shape of the government's budget. Consequently, the Reagan program was first met with skepticism: efforts to cut established programs with entrenched constituencies would fly in the face of vested interests expert at protecting their programs. The Stockman ax would be blunted by platoons of lobbyists and parochially minded congressmen intent on protecting what Stockman once called the "social pork barrel."

In the end, Reagan was more successful than most observers expected. The resounding 1980 electoral victory of the Republican party and its successful takeover of the Senate certainly helped Reagan achieve much of his political agenda. Reagan also experienced an unexpected wave of congressional cooperation in the aftermath of the attempt on his life. As a result, and in contrast to Thatcher's effects on the NHS, Reagan's actions proved to be more harsh than his rhetoric. In Reagan's first year the clientele groups of the targeted health programs were caught off guard, and he achieved many of his proposed cuts, especially for discretionary programs.

Reagan's plans to encourage free-market competition and stimulate private sector growth in the financing and delivery of health services were also translated into an array of programmatic and regulatory initiatives. The Medicare voucher proposal, advocated by many free market economists as a way to introduce competitive principles to the Medicare population and contain Medicare spending, was one of the first Reagan proposals to surface. Under a voucher program, persons eligible for Medicare would be entitled to receive a voucher worth some specified amount to purchase a qualified private health insurance plan. If the voucher exceeded the cost of the insurance premium, the person would be able to pocket the difference; if it was less, the person would have to pay the difference out of pocket. The key to the voucher alternative would be convincing the elderly that they would obtain better coverage in the private market than that available from Medicare.[64]

Critics of the voucher proposal argued that it would result in adverse selection. Persons needing the most care or having the highest risk of medical problems would tend to remain with Medicare, while those in better than average health would opt for the voucher program. Thus the average per capita cost for beneficiaries still enrolled in Medicare would probably rise, causing the system's costs to climb. This would defeat the principal rationale for the voucher program. But to hold down costs, the value of the voucher would probably not be allowed to keep pace with inflation. This would result in additional out of pocket costs for beneficiaries or lesser coverage. In effect, by "privatizing" Medicare, vouchers would result in reduced access to care for those unable to afford the increased out of pocket costs, and a residual Medicare program overburdened by the needs of the most vulnerable—the disabled, renal patients, and the sickest of the elderly.[65] In short, the voucher plan would transform Medicare into a two-class system of care, thus defeating its original purpose of universal and equal access to care for America's elderly and disabled.

The voucher proposal was introduced for the administration by Representatives Stockman (before he moved over to the Office of Management and Budget) and Gephardt (D., Mo.); it was first given serious consideration by the House Ways and Means Committee in its efforts to meet tax and spending targets set in the fiscal year 1983 budget resolution. Although the proposal was embraced by conservative Republicans, it also received the support of many Democrats concerned with budget deficits and exploding Medicare costs, and it took the efforts of liberals in the House-Senate conference on the tax bill to defeat the measure. Despite its defeat, in late 1982 the Department of Health and Human Services decided to encourage vouchers incrementally by awarding a collection of grants, contracts, and waivers of standard Medicare reimbursement methods, for the development of competitive Medicare and Medicaid demonstration projects.[66]

A more comprehensive pro-competition package was belatedly announced by Reagan in his 1984 budget submission to Congress. Included in the package was a program of voluntary vouchers for Medicare beneficiaries. It also contained a change in a major tax expenditure which excludes employer contributions to workers' health insurance premiums from taxable income (estimated to cost the government $29 billion in revenues in 1984). According to the administration, this tax subsidy "stimulated excessive health insurance coverage and contributed to health care cost inflation, because consumers have no incentives to hold down costs if they bear only a very limited part of the costs directly."[67] Reagan's proposal was to place a cap on the amount of the employer's contribution which would be tax-free. It is interesting to note that while Reagan was pushing to close this loophole in order to hold down health costs, the Thatcher government was adopting the tax break as a means to stimulate private medicine.

Reagan's competition package failed to obtain congressional support, and the voucher and tax provisions died with the ninety-eighth Congress. The Administration proposes them anew in each annual budget submission but Congress to date has given them icy receptions. Meanwhile the administration was (and continues to be) successful in pushing less sweeping "pro-competitive" and privatization measures through Congress, as can be seen by examining the changes to the federal health planning program and the professional service review organizations (PSROs).

The health planning program had been established in 1974 to encourage a more rational distribution of health care facilities and technology. The most visible and controversial aspect of the program was the certificate of need process used by state and local health systems agencies to approve or reject construction of facilities and the purchase of major medical equipment. The program was extremely unpopular with medical providers and had failed to achieve a very convincing record of containing costs.[68] Health planners and consumer advocates, however, believed that the program played a critical role in the allocation of new facilities and in giving consumers an effective way to participate in local decisions on health matters.

PSROs were groups of physicians organized to determine whether medical treatment under Medicare and Medicaid was necessary and of high quality. Although they had been created to monitor the quality of care received by federally insured patients, these review organizations gradually were viewed as a way to hold down the utilization of services. Both the health planning and PSRO programs were viewed by the administration as vestiges of an outmoded and ineffective regulatory program to hold down health care costs.

With each successive Reagan budget, these programs faced termination. Through compromise between the administration and the Congress, they were gradually reconstituted into very different and significantly less ambitious entities. In 1981, funds for the health planning system were reduced from about $130 million a year to $64 million. In 1982, the program narrowly escaped death or transformation because the House and the Senate failed to reach agreement on what to do with it. In the years since 1982, a divided Congress has helped to forestall dramatic changes in the program. Its survival has also been aided by the lingering concerns of conservatives and liberals alike that the program, however flawed, remains the only regulatory check on excessive hospital development and wasteful duplication of services and technology. But funding cuts have reduced the program to a shadow of itself, and the planning system has largely become dependent on state and local support for its survival.[69] As of late 1986, health planning is slated for termination unless Congress provides a last minute extension through the appropriations process.

The PSROs experienced a more definitive fate. Congress, in passing the 1981 Omnibus Budget Reconciliation Act, rejected Reagan's proposal to terminate these boards, but reduced federal funding and gave the federal government the authority to end funding for any PSRO found ineffective or inefficient.[70] In the following year, Congress agreed to Reagan's request and repealed the PSRO program. In its place, Congress provided for peer review of Medicare claims by physician review boards under contract with the Department of Health and Human Services.[71] This "contracting out" of operations once performed by federal entities was a standard administration reform measure, ideologically consistent with the conservative belief that the private sector would perform more efficiently.

Given the antigovernment stance of the Reagan administration, it is interesting to reflect on its efforts to "reform" Medicare. Because of Medicare's popularity and entitlement status, it had fared relatively well in Reagan's budget proposals, especially compared to discretionary health programs. Nevertheless, the administration was anxious to contain the growth in Medicare spending and began searching for cost containment measures early in its tenure.

There was a general consensus among health experts that the existing reimbursement system, in which providers billed Medicare for services on a reasonable cost basis, created perverse incentives for providers to charge whatever the market (in this case, the government) would bear. And most analysts believed that containing costs required a change to a prospective payment system in which providers would be given positive incentives to hold down charges to Medicare. There was far less consensus on the specifics of such a system. In his 1981 budget, Reagan proposed a modest cut ($1 billion) in Medicare and increased cost-sharing for beneficiaries. Congress gave Reagan what he requested and more, partly to allow it more negotiating leverage to reject certain of Reagan's Medicaid cuts. The 1982 budget battle resulted in far more substantial changes for Medicare. Reagan again came in with increased cost-sharing for beneficiaries and other changes that would add to the burden of Medicare patients. The Congress, increasingly concerned about the budget deficit, the financial status of the Medicare trust fund, and the failure of hospitals to hold down price increases, took matters into its own hands and passed new limits on Medicare reimbursement for hospitals. It also required the Department of Health and Human Services to submit within five months a plan for prospective payments to hospitals and nursing homes.[72]

In December 1982, the administration sent its prospective payment proposal to Congress. It was incorporated into congressional action on a fast-tracked social security reform package, and a modified version of this sweeping change in Medicare reimbursement was enacted in April 1983. The fast-track process prevented the customary stalling tactics of the relevant special interest groups from having much influence on the outcome. Indeed, because the 1982 reimbursement limits were viewed by many hospitals as extraordinarily severe, their lobbyists were instructed to accept the new prospective payment system as a lesser evil. With certain major exceptions, such as Blue Cross, the Catholic Health Association, and the American Medical Association, the health lobbies supported the proposal and helped it through the legislative obstacle course.[73]

The speed with which this proposal became law defies conventional wisdom about the cumbersome and protracted nature of the legislative process.[74] Here was the most sweeping reform of Medicare to come along since it was established. Yet Congress was able to overcome its usual penchant for parochial politics and incremental change and enact this proposal in a matter of months. The reasons for this dramatic departure from congressional norms are detailed elsewhere.[75] In short, however, prospective payment sped through Congress because Congress felt compelled to finally do something about rising health care costs, and because the relevant health care groups were either supportive of the change or too divided within their own camps to mount effective opposition. In addition, prospective payment had become all things to all people. Conservatives believed it to be a pro-competitive, free market measure; liberals believed it to be just the right dose of regulation to control Medicare's hospital costs.

The newly enacted law provided that over four years, medical reimbursement for hospital operating costs would be converted to a system of payments made at predetermined, specific rates which represent the average cost, nationwide, of treating a Medicare patient according to his or her diagnosis.[76] The 467 diagnoses in the classification scheme used to group inpatients were known as Diagnosis Related Groups [DRGs]. The rates would be adjusted to reflect differences in labor costs and other relevant factors that vary by region and degree of urbanization, but the key to the new system was that through adjustments to the DRGs, the federal government would now be able to establish an annual fixed limit on how much it would spend on hospital reimbursement under Medicare. The DRGs were to be fashioned after those used in New Jersey, which had a relatively new program encompassing both public and private payers, but one not conclusively evaluated for its effects on costs or quality of care. In fact, the new prospective payment law provided that states like New Jersey with their own cost containment programs could obtain a waiver of the federal DRG system. This provision for state waivers had not been supported by the administration, which preferred a uniform national DRG rate.[77]

The DRG payment system is of particular interest because it is an anomaly within the Reagan administration's larger health care program. Here was an administration dedicated to privatizing and decentralizing health care, to restoring market forces in a sector perceived as hampered by ineffective and inefficient government subsidy and regulation. Yet this very same administration was responsible for increasing government control over hospital financing and physician behavior. The DRGs provide the government with the ability to control the distribution and use of expensive new technologies and to influence the nature of the medical marketplace. This will become even more true if and when capital costs are phased in under the prospective payment program. Already, the government has used the DRGs to make severe cuts in what it otherwise would have paid hospitals for Medicare patients, and its ability to set different rates for each diagnosis will encourage hospitals to alter their policies to admit more patients in the most profitable DRGs. Hospitals will begin to select a "mission" to provide those services at which they are most efficient, and those hospitals operating at the margins will either close down or seek out mergers or takeovers.[78] The nonprofit hospitals serving large numbers of charity patients are at a particularly high risk of this fate. Although the Department of Health and Human Services is required under law to account for high charity caseloads in their rate-setting, it has resisted making such adjustments. If the worst-case analysis proves correct, many public and nonprofit hospitals may be forced to close or reduce their charity loads. Then the uninsured poor may find themselves with severely reduced access to hospital care.

The DRGs are also expected to have a major influence on the way in which hospital physicians practice medicine. The new payment system is making hospital administrators extremely cost conscious, and they are expected to try to reduce the intensity of services and length of stay for Medicare patients. Because physicians control over 70 percent of health care expenditures, they are being warned that their style of practice will be scrutinized. If they are found to be "excessive" in their use of services for patients, they could have their hospital staff privileges restricted.[79]

In short, DRGs allow the federal government to establish limits on care provided to Medicare patients. Such limits can be viewed as a form of medical rationing, in which political decisions become increasingly important in determining who gets what and how much medical care. Because the DRG system could become the basis for a federal all-payers, cost containment program, its potential as an instrument for the rationing of all health resources is evident.[80] In the words of Senator Hatch (R. Utah), chairman of a major committee with jurisdiction over health issues:

> The required use by all payers of the Federal diagnosis-related-groups . . . and the specific payment rates set by HHS is nothing less than a design to discard the free-enterprise system in favor of a program of national controls which would turn health care in the United States into a Federal public utility. . . . It is one thing for the U.S. Government to act as a prudent purchaser of health care in a competitive marketplace with other purchasers of care. It is quite another thing for health-care providers to be required to accept as payment in full from all private citizens and third-party payers rates dictated by a Federal Government agency. This has the effect of replacing the marketplace.[81]

In the absence of an all-payers cost containment program, further growth of medical expenditures is likely to consume an increasing share of America's GNP. Unless there evolves a national commitment to permit an unlimited use of health resources, such growth is likely to produce painful responses. For the federal programs of Medicare and Medicaid, difficult decisions to curb benefits and limit eligibility for expensive medical procedures may be necessary. This is already the case in Britain. It is also already true in the United States for certain forms of organ transplantation.

Aaron and Schwartz[82] have studied the way decisions are made in Britain regarding the allocation of several expensive medical therapies and equipment, and they have suggested the relevance of these decisions to the American health system as it grapples with such immediate problems as the diminishing Medicare trust fund. In Britain, many of these decisions result in trade-offs between quantity and quality of care. To afford high quality care, choices have to be made about limiting the availability of hip replacements, transplants and certain diagnostic procedures. The Reagan administration's budget cuts and program changes have set the stage for a national debate on the limits to health care; future administrations are likely to face more wrenching decisions.

CONCLUSIONS

This analysis reveals that under conservative political rule, the British and American health systems have reacted in similar ways to a set of shared perceptions of why their systems are in crisis. The Thatcher and Reagan governments have attributed this crisis largely to excessive government regulation and control over health care, a commodity that they believe is best left to the free market. In their view, inefficiencies are pervasive within the health systems and have led to excessive demand, uncontrollable costs, and increasingly scarce resources.

Critics of the Left might argue that the conservative agenda for responding to problems plaguing the American and British health systems is fundamentally flawed because it responds to the wrong set of problems with the wrong set of policies. But this is beside the point for this discussion. The fact is that conservative ideology and leadership have produced the expected response: both nations have pursued policies to encourage penetration of free-market forces into their health systems. This response has primarily taken the form of privatization and, to a lesser extent, decentralization of the political control over the day-to-day operations of health programs.

In Britain, these policies have placed the NHS in a more tenuous position than at any time in its history, as private sector medicine has assumed a more substantial role in the delivery of care. Accordingly, the striking contrast between Britain's system of universal, comprehensive, and state-financed health care and America's system of mixed public-private, fee-for-service medicine has eroded. The result is that ability to pay has become increasingly important to access to care in Britain, making it much more similar to its American counterpart. The new DRG prospective payment program in the U.S., which will result in tighter government controls on the hospital sector and will open the door to system-wide cost controls, promotes convergence in another way. While this is not a free-market response to the problem of inflation in health costs, it is a response that draws the American health system closer to that of Britain. To the extent that the DRGs enable the federal government to control annual expenditures of health care, they approximate the British government's budgeting for the NHS.

Both socioeconomic factors and ideology must therefore be given a role in explaining the tendencies toward convergence. Had there not been an explosion of costs and intense pressures on national budgets, it is likely that the natural inertia of policies and institutions would have kept the two systems widely divergent. At the same time, while Labour might have been forced by economic conditions to hold down expenditures on the NHS, it probably would not have pursued policies to privatize medicine. In the United States, the picture is not as clear, but a second Carter administration probably would not have sought major cuts in discretionary health and entitlement programs. Most likely, however, it would have continued to seek systemwide cost containment and policies to stimulate competition.

Yet the moves toward convergence can be easily overemphasized. There is still a contrast between Britain's system of universal, comprehensive, and state-financed health care system and America's mixed, public-private, fee-for-service medicine. The ideological base which supports each[83] and the institutional apparatus have changed only marginally in the Thatcher-Reagan years.

Two long-term factors, however, may push the two countries closer together in the provision of health care. One is the increased demand generated by the aging populations of both countries. The other is the nature of modern medicine, in which developments in technology, increased specialization, and the dominance of the medical model of care are likely to continue. Taken together, these are powerful forces, operating in all industrialized societies, not only the United States and the United Kingdom.[84]

NOTES

The opinions expressed in this chapter are solely those of the author and do not necessarily reflect the views of the Senate Special Committee on Aging.

1. See, for example, *The Equitable Healthcare Survey: Options for Controlling Costs,* conducted by Louis Harris and Associates, New York, 1983. Included among the findings of this national survey of 1501 adults, 100 physician leaders and other health care professionals, was a general consensus that the health care system needs fundamental reform for the system to work better, and that high costs and limited access to care were foremost among the respondents' concerns.
2. David Hale, "Reagan vs. Thatcher," *Policy Review* (Winter 1982): 92.
3. Ibid., 93.
4. Rudolph Klein, "The Politics of Ideology vs. the Reality of Politics: The Case of Britain's NHS of the 1980s," *Milbank Memorial Fund Quarterly/Health and Society* 62 (1984): 82–109.
5. Klein provides an excellent analysis of the place of the NHS in postwar British politics, discussing the unique status of the NHS among health systems for which it serves as "an instrument for the deployment of paternalistic expertise, rather than a system of health care responsive to consumer demands (whether articulated through the political or economic market) . . . consistent with its founding ideology, Britain's NHS is designed to insulate decisions from either individual or political demands so that they may be taken according to rational criteria based on scientific or professional knowledge." See Klein, "Politics of Ideology," 86.
6. Ibid., 89.
7. Henry J. Aaron and William B. Schwartz, *The Painful Prescription: Rationing Health Care* (Washington: Brookings Institution, 1984).

8. Samuel Mencher, *British Private Medical Practice and the NHS* (Pittsburgh: University of Pittsburgh Press, 1968), 10.
9. Department of Health and Social Security, *Annual Report 1977* (London: Her Majesty's Stationery Office (HMSO), 1978).
10. Steven Jonas and David Banta, "The 1974 Reorganization of the British National Health Service: An Analysis," *Journal of Community Health* 1 (1975): 93.
11. National Health Service Act 1977, *Use of Hospital Accommodation and Services in England for the Private Practice of Medicine* (London: HMSO, 1977.)
12. Klein, "Politics of Ideology," 82–109.
13. Ibid., 104.
14. John Lister, M.D., "Shattuck Lecture—The Politics of Medicine in Britain and the United States," *New England Journal of Medicine* 315 (17 July 1986); 168–174.
15. "National Health Service: The Knives are Out," *New Statesman* 104 (15 Oct. 1982): 9.
16. This notion overlooks the fact that NHS demand has largely increased because of demographic changes. The British population is aging and the elderly require more care.
17. Geoffrey R. Weller, and Pranal Manga, "The Push for Reprivatization of Health Care Services in Canada, Britain and the United States," *Journal of Health Politics, Policy and Law* 8 (Fall 1983): 497.
18. Ibid., 498.
19. "The National Health Service: Royal Commission's Report." *Survey of Current Affairs* (London: British Information Service, 1979), 251.
20. "National Health Service: The Knives are Out," 10.
21. Conservative Research Department, "Health and Social Services," *Politics Today* 16 (7 October 1985): 313.
22. Department of Health and Social Security, *Patients First*, (London: HMSO, 1979), 2.
23. *Health Services Act 1980*, annotated version, chap. 33, (London: HMSO, 1980), 53.
24. British Information Service, *Health Services in Britain* (London: Central Office of Information, 1977).
25. Klein, "Politics of Ideology," 82–109.
26. Health Services Act 1980.
27. John Lister, M.D., "The British Medical Scene Since 1980," *New England Journal of Medicine* 308 (3 March 1983): 532.
28. Timothy Harper, "Guess Where Fee-For-Service is Flourishing Now," *Medical Economics* 62 (10 June 1985): 143.
29. Jonathan Spivak, "Private Health Care in Britain," *Wall Street Journal* (21 August 1979).
30. "In Brief: BUPA—New Insurance Scheme," *British Medical Journal* (10 Feb. 1979). See also, Mencher, *British Private Medical Practice and the NHS*.
31. Mencher, *British Private Medical Practice and the NHS*. See also, J. Robson, "The NHS Company Inc? The Social Consequence of Professional Dominance in the NHS," *International Journal of Health Services* 3 (1973): 413–26.
32. Lister, "British Medical Scene," 532.
33. Klein, "Politics of Ideology," 82–109.

34. Aaron and Schwartz, *The Painful Prescription*.
35. "In Defence of our National Health," *New Statesman* 104 (24 September 1982), 2.
36. "Thatcher's Think Tank Takes Aim at the Welfare State," *Economist* (18 September 1982), 57–58.
37. Ibid.
38. John K. Iglehart, "The British National Health Service under the Conservatives," *New England Journal of Medicine* 309 (17 November 1983), 1265.
39. Ibid.
40. Klein has observed that this pattern of expenditures suggests "that national economic performance, rather than party ideology, may be the deciding factor in determining the NHS budget." Such an observation conforms with the basic notion of convergence as economically determined. See Klein, "Politics of Ideology," 94.
41. Ibid.
42. "Health Service: Still Growing," *Economist* (2 April 1983).
43. "Health Service: Sick Statistics," *Economist* (4 June 1983), 47–48.
44. Ibid.
45. Iglehart, "British National Health Service," 1264–8.
46. John K. Iglehart, "The British National Health Service under the Conservatives—Part II," *New England Journal of Medicine*, 310 (5 January 1984), 63–67.
47. "National Health Service: Management But No Objectives," *Economist* (24 March 1984), 55–56.
48. Lister, "Shattuck Lecture," 168–74.
49. Beth C. Fuchs, *Comparative Health Policy: A Humanistic Evaluation of Health Policy in Great Britain and the United States,* unpublished dissertation (University of North Carolina at Chapel Hill, 1980).
50. Iglehart, "British National Health Service—Part II," 63–67.
51. Harper, "Guess Where Fee-For-Service," 143.
52. Conservative Research Department, "Health and Social Services," *Politics Today* 16 (7 October 1985).
53. Harper, "Guess Where Fee-For-Service," 143.
54. Lister, "Shattuck Lecture," 168–74.
55. J. L. Bernard, "National Health Service Facing Severe Crisis," *Journal of Commerce* (10 November 1982): 4A.
56. Mounting inflation would have produced significant adjustments in the American health sector even in the absence of any fundamental policy change produced by the 1980 presidential election. Plagued by skyrocketing health insurance premiums, businesses had begun to exercise their purchasing power to stimulate competition among medical providers. Doctors and hospitals were creating new forms of organizations to sell their services at competitive prices, and health maintenance organizations were becoming an established form of prepaid health care. States were experimenting with various cost-containment measures; and threatened by cost controls by the Carter administration, the hospital industry had even begun a voluntary program to contain costs. But such changes were more marginal than systemic and their effectiveness in lowering inflation was largely unproven.
58. Office of Management and Budget, *Fiscal Year 1982 Budget Revisions* (Washington: Executive Office of the President, 1981).

59. Hale, "Reagan vs: Thatcher," 91–109.
60. Mark Freeland and Carol Schendler, "Health Spending in the 1980s: Integration of Clinical Practice Patterns with Management," *Health Care Financing Review* 5 (1984): 1–68.
61. Office of Management and Budget, *Fiscal Year 1982,* M–2.
62. Congressional Budget Office, *An Analysis of President Reagan's Budget Revisions for Fiscal Year 1982: Staff Working Paper* (U.S. Congress, March 1981). Grants to states and local governments for all programs, not just health, made up half of the portion of the budget that was recommended for cuts under Reagan's budget proposals for Fiscal Year 1982.
63. Office of Management and Budget, *Fiscal Year 1982.*
64. Glenn R. Marcus, *Health Insurance: The Medicare Voucher Proposals* (Washington: Library of Congress, Congressional Research Service, Issue Brief, 1983).
65. Ibid.
66. Ibid.
67. Office of Management and Budget, *Budget of the United States Government Fiscal Year 1984* (Washington: U.S. Government Printing Office, 1983).
68. Aaron and Schwartz, *Painful Prescription.*
69. Congressional Quarterly, *1981 Almanac* (Washington: Congressional Quarterly Press, 1982). See also Congressional Quarterly's *Almanac* for the years 1982 through 1985.
70. Ibid.
71. Congressional Quarterly, *1982 Almanac* (Washington: Congressional Quarterly Press, 1983).
72. Ibid., 471.
73. John K. Iglehart, "Medicare Begins Prospective Payment of Hospitals," *New England Journal of Medicine,* 311 (November 17, 1984), 1428–32.
74. Beth C. Fuchs and John F. Hoadley, "The Remaking of Medicare: Congressional Policymaking on the Fast Track," paper presented at the annual meetings of the Southern Political Science Association (Savannah, Georgia, 3 November 1984).
75. Ibid.
76. Janet Lundy, "Health Care Cost Containment" (Washington: Library of Congress, Congressional Research Service, Issue Brief, 1983).
77. Iglehart, "Medicare Begins Prospective Payment," 1428–32.
78. Carolyn Phillips, "Medicare's New Limits on Hospital Payments Force Wide Cuts," *Wall Street Journal* (2 May 1984), 1, 23.
79. U.S. Congress, Senate Special Committee on Aging, *Quality of Care Under Medicare's Prospective Payment System,* Vols. 1 and 2 (Washington: U.S. Government Printing Office, 1986).
80. The legislation creating DRGs required the Department of Health and Human Services to report to Congress by the end of 1985 on the application of DRGs to reimbursement of all payers for inpatient hospital services. As of late 1986, the report had not been given to Congress. However, the enthusiasm for such efforts appeared to be waning with increasing consumer concerns that DRGs result in reduced quality and access to care.
81. U.S. Congress, *Congressional Record* (Washington: U.S. Government Printing Office, 1983), S3346.
82. Aaron and Schwartz, *Painful Prescription.*

83. Anthony King, "Ideas, Institutions, and the Policies of Governments: A Comparative Analysis," *British Journal of Political Science* 3 (July and October 1973): 291–313; 409–23.
84. Clark Kerr, *The Future of Industrial Societies: Convergence or Diversity* (Cambridge: Cambridge University Press, 1983). See also Harold L. Wilensky, *The Welfare State and Equality* (Berkeley: University of California Press, 1975).

Housing Policy:
Converging Trends,
Divergent Futures

Nathan H. Schwartz

For the first time since the emergence of a "universalistic" British welfare state in the 1940s,[1] the principles of British and American social welfare policy seem to have converged. Both the Thatcher and the Reagan administrations are committed to reducing the size of the welfare state and reducing the role of government. This essay compares one area of social welfare policy—housing—in Great Britain and the United States. Examining the results of policy initiatives in housing policy can help us understand whether the convergence in principles has resulted in a convergence of policy outcomes, as well as helping us speculate upon the future of housing policy in the two countries. This essay will explore these questions by examining the structures of policy in both countries—the incentives to action built into the policies, the ways that housing policy affects different classes of recipients, and the roles of the political and administrative institutions in formulating and implementing housing policy.

Running through this essay are three themes about the comparison between housing policy in Great Britain and the United States. The first is that there are great similarities in the trends in housing policy in both nations. Some of those trends predate the Reagan and Thatcher administrations; other trends, especially those oriented towards cuts in expenditures on housing policy, are new.

A second theme in both countries is the bifurcation of housing policy between owner-occupied housing and "subsidized" housing for those unable to become owner-occupiers. Housing policy can be considered bifurcated because the subsidies for these two kinds of housing are different and the instruments used to implement each kind of policy are quite different. This bifurcation can be seen in policy outcomes which increasingly often favor the middle and upper classes while disadvantaging lower-income groups.

The third theme of the essay is that the great differences in the configuration of housing policy and politics are likely over time to lead to policy divergence rather than long-term convergence. In sum, the British case, even in times of cutbacks, shows a reliance on traditional implementation mechanisms, especially local government, to implement both owner-occupier and subsidized housing policy. This reliance reinforces the concern of political parties at both the local and national level with housing as a major issue. In the United States, in contrast, the combination of budget cuts and other trends in housing policy can be seen as continuing a general trend toward the deinstitutionalization of housing policy. Housing policy becomes increasingly removed from the sphere of direct government activity (even though in areas like the mortgage interest deduction, the cost to government may continue to rise), *and* the likelihood of political activity is diminished.

SUBSIDIZED HOUSING

A distinction is usually drawn between "subsidized housing" and other forms of housing, such as owner-occupied or privately owned rental housing. However, as later sections of the essay will demonstrate, tax breaks (such as the mortgage interest deduction on personal income tax) and other forms of aid to home owners represent a bigger drain on the national treasuries of Great Britain and the United States than so-called "subsidized housing." With the reader cautioned that "subsidized housing" is not the only housing to receive subsidy, the term "subsidized housing" will be used here to denote programs of housing aid not connected with home ownership, as is common in the literature. This section of the essay will examine the trends in subsidized housing programs in both countries. While there are common trends in policy, what is striking is that, with the exception of the massive cuts in financial aid for subsidized housing, these trends predate the Reagan and Thatcher administrations.

The basic trend in subsidized housing policy in both countries is the movement away from direct government provision of housing toward greater subsidies to the private sector to provide such housing. In both countries, the "traditional" method of providing subsidized housing has been through national government financial subsidies to local governments for building and managing public housing (in the United States), or council housing (in Great Britain). In recent years the trend has been away from using a unit of government as landlord.

In the United States, this movement away from government as the direct provider of housing started with the 1959 Housing Act, which provided federal loans to nonprofit groups to provide housing for the elderly and handicapped. The 1968 Housing and Urban Development Act furthered the trend in its section 236 program, which provided subsidies to reduce the interest rates on mortgages for nonprofit groups to build low-income housing. The major housing program of the 1970s, the section 8 program of the 1974 Housing and Community Development Act, also provided subsidies to landlords in the private sector to provide housing to those in need. The Reagan administration's "housing voucher" program (a limited version of which was adopted in 1984), in which those deemed eligible for housing subsidies would receive a cash grant to help enable them to afford housing, assumes that housing will be found in the general housing market.

British policy has followed a similar course, emphasizing greater subsidies to the private sector at the expense of housing programs directly administered by the public sector. As later sections of the paper will detail, much of this aid has been in the form of massive aids to home ownership, including aid directed at those in the bottom income brackets of home ownership. In addition, with the 1974 Housing Act, the British government breathed life into the voluntary housing movement—nonprofit associations that provided housing—by providing subsidies to the associations to provide housing for those in need of special facilities (such as senior citizens and the handicapped) as well as for those in general need of subsidized housing.[2] In addition, the British government has provided rent subsidies to tenants in private rental housing who do not have incomes deemed adequate to cover market rents.

One major difference between the two countries is in the institutional framework of such policy. The United States case, especially when considering the housing allowance proposals, represents a trend toward total reliance on the private housing market. In that approach, new provider institutions are not created; rather, the goal is to help families in need to purchase housing in the private housing market. In the British case, the trend away from the use of governmental institutions is reflected in provision of incentives for the formation of nongovernmental institutions to provide these services. So while both countries are headed toward less direct government provision of housing, the British case is characterized by the development of alternative institutions, while the American case represents increasing reliance on market mechanisms.

A second trend evident in both countries has been to base the rents of subsidized housing on the tenant's income rather than on the actual cost of the housing. Originally, public or council housing rents were based on the actual cost of the housing to the local housing authority, minus the subsidy from the national government. The trend, however, has been toward basing a family's rent on some standard of what they can afford to pay, rather than on the actual cost of the housing.

In the United States, this trend toward basing subsidized housing rents on income rather than cost of housing was first evident in 1969 when the Congress adopted legislation that limited the rents in subsidized housing to a maximum of 25 percent of family income. The difference between that rent and the actual cost of the housing was to be covered by government subsidy. In part, this policy can be seen as the result of rising costs of construction, which made new units, even those receiving mortgage interest subsidies, too expensive for poor families. Great Britain has followed similar policies, instituting a system of "fair rents," where the rents for council housing were to reflect the market rents for housing in the area, but tenants were eligible for subsidies to make up the difference between those rents and what they were deemed able to afford.

A third trend is from the subsidizing of units to subsidizing individuals. In the past, American policy aimed at encouraging the provision of units of subsidized housing; the government signed long-term contracts with public housing authorities, nonprofit groups, or private landlords, guaranteeing that subsidies would be available to them when they housed eligible families. The change to subsidizing individuals began with the section 8 program of the 1974 Housing and Community Development Act. At its clearest, this trend is represented by the housing voucher program proposed by the Reagan administration and for which Congress approved a small appropriation in 1984. This program provides recipient families with a direct cash payment as housing aid once they have obtained housing that meets certain quality standards.

This trend toward subsidizing the individual, rather than the housing unit, is also evident in Great Britain. The "fair rent" policy (in which subsidized housing is rented at "market rent" and low-income families are eligible for rent subsidies) is evidence of this trend, especially since this program also aids residents of property rented from private landlords.

It should also be noted that the British subsidy is much broader than the American, in that in Britain all those who meet the income qualifications can receive the housing payment, while in the United States the number receiving housing subsidy is restricted by the amount of money apppropriated. In the United States, this trend furthers the move away from special institutions with responsibility for providing housing to use of the market alone. That move seems to offer the individual more choice, but also assumes that the market will respond. However, in a situation where the number of people who receive such subsidy is dependent on appropriations and each "housing voucher" is only for five years, there would seem to be great uncertainty about the likely demand for such housing. Under those conditions it is unclear whether the market will move to provide low-income housing meeting minimum standards, given the current costs of credit and the uncertainties of subsidy; developers may doubt either that there will be sufficient numbers of renters or that the program will be around long enough to allow them to pay back their costs.

THE FINANCE OF SUBSIDIZED HOUSING UNDER REAGAN AND THATCHER

One common aspect of both the Reagan and Thatcher administrations has been a massive reduction in aid for subsidized housing. This has meant a reduction in the creation of new subsidized housing and in the size of subsidies received by individuals. The reduction in aid has been part of a philosophical goal of paring down the welfare state and also of an economic goal of reducing government spending.

The cuts under Reagan have been massive. That is not to say that considerable variation did not exist before Reagan. For example, while the fiscal year 1977 appropriation was sufficient for an estimated 373,000 units to be added to the subsidized housing stock of the United States, by the end of Jimmy Carter's administration (fiscal year 1982) the problem of fiscal constraints had led that administration to request only 260,000 additional units.

Nevertheless, the cuts under Reagan have been massive and sustained. When Reagan took office, the Carter budget proposal for approximately 260,000 units for fiscal year 1982 was pending. The Reagan administration proposed cutting this to 175,000 units; a Congress eager to please cut this figure back even more to approximately 142,000 units.

On the surface, the 1983 budget, the first budget originating with the Reagan administration, called for a slight increase over the 1982 budget to 219,000 units of subsidized housing. However, this number considerably overstates the actual number of units that would be added to the stock of subsidized housing. After subtracting the number of units that were simply units under one program converted to another program, as well as subtracting the cancellations proposed for units approved in earlier years but not yet constructed, this budget called for an actual decrease in the number of subsidized units available.[3] Similar budgetary magic took place in the 1984 requests where the budget called for the funding of 90,000 additional units; after subtracting the conversions of existing units of subsidized housing from one program to another, the actual number of new units being added to the stock of subsidized housing was only 63,000 units.[4] Legislation pending before Congress in the summer of 1986 would eliminate funds for the construction of new public housing entirely, reserving available funds only for the renovation of existing units.

In Great Britain, similar cuts in expenditure and construction can be found. For example, while James Callaghan's 1977 budget called for £ 1.263 billion to be made available for local authorities to construct new housing, Prime Minister Thatcher's budget for 1984–85 called for only £.650 billion for the same purpose.[5] The effect of these budget cuts can be seen in the ability of the subsidized housing program to meet the needs for such housing. The 1977 consultation paper, "The Housing Policy Review," presented by the last Labour government, included estimates of how many units of housing would have to be provided by the public sector in order to meet the projected needs for such housing. These projections assumed that such needs would decline, for example, from 161,000 units in 1976 to 122,500 units in 1981. But the effect of the budget cuts has been a massive shortfall relative to those needs projections. For example, in 1977, under the Labour government, 180,000 units of council housing and housing association housing were started, a "surplus" of 19,100 units over what the Green Paper had projected. In 1978, still under Labour, cuts in the housing budget meant that only 110,000 units were begun, a deficit from projected needs of 49,100 units. But by 1981, well into Thatcher's first term, when the 1977 Green Paper had projected needs for only 122,500 units (a reduction of 37,500 units from the 1978 level), funds were only available for starting 40,200 units, a shortfall relative to the need projections of 82,300 units.[6] Thus Thatcher's government has made substantial cuts in funding of council housing and association housing. Rhodes has reported that "the clampdown on capital expenditure for new council housing looks set to re-create a gross housing shortage in the United Kingdom . . . by the mid-1980s."[7]

In addition to cutting the number of subsidized housing units added to the housing stock, both Reagan and Thatcher have sought to shift more of the cost of subsidized housing to the recipients. In its first year in office, the Reagan administration gained congressional approval to raise from 25 percent to 30 percent the proportion of income that recipients of housing subsidies were expected to pay as rent.

For the fiscal year 1983 budget, the Reagan administration proposed adding the cash value of food stamps received by a family to the calculation of its total income, thus raising its total income and increasing the 30 percent of income the family would pay as rent. Analysts at the Urban Institute have estimated that the rise in rent to 30 percent of income, plus the addition of food stamps to the calculation of income, would result in a reduction of 44 percent of the benefits received by those in public housing.[8] By this time, however, the Congress was not as willing to adopt any administration proposals and refused to go along with these changes.

In addition, concerns with controlling the federal budget deficit have led to the adoption of measures that also have the effect of cutting housing programs. The Reagan administration's concern with the particular budgetary implications of housing subsidies was clear in the fiscal 1983 budget, which identified two items of particular concern to those who write budgets. The first is that all the programs "involved long-term subsidy commitments that result in uncontrollable budget outlay increases for many years."[9] This statement refers to the fact that most housing subsidy programs commit the government to subsidize a housing unit in some manner for fifteen to forty years. The second budgetary defect noted was that since the "tenant's rent contributions are capped by law, any unanticipated cost increases are borne solely by the Federal Government."[10]

The response to these budgeting concerns can be seen in the new housing voucher program. First, to eliminate the long-term commitment (which appears in the budget the year the commitment is made), the period of subsidy guarantee has been reduced to five years. While reducing the initial budgetary commitment, this action does not reduce the actual outlays per year for each family receiving subsidy. It does create an almost invisible cut in the number of subsidized units. As subsidies expire on particular units, the approval of seemingly "new" subsidies is really only renewal of old subsidies, not additions to the total. In this case, reducing the subsidy period to five years greatly increases the number of subsidies that can be seen simply as renewals rather than additions to the total. The budgetary legacy of this action will be to require approval in the future of many more units per year simply to keep the number of families receiving subsidy the same.

The response to the problem of lack of control over the level of subsidy has been again addressed in the new housing voucher program. The housing vouchers to be given to families are of a fixed size, varying only by family size, not by income. A family with no income receives the voucher for the same amount as a family of the same size but with an income at the program's upper limit. While this provision makes the program insensitive to differences in family income, it also makes the cost of the program absolutely predictable: changes in family income or cost of rent that would have led to changes in subsidies in previous programs are eliminated by fixed-size vouchers. Similarly, however, it means that the program no longer represents an attempt to provide similar access to housing; relatively better off families are in a better position. It should also be noted that this program is not universal; like other subsidized housing programs in the United States, it does not provide funding for all those who qualify. Thus there remains the basic inequity between the poor receiving benefits and those eligible but not receiving benefits.

The Thatcher government has also attempted to shift more of the cost of council (public) housing to those receiving benefits. In January 1984, the government sought to reduce housing aid by almost 230 million pounds. Commenting on this proposal, *The Economist*, hardly known as a champion of the welfare state, characterized the proposal as "bashing the poor," arguing that the "burden of the proposed saving—230 million pounds a year—was laid unfairly and squarely on Britain's poorest," as well as increasing the incentives for low-paid workers to go on the welfare dole because of the way the cuts were to be implemented.[11] Later the government, in the face of a backbench revolt on the issue, reduced the cuts to £185 million—still a major reduction.[12]

It is clear that both Reagan and Thatcher have attempted to shift the burden for an increasing proportion of the costs of subsidized housing to those receiving the subsidies. The next section of the essay, which examines government aid to the owner-occupier sector, will show that home buyers and home owners have not been expected to bear the burden of similar cuts.

SUBSIDIES FOR OWNER-OCCUPIERS

In contrast to the cuts in aid for subsidized housing, subsidies for owner-occupiers continue to grow in both countries. In the United States, the primary subsidy to home owners is the mortgage interest deduction from personal income tax which allows them to deduct from their taxable income the interest payments they have made on their mortgage. This is an off-budget item—Congress does not have to approve subsidies that take the form of a tax break on the same yearly basis that is required for direct expenditures, such as the funds for what we have termed "subsidized housing." The government's calculation of the size of this tax break reveals that the cost of the mortgage interest deduction is considerably higher than the amount spent on "subsidized" housing and is growing at a much faster rate. In 1977, the cost of subsidized housing to the federal government was $2.968 billion, and had grown by 1984 to $9.467 billion, an increase of 219 percent.[13] The loss to the United States Treasury of the mortgage interest deduction was $5.435 billion in 1977, growing to $22.735 billion by 1984, an increase of 318 percent.[14] So in 1984, the size of the home-owner subsidy was 2.4 times as great as the subsidy to "subsidized housing," while its cost was increasing 45 percent faster than the cost of "subsidized housing."

The figures for Britain show a similar emphasis on aid to the owner-occupier sector, despite a much larger subsidized sector. Britain grants home owners relief of mortgage interest much as the United States does, except that mortgages for second homes are excluded, and tax relief only applies to interest on the first £30,000 of a mortgage.[15] The costs of these deductions (and other aids to home owners to be discussed below) are also substantial. During the Thatcher administration, the relative positions of subsidies to "subsidized housing" and those to owner-occupiers have reversed—aid to owner-occupiers becoming larger than aid to those in subsidized housing. For example, in 1979–80, general subsidies to public sector tenants and rebates to renters came to a total of £1.915 billion, 174 percent more than the £1.100 billion of mortgage tax relief. By 1981–82 the balance was estimated to have switched in favor of mortgage tax relief, coming to an estimated £1.3 billion, as compared to £1.28 billion for general subsidies to public sector tenants plus rent rebates.[16]

In addition to the mortgage interest deduction, the British government provides two other aids to home ownership. One takes the form of "renovation grants," which are direct grants covering 50 percent to 90 percent of the costs for improvement of existing housing, repairs, and provision of standard amenities (bath, water, etc.).[17] These grants are available both to individual home owners and to local governments with funding divided roughly between the two. Under the Thatcher administration, the amount of money available in this category has jumped considerably: in 1977–78 (under the previous Labour government) it was £440 million; under the Thatcher government in 1982–83 it had jumped 168 percent to £1.18 billion.[18]

The other way in which the British government aids home ownership (beyond the mortgage interest deduction) is by offering council house occupants the right to buy the unit that they occupy, a policy pushed by the Thatcher government. Despite some local government resistance to such sales (the policy ultimately being upheld by the courts), much council housing has been sold. In the period from May 1979 to August 1983, 525,000 families had purchased their council housing and another 150,000 requests to purchase were awaiting action. To make the purchase of these units attractive, the government has made these council houses available for substantially less than their full valuation; it has been estimated that the discount from full valuation is 43 percent.[19] The policy of selling the property at a substantial discount has also come under much attack from critics, including some Conservative members of Parliament who have suggested that in the long run the policy will cost government more than it will save, as well as potentially harming the housing situation of the elderly, large families, the disabled, and ethnic minorities.[20] In addition, there appear to be limits on how many units will actually be purchased; many council house tenants, while wishing to own their own housing, have no desire to own the council house they reside in.[21]

In conclusion, it is clear that government policy in both countries heavily subsidizes owner occupation just as it subsidizes the category of "subsidized housing." In both countries the absolute cost to the government of aid to home owners is greater than the cost of aid to subsidized housing. Furthermore, the aid to home owners has been increasing at a greater rate than aid to subsidized housing, further emphasizing existing disparities between the forms of housing. In short, owner occupation holds a more prominent place in government policy and receives ever larger government subsidies relative to so-called subsidized housing.

THE DEMOGRAPHIC CONTEXT OF HOUSING POLICY

While the basic trends in housing policy in Great Britain and the United States are very similar, the likeness does not necessarily constitute proof of the convergence of policy. It is also necessary to look at the context of policy to see if other key determinants are also similar. This section looks at the demographic configuration of housing tenures and the political and institutional configuration of housing politics. Both these factors can help us to predict plausible futures for housing politics in these countries. The configuration of housing tenure signals the configuration of potential political forces concerned with different kinds of housing policies, while the examination of the political and institutional configuration of housing politics can help us develop an understanding of what issues are likely to be represented in policymaking.

As the earlier sections of this essay have shown, different kinds of housing receive different kinds and levels of support from the tax system and housing subsidy programs. Assuming that people may show concern about policies that affect them, the distribution of the population in different kinds of housing may well constitute one signal about the politics around specific housing policies. Rex and Moore have suggested that housing tenure is the key determinant of political orientation toward local politics and assert that housing tenure is the determinant of conflict in local politics.[22] Hence, the distribution of the population in different housing tenures can signal the potential demographic dimension of support for or concern about policies supporting different housing tenures as well as the potential effect of different policies aimed at different tenures.

One of the basic differences in the context of policy in Great Britain and the United States is the existing distribution of housing tenures. In both countries, owner-occupiers (including those people who are paying off mortgages on the house they live in) constitute the largest housing sector; in Britain that sector comprises 56 percent of all housing units, while in the United States that sector accounts for 65.5 percent of housing. The biggest difference is in the publicly owned sector: public housing in the United States accounts for only 1.6 percent of total housing units, while British public housing (council housing) accounts for 31 percent of all housing. Housing rented from private landlords accounts for 32 percent of American housing, while accounting for only 13 percent of the British supply.[23]

These differences in the distribution of housing tenures have several important political implications in terms of the *potential* for political action on the basis of the size of the group in a particular housing tenure. First, the size of the owner-occupier sector in both countries makes it unlikely that policies worsening its position would be adopted—one takes on majorities only in extraordinary times. Secondly the size of the public housing sector in Britain makes its inhabitants potentially an important political force, while in the United States, where public housing comprises less than 2 percent of the housing stock, the inhabitants are unlikely to be an important force in national politics. In contrast, it is more likely that the private rented sector (landlords and tenants) might be a significant political force in the United States, given that the sector represents almost a third of the housing supply, while in Britain this sector accounts for a much smaller part of the housing supply.

The political significance of a housing tenure also seems related to the social characteristics of existing housing tenures and the political context of action. In a comparison of the United States, Australia, and Great Britain, McAllister found that only in Great Britain was housing tenure associated with voting patterns, with owner-occupiers much less likely to support the Labour party than council house occupants.[24] He suggests that one reason for this stems from differences between the social composition of housing tenures in each country: in the United States and Australia, it is relatively easy to move from renting to home ownership and the social composition of the two tenures is similar, while in Britain the council house tenant is socially distant from the owner-occupier.[25] In addition, the political context becomes important in determining the political significance of housing policy. Assessing the effect of housing sectors on electoral outcomes, McAllister suggests that a political party consensus favoring home ownership in Australia and the United States reduced the relation between housing tenure and party support, while in Britain the party division over council housing was reflected in the great difference between owner-occupiers and council house tenants in party identification.[26]

Going beyond the electoral consequences, the effect on policy of the system of housing tenures is conditioned by other aspects of the political context including: the institutions that make policy and their responsiveness to particular housing sectors; the actual organization of a sector for political activity; and the access of other groups involved in the sector, such as the providers or developers who may be very well organized to gain representation of their interests even though the people who live in that form of housing are not numerous or well organized.

The importance of a particular housing sector in a comparative analysis is that it identifies different forces that may be mobilized in response to different policies. For example, initiatives to eliminate public housing in the United States and Great Britain face very different potential responses. In the United States the population in public housing is small and not likely to have much political power; in Great Britain roughly one-third of the population lives in public housing and thus has a potentially great effect on the politics of the issue. With an eye to the potential power of those affected, an analysis of the attempts to eliminate or reduce the role of public housing in both countries becomes relatively straightforward. Given the small size of the public housing sector in the United States, it is no surprise that the American approach has not involved any particular measure to provide better housing to those affected by the downgrading of public housing, while in Britain the policy has been successful while pursued in terms of making the inhabitants of public (council) housing into home owners, a more desirable status. American policymakers did not have much to worry about in terms of public reaction, and British policymakers have gained wide acceptance of a policy that made the change attractive to many of those affected.

THE POLITICAL AND INSTITUTIONAL CONTEXT OF HOUSING POLICY

If the current convergence of policy trends is likely to be long-lived, the institutional and political factors that affect housing policy should reinforce the trends under analysis. In examining the political and institutional aspects of housing policy, this section will first look at subsidized housing and then at the owner-occupier sector.

In Great Britain, the key institutions in the provision of subsidized housing are central government and local governments. Central government provides the finance and basic guidelines for the creation and administration of council housing within certain limits; local government builds and administers council housing, approves grants to "housing associations," and, as will be discussed later in this section, hands out improvement grants to home owners, and in some cases directly provides mortgage money for those wishing to become owner-occupiers.[27] While the mix of aid may differ, both Labour- and Tory-controlled local councils are likely to be active on the issue; Labour councils are more likely to be active in the provision of council housing, but both provide improvement grants and other aids to owner-occupiers as well as approving government grants to housing associations.

Besides the major role of local authorities in providing subsidized housing, the politics of housing are also very important at the local level. It is important to remember that not only is council housing controlled by local governments, but also the approvals of funding for the voluntary housing associations, the nongovernmental agencies providing housing, as well as various direct grants for owner-occupiers. So in institutional and political terms, local government is a focus for British housing policy.

As the primary institution implementing housing policy, local government gains additional significance as the potential political and organizational focus for housing policy concerns. Concentrating the implementation of housing policy in this one institution holds the promise for a concentration of political action and organization that is not possible when the implementation of policy is spread among many different institutions within and outside of government. But while the structure of housing policy implementation concentrates local concerns about housing policy around local government, there is no guarantee that this concentration of local concerns will affect national policymaking. Significant ties need to exist between local government and politics with national government in order for the concentration of policy implementation at the local level to have an effect on national policymaking.

The general character of recent relations between center and local governments seems to minimize the influence of local government over national policymaking, but it is oversimplifying that relationship to ignore significant connections between central and local government that do give local government important forms of influence. Starting in the 1970s and furthered by the Thatcher government, central government has radically extended its powers over local government finance.[28] These powers used by the Thatcher government to control local finance include: requiring central government approval of capital expenditures by local government; setting cash limits on central government aid to local governments; and the Local Government and Planning and Land Act of 1980, which gave the government the seeming ability to determine the appropriate levels of spending by each local authority and to penalize severely any that exceeded these levels.[29]

The extension of such control has been seen as detrimental to local government. R.A.W. Rhodes has argued that when central government's approach to dealing with local government finance is based on a strategy of control, "the outcome will be unintended consequences, recalcitrance, instability, ambiguity and confusion: in short, the *policy mess* that has become the defining characteristic of British central-local relations."[30] Douglas Ashford has attributed part of the problem to a lack of connection between central and local governments: ". . . there is no clear institutional link between levels of government that, on one hand, keeps central politicians honest and, on the other hand, enables local politicians to influence decision-making at higher levels."[31] Ashford argues that British central government policy toward the finance of local government suffers from an approach based on national party conflict and that the result is to leave local governments at the whim of central government without corporate interests of local government as a whole being adequately represented within the system.[32]

However, care must be taken in extending the analyses offered by Ashford and Rhodes. They do not seem to be useful if used as the basis for a conclusion that local government and politics do not have a voice in central government policymaking. What Ashford and Rhodes are suggesting is that there is no single institution representing local government with a clear and constitutionally powerful voice in affecting central policymaking. Instead, there is a host of different institutional connections between local and central governments that provide local government with a chorus of voices. None of these institutional connections bestows decisive influence on local government, and only rarely do all the elements of British local government seek similar goals. In addition, the influence of local government varies depending on the issue and the specific connection used to exercise influence; nevertheless, local influence exists.

One of the important links between local policy issues and national policy is through party organization. It is clear that, to varying degrees, governments listen to their partisans from local government through their party organizations. Gyford and James explain one indicator of this connection as the important role of local government sections within the major parties and the prominent place of doctrines of local government within the smaller parties.[33] A second indicator of the importance of the party connection is their finding that local government officials are appointed to important national government positions, indicating those officials' importance both as local policy spokespeople and as members of the party.[34]

A third indicator of the importance of the party connection is that, on occasion, national government has backed off from certain positions when the national party has lined up behind the affected local authority. In general, local government and party officials (especially in the Conservative party) are not keen to embarrass a national government of their own party, but this is not always the case.[35] In 1975 the Labour-controlled South Yorkshire County Council came into conflict with the national Labour government over the issue of public transit fares. Ultimately the national government settled on a compromise which relieved it of subsidizing the (low) fares which the council had implemented, but without the original aim of forcing the county council to change its policy and raise fares (the county being willing to subsidize the fares out of local taxes). Gyford and James consider that the ultimate position taken by the government was the result of Labour party pressure put on the government.[36] Hence, the connection through the political party between center and local government can be an important avenue of influence for local government.

Another important institutional connection providing local government some influence on national policymaking comes from the influence of local government and local parties on parliamentary activity. Even given the strength of a prime minister like Margaret Thatcher, possessing a solid majority in Parliament, there is the possibility, or threat, of a backbenchers' rebellion threatening the government's majority. A rebellion occurred when the Thatcher government, as part of its attempt to control local government spending, attempted to enact legislation requiring local authorities to hold a referendum before levying additional taxes to overcome reductions in central government grants.[37] According to Gyford and James, the power of local Conservative government leaders was manifest in their ability "to persuade nearly forty Conservative MPs to make known their hostility to the rates referendums proposal, thereby removing the 'environmental constraint' of a guaranteed government majority and enabling discussions to take place on alternative legislative proposals."[38] Despite the strong intentions of the Thatcher government, Conservative local governments were able to exercise influence over central government policymaking. While this connection is clearly in evidence where commonality exists in party affiliation, there is also good evidence that Members of Parliament are often willing to plead the case of their local authority to the government regardless of party affiliation.[39]

Another set of institutional connections between local governments and central governments is the associations representing the different kinds of local authorities: the Association of County Councils (ACC), the Association of District Councils (ADC), and the Association of Metropolitan Authorities (AMA). While these organizations are often in conflict because of different political affiliations, Rhodes has characterized them as the "national community" of local government because of their frequent contacts with each other and their many shared activities.[40] Rhodes has also argued that there are three policy areas in which this "national community" is prominent: "alterations to the structure and functions of local government, negotiations over central grant and decisions on pay increases for local government employees."[41] While the Thatcher government has not been interested in a process of negotiating central grants, clearly it takes the associations seriously. For example, the government made a set of technical amendments to the 1980 Local Government Planning and Land Bill apparently in order to gain the support of the Conservative-controlled ACC at the point where the bill was being considered by the House of Lords.[42] Not unlike the connections discussed before, this is another avenue of significant (although not decisive) influence used by local government.

In addition, with regard to many of the issues of local policy such as housing (or finance), national governments and their local partisans often share a general ideological perspective. For example, years before the election of the Thatcher government, a number of Conservative-controlled local authorities began selling council housing—their actions building broad Conservative party support for such activity that culminated in the 1980 Housing Act.[43] A shared position may act as a constraint on central government policymaking. The example of council housing sales indicates an even more active role for local government; what constitutes appropriate policy for national government may be set, in part, by the previous action of local governments which defines and builds political support around particular policies.

What is clear from the preceding analysis is that there are many channels through which local government exercises influence on national policy. The influence of local government is limited by the lack of a clear constitutional role in national policy and by the lack of institutions which effectively speak for local government as a whole in the national arena.

While local government speaks with many voices through many different channels, it is important to note that at the national level there is not much coherence in the perception of local government. Gyford and James have suggested that three distinctly different views of local government are held within the national parties and that these views cut across party boundaries, suggesting that rarely can we assume continuity of view within any single party.[44] In addition, shifting coalitions within the parties make it difficult to assume a clear continuity of party policy toward local government.[45] Thus, while local government speaks to national government without one clear voice, it also appears that the parties lack a clear voice on local government issues. That lack of a clear national voice emanating from the parties may in fact serve to enhance the influence of those local voices within the parties: the concerns of those from local government become important because these participants from local government are important as potential supporters in intraparty conflict.

In Britain, as described above, there is both a clear institutional center for the implementation of housing policy (local authorities) and a set of connections from the implementing authorities to British central government, which formulates and funds the policy. This configuration provides a focus for politics at the local level, and also the institutional mechanisms (through political parties, local government ties with members of Parliament, etc.) for the translation of those local politics into national politics.

In the United States, there appears to be less effective institutional support behind subsidized housing. For local government, public housing is much less important politically than council housing is in Great Britain. In addition, while local government may have a role in determining eligibility for public housing, section 8 units, and for approving construction of certain types of subsidized housing, housing policy does not seem to have become a general focus for political activity—in line with the much smaller role of the American government in providing housing. In addition, working against its role as a potential institutional center for housing, local government in the United States has little direct role in providing aid and encouragement for home ownership, in contrast with the British case.

In addition, the connection of local government to central government seems much weaker in America than in Britain. First of all, the role of party membership in policymaking is much weaker. It is not clear that local parties carry much clout with national parties on issues of local governance, and even if local governments have influence over the national parties, it is not clear that the national parties have much influence over national policy. Furthermore, it is not clear that local governments have been very effective in influencing the activity of specific Congressmen. While Congress has not gone along with all of President Reagan's proposals for budget cutting, nevertheless it has gone along with major cuts in the subsidized housing programs. Perhaps the relatively small size of these programs meant that cities were putting other issues first in their attempts to fight Reagan's social budget cuts. Still, doubt is cast on the role of local governments as a clear and effective institutional center for policymaking.

Traditionally, the groups seen as having a incentive to support subsidized housing in the United States have included advocacy groups for the poor, housing finance institutions, and the housing construction industry. In fact, the initiation and expansion of subsidized housing programs in the United States often seems motivated not simply by concern for the needs of the poor, but by the needs of the housing finance and construction industries in periods of recession or depression.[46]

Interviews with staff members of housing advocacy interest groups and staff (from both parties) of congressional housing committees during the summer of 1984 produced very similar views about the relative influence of these different groups on current housing policy decisions in Congress. None of those interviewed felt that advocacy groups for the poor had proven able by themselves to influence Congress or the administration on issues of subsidized housing.

Those interviewed also argued that the home builders' lobby was no longer supporting the building of public housing as a way of boosting the industry. This disinterest was attributed to a concern with the effect of federal spending on the mortgage interest rate, which affects private demand for housing. Those interviewed (none of whom were members or staff of the National Home Builders Association) described the home builders' support for budget cuts that might reduce the federal deficit, based on the hope that this reduction would result in lower mortgage interest rates and an increase in demand for private sector housing. In other words, the home builders were perceived as having decided that a trade-off existed between subsidized housing and private market housing, their hopes resting with private home building.

The basic trends in housing policy noted earlier may well reinforce this lack of interest in subsidized housing on the part of the construction industry. As housing subsidies are increasingly oriented toward subsidizing individuals and not units, the subsidies for new construction seem increasingly dependent on whether new construction is directly competitive in cost terms with existing housing, which is rarely the case. The Reagan housing voucher plan goes to the logical conclusion of this approach, providing no special subsidies for new construction, based on the assumption that sufficient housing is already available. In a situation where the normal operation of housing programs does not benefit the construction industry, builders' interest in it may well wane.

Housing policy trends in the United States, moving away from direct government action and toward the use of market mechanisms, mark a deinstitutionalization of housing policy in the political sense—government action increasingly often uses forms that Lester Salamon has termed "automatic." Salamon has defined this type of "automatic" implementation mechanism as "one that utilizes existing structures and relationships (e.g., the tax structure or the price system) and requires a minimum of administrative decision-making."[47] Housing policy increasingly often becomes removed from the sphere of direct government activity, even though in areas such as the mortgage interest deduction, the cost to government may continue to rise. The political result of this deinstitutionalization may be to weaken political activity around housing issues. Salamon has hypothesized, "The more automatic the tool of government action, the less certain the achievement of program purposes, the greater the leakage of program benefits, and the more problematic the generation of needed political support."[48] Especially for those who are not already well organized, the clear institutional presence of the state may serve to provide a focus for political activity; without that organizational focus, such activity may be seriously reduced. In the United States there seems to be no major institution or set of institutions capable of bringing the issue of subsidized housing to the fore of the policy agenda, much less of making major gains in policy. In the current situation, even a crisis in housing—such as a collapse of the credit market or a major downturn in the housing construction industry—would most likely lead to aid for home owners through devices like loan guarantees rather than through an expansion of subsidized housing programs.

Unlike the great differences on the political and institutional contexts of subsidized housing policy in the two countries, the contexts of policy governing owner occupation are quite similar. In both countries the predominant form of aid for owner occupiers is mortgage interest relief. In addition to being increasingly expensive for central governments, this is also an invisible form of aid in terms of budgeting. As a tax expenditure—funds not collected (as opposed to funds spent by government)—mortgage interest relief does not require annual approval as part of the budget. As a result it does not face the cuts in lean budgets in the same way that the "on-budget" parts of subsidized housing do. Mortgage interest relief is a program that grows by itself, not requiring legislative or executive affirmation.

It is not the case, however, that the provisions of the mortgage interest relief are never changed. For example, tax reform legislation pending before Congress in the summer of 1986 (and approved by conference committees of both houses) called for limiting the mortgage interest deduction to first and second homes. This change had the appearance of making the Congress appear serious about eliminating loopholes that favored the rich. But the legislation avoided alienating the vast majority of home owners, the construction industry, and housing finance institutions. The great political strength of the housing interest deduction is indicated by the fate of similar deductions for interest paid on other forms of consumer credit (including car loans and credit card payments) which would be eliminated by the new bill. The 1986 legislation, if adopted, may also inadvertently reduce the cost of the mortgage interest deduction to the Treasury; by reducing rates of taxation, the legislation will reduce the relative benefit of the mortgage interest deduction.

It is difficult to imagine any political force capable of dislodging mortgage interest relief. The shared interests of builders, construction workers, banks, and much of the middle and upper classes, plus a widely shared ideology of the benefits of home ownership, make it difficult to conceive of an elected executive or legislature willing to take on the issue in either Britain or the United States. Thus, in both countries we can easily conceive of this growing financial aid to the middle and upper classes continuing.

The mortgage interest deduction does not directly involve the administrative activity of any housing agency of government. In terms of its relation to the institutions of housing policy, the mortgage interest deduction certainly does not seem to involve home owners in any concerns shared with people living in other forms of housing. In that sense, the lack of shared institutions reinforces the political fragmentation of housing policy. But it should be noted that while the American home owner is aided largely through the mortgage interest deduction, many British home owners receive other forms of aid that do come through institutions that implement other forms of housing policy. As noted earlier in the paper, British local governments administer home improvement grants, and the sale of council housing, and in some cases provide loans to home owners. In that sense, British policy towards home owners can be seen as reinforcing the definition and relationships of existing housing institutions, specifically local government as the implementing agency receiving basic funding and approval by central government. This is certainly not the case in the United States, where policy toward home ownership shares little of the institutional configuration of subsidized housing.

In summary, an analysis of housing tenures and the political and institutional contexts of policy reveals great differences between Great Britain and the United States. The American case exemplifies the deinstitutionalization of policy, as government action stresses the use of the private market as the provider of housing. This pattern is reinforced by a distribution of housing tenures where there are relatively few Americans in public housing and no clear institutional center that can focus political support for subsidized housing. In Great Britain, the institutional constituents of housing policy are clearer and more focused. Local government serves as the prime implementation agency for housing policy, not only providing council housing but also approving grants for voluntary housing associations and grants to home owners. This role is reinforced by the relatively large number of British residents in council housing and/or dependent on government housing grants, which makes British local government a focus for concern about housing. Furthermore, local governments seem to have clear and well-articulated mechanisms for influencing the decisions of national government and the national parties on such issues.

DIFFERING FUTURES FOR HOUSING POLICY

Thus far this essay has found both major similarities and differences in housing policy and politics in the United States and Great Britain. This section will summarize those findings and then assess their import for future housing policy in the two countries.

The first theme of the essay was that current trends in housing policy are quite similar in both countries. In the area of subsidized housing, both countries seem to be moving away from direct government provision of housing to subsidization of nongovernmental housing providers; in both countries, rents for subsidized housing are increasingly often based on the income of the tenant rather than the actual cost of the housing; and in both countries there has been movement toward subsidizing individuals rather than housing units. In both countries owner-occupied housing receives substantial subsidies.

A second theme was that housing policy is bifurcated between measures supporting owner occupation and those supporting subsidized housing in both Great Britain and the United States. There often appears to be little attempt to compare, much less to harmonize, the policies in those two sectors. Characteristic of this difference has been that while subsidized housing expenditures have been reduced in both countries as part of government budget reductions, the cost of the subsidies to home ownership continues to rise without any substantial check.

In both countries, subsidized housing is implemented typically through annual expenditures, while much of the aid to owner-occupiers is through tax deductions which do not require yearly approval. The effect is that subsidized housing is much more vulnerable to budget cuts than is owner-occupied housing. This difference is reflected in the politics of housing, where the mortgage interest deduction seems almost invulnerable in both countries, while subsidized housing programs, as part of the welfare state, are fair game for attack. In fact, considering the budget cuts for subsidized housing in each country, home ownership has become more costly than subsidized housing to both governments. This bifurcated policy represents an increasing emphasis on state aid to the middle and upper classes, rather than to those at the bottom of the income ladder.

The third theme of the essay is that the configuration of housing tenures and the institutions and politics of housing are very different in the two countries. It was noted in the American case that there is no clear focus, or set of institutions, to handle housing policy. This lack of focus has been accentuated by moves to depend on the market for the provision of all forms of housing, further weakening any institutional base for housing policy.

On the other hand, Great Britain has not seen the same general movement toward use of the private market as the sole provider of housing. In subsidized housing, some of the move away from direct government provision has been to the provision of housing through other institutions, such as voluntary housing associations. These institutions have a primary orientation toward providing subsidized housing, since their reason for existence is housing provision. Even in the owner-occupier sector, government institutions have been directly involved in activity, whether through sales of council houses or through direct grants to home owners for certain kinds of improvements. The result is that in Great Britain a clear network of institutions involved in housing policy still exists, with central government providing much of the finance and local government having a major role in the implementation of virtually all policy, including the direct provision of council housing, approving the activity of local voluntary housing associations, and granting funds to owner-occupiers for home improvement. National and central government are linked together on these issues, not just because of their joint roles in the implementation of policy, but also by political parties which span the gap between local and national government.

To determine the comparative futures of policy in each country requires determining whether the similarities in policy will, over time, render the differences in institutional and political structure meaningless, or whether the differences in institutional and political structure will make the policy similarities only a momentary phenomenon.

In the United States, there seems to be little political force behind policies for subsidized housing that utilize nonmarket institutions. Thus, given existing trends, any expansion of housing subsidies would likely be in the form of housing vouchers or other forms of aid which follow current noninstitutional forms, relying on the private housing market for the primary provision of housing. Furthermore, if institutional self-interest is a factor in the continuing existence of political pressure on an issue, these noninstitutional solutions may also imply a continuing political weakness in support of housing subsidies, unless landlords renting to those receiving subsidies were to organize.

On the other hand, the owner-occupier sector can look after itself—the institutional interest of housing finance institutions in home ownership and the desire of Congress not to alienate a majority of households make cutbacks in support to owner-occupiers unlikely. It is also unlikely that a crisis affecting the owner-occupier sector, such as a credit crisis, would result in a turn to other institutions, such as public housing, to meet housing needs. It is more likely that more aid to financial institutions or directly to home owners would be the response.

The future of the British case is less clear. The sales of council housing, which simultaneously increase the number of the owner-occupiers while reducing the number of those in council housing, might be seen as directly shifting support (or concern) away from institutional·(nonmarket) forms of housing provision (government and voluntary associations) to market forms (home ownership). However, in comparison to the American case, this shift should have less significance for the politics of housing since even the expansion of home ownership involves local government to a much greater and visible extent than in the United States. For example, local government in Great Britain is responsible for providing improvement grants which make home ownership possible for many people. While there may be a shift from nonmarket forms of provision, in fact governmental institutions are still a clear provider of aid necessary to home ownership for many in that category. Furthermore, any increases in the cost of home ownership relative to the income of those paying off mortgages will increase their dependence on government aid.

In addition, there are certain categories of governmental or other non-market forms of housing provision which still receive widespread support. It is still the case that almost a third of British housing is provided by local authorities. So even a massive shift toward tenant purchase of those units is not likely to eliminate the importance of council housing to many voters. In addition, other nonmarket, institutional forms of housing provision, such as voluntary housing, are seen by many on both sides of the House of Commons as essential elements of housing policy. For example, the first Thatcher government was unable to get the statutory "right to buy" one's council house extended to voluntary housing, since many feared that this would reduce the available housing for certain groups, such as the elderly.

In short, housing is likely to remain a major political issue in Great Britain, as current trends do not eliminate local government as a focus of housing policy or disrupt the connections between local housing politics and central policymaking. Thus, it is possible in Britain, though not in America, to conceive of various kinds of housing crises being met with nonmarket mechanisms. It is possible to conceive of future support from both sides of the House of Commons for expansion of voluntary housing opportunities for special groups, such as the handicapped or elderly, and more aid to poorer homeowners. It is also possible that a future Labour government might support expansion of certain types of council housing. All these suppositions rely on the existing configuration of nonmarket institutions to provide housing aid, thus maintaining institutions that provide a focus for maintenance of subsidized housing programs.

In comparison, the future of housing policy in the United States seems tied to the ability of the private market to provide housing. Politically, the reliance on these market mechanisms produces ever-increasing growth in aid to home owners and undercuts the growth of institutional forces that could gain increased aid for others in need of subsidized housing. In Britain the balance of aid also favors the home-owning sector, and the institutional forces remain that make housing policy a central political issue and make policies aiding needy non-home owners possible.

NOTES

1. Derek Fraser, *The Evolution of the British Welfare State* (London: Macmillan, 1973), 192–3.
2. Peter Malpass and Alan Murie, *Housing Policy and Practice* (London: Macmillan, 1982), 9.
3. Nathan H. Schwartz, "Reagan's Housing Policies," in Anthony Champagne and Edward J. Harpham, eds., *The Attack on the Welfare State* (Prospect Heights, Ill.: Waveland Press, 1984), 158.
4. Nathan H. Schwartz, "Reagan's Housing Policies." (Birmingham, Ala.: Southern Political Science Association Meetings, 1983, mimeo), 19–20.
5. *The Government's Expenditure Plans: 1984–85 to 1986–87: Volume Two,* Cmnd. 9143—II (London: H.M.S.O., 1981), 50.
6. Environment Committee, House of Commons, *Session 1982– 83: Department of the Environment's Winter Supplementary Estimates 1982– 83: Minutes of Evidence,* HC 170-i (London: H.M.S.O., 1983), 19; Government Statistical Service (United Kingdom), *Social Trends No. 13: 1983 Edition* (London: H.M.S.O., 1983), 112.
7. R.A.W. Rhodes, "Continuity and Change in British Central-Local Relations: 'The Conservative Threat,' 1979–83," *British Journal of Political Science* (January 1984): 279.
8. Raymond J. Struyk, John A. Tuccillo, and James P. Zais, "Housing and Community Development," in John L. Palmer and Isabel V. Sawhill, eds., *The Reagan Experiment* (Washington, D.C.: The Urban Institute Press, 1982), 411.
9. Office of Management and Budget, Executive Office of the President, *Major Themes and Additional Budget Details: Fiscal Year 1983* (Washington, D.C.: Government Printing Office, 1982), 104.
10. Ibid.
11. *Economist,* 21 January 1984, 49.

12. *Economist*, 11 February 1984, 54–5.
13. Office of Management and Budget, *Budget of the United States Government: Fiscal Year 1983* (Washington, D.C.: Government Printing Office, 1982), 9–53; Office of Management and Budget, *Budget of the United States Government: Fiscal Year 1986* (Washington, D.C.: Government Printing Office, 1985), 5–115.
14. Office of Management and Budget, *Budget of the United States Government: Fiscal Year 1983: Appendix* (Washington, D.C.: Government Printing Office, 1982), 130; Office of Management and Budget, *Special Analyses: Budget of the United States Government: Fiscal Year 1986* (Washington, D.C.: Government Printing Office, 1985), G-44.
15. Alan Murie, Pat Niner, and Christopher Watson, *Housing Policy and the Housing System* (London: George Allen & Unwin, 1976), 172; Mark Boleat, *National Housing Finance Systems: A Comparative Study* (London: Croom Helm, 1985), 41.
16. Environment Committee, House of Commons, *DOE's Housing Policies: Enquiry into Government's Expenditure Plans 1981/82 to 1983/84 and the Updating of the Committee's First Report for the Session 1979/80*, HC 383 i–ii (London: H.M.S.O., 1981), xii.
17. Government Statistical Service (United Kingdom), *Social Trends No. 13: 1983 Edition* (London: H.M.S.O., 1983), 200.
18. *The Government's Expenditure Plans: 1983–84 to 1985–86: Volume Two*, Cmnd. 8789-II (London: H.M.S.O., 1983), 33–4.
19. *Sunday Times*, 14 August 1983, 2.
20. Environment Committee, House of Commons, *Council House Sales: Volume 1*, HC 366-I, (London: H.M.S.O., 1981), lxvi–lxvii.
21. London *Times*, 29 June 1983, 2.
22. John Rex and Robert Moore, *Race, Community, and Conflict: A Study of Sparkbrook* (London: Oxford University, 1967).
23. U.S. Department of Commerce, Bureau of the Census, *Statistical Abstract of the United States: 1982–83* (Washington: Government Printing Office, 1982), 751, 760; Government Statistical Service (United Kingdom), *Social Trends No. 13: 1983 Edition* (London: H.M.S.O., 1983), 114.
24. Ian McAllister, "Housing Tenure and Party Choice in Australia, Britain and the United States," *British Journal of Political Science* 14 (October 1984): 517–9.
25. Ibid., 518.
26. Ibid., 518–9.
27. Malpass and Murie, *Housing Policy and Practice*, 46–8.
28. Douglas E. Ashford, "At the Pleasure of Parliament: The Politics of Local Reform in Britain," in Donley T. Studlar and Jerold Waltman, eds., *Dilemmas of Change in British Politics* (Jackson, Miss.: University Press of Mississippi, 1984), 102–25; Mike Goldsmith and Ken Newton, "Central-Local Government Relations: The Irresistible Rise of Centralized Power," in Hugh Berrington, ed., *Change in British Politics* (London: Frank Cass, 1984), 216–33; Rhodes, "Continuity and Change in British Central-Local Relations," 261–83.
29. Ibid., 270–1.
30. Ibid., 283.
31. Ashford, "At the Pleasure of Parliament," 111.
32. Ibid., 105.

33. John Gyford and Mari James, *National Parties and Local Politics* (London: George Allen & Unwin, 1983), 87.
34. Ibid., 130.
35. Ibid., 161–5, 196.
36. Ibid., 138–47.
37. Rhodes, "Continuity and Change," 270–1.
38. Gyford and James, *National Parties and Local Politics*, 203.
39. Nathan H. Schwartz, "Race and the Allocation of Public Housing in Great Britain: The Autonomy of the Local State," *Comparative Politics* 16 (January 1984): 219–20.
40. Rhodes, "Continuity and Change," 263.
41. Ibid.
42. Gyford and James, *National Parties and Local Politics*, 164; Rhodes, "Continuity and Change," 279.
43. Gyford and James, *National Parties and Local Politics*, 130.
44. Ibid., 206–7.
45. Ibid., 204–5.
46. Nathan H. Schwartz, "Reagan's Housing Policies," in Champagne and Harpham, eds., *The Attack on the Welfare State*, 150–1.
47. Lester M. Salamon, "Rethinking Public Management: Third-Party Government and the Changing Forms of Government Action," *Public Policy* 29 (Summer 1981): 268.
48. Ibid., 269.

The Strength
of Policy Inheritance

Jerold L. Waltman

As discussed in the introductory chapter, there are three reasons to suspect that convergence should be occurring in British and American public policies in the 1980s. First, many economic and social trends in the two countries are closely parallel, meaning that there are similar economic and social problems for the state to address. Especially in the area of economics, not only is there the transition to a post-industrial economy, but also the rise in inflation accompanied by the slowdown of the 1970s. Thus, insofar as similar policy problems had to be faced, one might expect to find similar policy responses. Second, the 1980s brought Margaret Thatcher and Ronald Reagan to power. Both offered proposals cut largely from the same philosophical cloth, while also expressing strong mutual admiration. Third, evidence accumulated that the nations' party systems were exhibiting similar trends, an idea which could be stretched to include other political institutions as well.[1] If institutions are evolving in similar directions, logically, analogous policies are likely to follow.

Yet the essays in this book have not uncovered a high degree of convergence. It could be, of course, that the models are wrong, that the policy influence of socioeconomic change, executive policy preferences, and institutional convergence is weak. Or, alternatively, the influence of these variables may be pronounced but not strong enough to overcome indigenous factors. For several reasons, the second scenario seems to fit better the cases examined here, with the weight of the policy inheritance being especially significant as a barrier to convergence. After a brief review of the findings, I will return to this point.

259

260 Jerold L. Waltman

PATTERNS OF CONVERGENCE AND DIVERGENCE

Jeffrey Freyman's detailed treatment of industrial policy indeed stresses some broad thematic similarities, rooted primarily, he suggests, in the environment. That is, the aging industrial base and the international position of both countries present many of the same choices. Yet, using Freyman's useful distinction between the *direction* and the *content* of policies, we see convergence only on the first dimension. Both nations' governments, of course, want to improve their country's competitive position and encourage growth. But what they have done in subsidies, tariffs, retraining schemes, and taxes varies markedly. Even the degree to which they engage in a coordinated set of actions that might be labelled an industrial policy differs in scale. The governing factors in this case, it appears, are the political culture and, related to that, the policy inheritance. British political beliefs have long tolerated or mandated extensive government penetration of the economy far more than those of Americans. The American liberal ethos, as analyzed by Louis Hartz,[2] has blocked anything other than piecemeal, ad hoc initiatives. Thus, the past and present come together in that the British have more already fashioned instruments and greater latitude in their use.

David Robertson found that even though both administrations gave similar reasons to explain the failure of existing policies, their actions led to actual manpower policies that were further apart by the end of 1985. On one hand, the British pursued a more activist strategy in trying to force draconian measures on the unemployed. Forced by political factors to relent from the strategy's more controversial aspects, they nevertheless pushed for much greater interventions in labor markets than did the Reaganites. The reasons were both institutional and the result of short-term political considerations. Despite similar unemployment rates, the structure of labor law and the implementing institutions are quite dissimilar in the two societies. The greater role of trade unions in Britain, as well as European Community membership, presented a different set of givens than the Americans had. Thus, while some elements of the environments of the political systems may have pulled policy in similar directions, other factors worked in the opposite direction. Not experiencing an American-type economic upturn, and en-countering the riots of 1981, made the electoral calculus different for Thatcher's party. Most previous research indicates that governments of every persuasion try to affect the economy favorably immediately before an elec-tion.[3] Hence, engaging in positive steps to treat unemployment meshed well for Thatcher with other efforts to blunt criticism of economic management. (In this case, it appears likely that the moves on the unemployment front were a substitute for the reflation that is more typical.)

In the area of taxes, we saw that similar economic analyses were put forth to justify cutting income tax rates, ostensibly for everyone but mostly for the well-to-do. However, Howe concomitantly raised the VAT to cover the shortfall, while Reagan steered clear of excise increases until much later and then only concurred in modest upward adjustments. The differences these paths made, when coupled with expenditure policies, on the deficits and the distributions of wealth were significant enough to discount the convergence thesis. The resulting budgetary differences are largely attributable to Howe's belief that substituting consumption for income taxes would not damage the structure of investment incentives, compared to Reagan's view that the total level of taxation was of equal importance, and also to the complex institutional structure of American politics. It is doubtful, on a careful reading of the evidence, that Reagan could have gotten consumption taxes increased enough in 1981 to cover the shortfall in income levies even had he so desired. Howe was fortunate, though, in having such a policy instrument as the VAT at hand; had he been faced with increasing excises on specific goods by the magnitude required to offset the income tax losses, he might have faced serious trouble (witness the petrol tax fight). Hence, again, the constitutional structure—in that previous decisions had left general consumption taxes to the states—all but precluded certain options for the Americans.

Energy policy is instructive for both patterns of convergence and divergence are noticeable. Both administrations propounded "free market" solutions, pressing the case for more production, seeing in each instance not only a confirmation of their ideology but also a path to energy independence. But even with a broadly similar set of environmental variables—the four-fuel base—there were distinct differences of "accent," as Rudolph puts it. The energy needs and the mix of the base make the technical requirements different (and make the United States's time table for another crisis shorter). Moreover, the institutional structure—meaning here the character of interest groups and the processes of policymaking—are sufficiently different to make exactly synonymous outcomes unlikely. Thus, while the broad contours of energy policy are similar, especially compared to other Western nations, the specifics vary significantly.

Richard Flickinger's essay on consumer policy points to the difficulties with simplistic convergence theories. The similarities in the economic systems of the two countries mean that the type of protection consumers receive, if they are to receive any, must also be roughly similar. At the same time, the marked variances in political values and institutional structures translate into pronounced differences in the accepted role of the state and the methods of implementation. Furthermore, deriving in large measure from periodic "reform cycles" (which never seem to change the underlying suspicion of government) and entrepreneurial politics, American policies are more open to short-term change than British. Even though, for example, both Thatcher and Reagan have sought to rely more on market forces, Thatcher has actually accomplished less. The differences in process, then, are enough to make this case one of only qualified convergence, in which convergence may come and go.

Pensions policy stands out from the others. After the adoption in 1975 of the earnings-based scheme, the systems have displayed convergence. In part, this is a derivative of the characteristics of the policy and the "life cycle" it seems to go through everywhere. More important, though, may be the fact of subsystem autonomy and the prevalence of similar processes within those subsystems. That is, the bureaucratic expertise model of policymaking is dominant in the pensions policymaking process of both countries. The traits of this model—technical dominance and elite recruitment to policymaking positions—not only pull the systems in converging directions but also facilitate the sharing of information across national boundaries. Heclo demonstrated earlier that these types of systems are especially prone to "social learning" as well as to the influence of bureaucracy-based experts.[4]

Health care demonstrates better than any other issue the importance of policy inheritance. Free market medical care is an icon for both administrations. However, the existence of the National Health Service and its popularity considerably narrows the scope for the introduction of free market principles. At the margins, through altered insurance policies and budget manipulation, some changes can be wrought in Britain. However, the already private system in the United States, along with the cumbersome administrative machinery of the few government health programs, make Reagan's task radically different. Securing an American-type system in Britain would be little short of revolutionary. Thus, there is strong convergence in intent, some small convergence in policy specifics, but mostly divergence, and still a wide divergence in actual governmental policies.

Nathan Schwartz's analysis of housing policy testifies to the strength of the institutional structures which surround a policy area. Although there is a convergence in the fact that a bifurcation exists in both countries between the owner-occupied and subsidized categories, otherwise the differences are pronounced—even in the face of similar ideological predispositions. Both sets of leaders talk of an "opportunity society" and, in Britain especially, of creating a nation of property owners.[5] But the positions of the housing construction industry in the United States and the local authorities in Britain do not have parallels in the other nation. Thus, even with sales of council houses, the remaining role of local governments and the links they maintain with central authorities would seem to preclude the emergence of a housing pattern like that of the United States.

TABLE 1: *Convergence versus Divergence*

Policy	Intent	Content	Resulting Policies Similar Overall
Industrial policy	C	C/D[1]	No
Labor Market	C	D	No
Taxes	C	C/D[2]	No
Energy	C	C/D[2]	No
Consumer policy	C	C	Yes
Pensions	C	C	Yes
Health Care	C	D	No
Housing	C	C/D[3]	No

[1] Direction convergent, content divergent
[2] Both convergent and divergent elements present
[3] Use of owner occupied and subsidized convergent, otherwise divergent

In sum, except at the most general level, convergence turns out to be rather weak, at least in the policy areas examined here. Table 1 presents a summary of the case studies. The *Intent* column refers especially to the Thatcher-Reagan period and the *Content* column primarily to the policies adopted during their tenures. Convergence, even in the limited sense of moving in the same direction, suffers a serious setback as illustrated by these two columns alone. However, the third column which compares the combination of old and new policies—the "policy mix" if you will—leaves no doubt that a convergence in the actual structure of governmental policies has not occurred. What accounts for these results? Equally important, why are consumer policy and pensions exceptions?

CONVERGENCE AND PUBLIC POLICIES

If the pressures for convergence are powerful, why have we found less of it than might be expected? Some tentative answers can be provided by more closely examining the reasons to believe convergence should be occurring.[6]

Twenty years ago A.F.K. Organski published his widely read *Stages of Political Development*, in which he posited that modern societies were moving toward socioeconomic structures and political institutions which would pull them all in a similar direction.[7] Most partricularly, centralized bureaucracies resting on expertise would articulate, process, and legitimate public concerns and policies. These formulations fit in well with those of other theorists such as Galbraith, and earlier Mannheim, who had foreseen a future based largely on planning.[8]

Organski's thesis is easily linked to the concept of postindustrialism. To the extent that one can formulate a model affecting public policy from the disparate works on postindustrialism, it takes the following contours: Economic and social changes occur first. In the economy, a shift takes place away from older industrial and capital intensive enterprises to newer, service-oriented, and knowledge-intensive sectors. White-collar jobs become more numerous, creating a higher standard of material living for more people and bringing demands for ever higher levels of education. Social attitudes alter as a concern for materiality only adds a "quality-of-life" dimension. Politically, two trends are of fundamental importance. First, these socioeconomic changes will shape the political agenda. Second, the increasing complexity of the economy and society will lead to increasing bureaucratization. Policymaking processes will come to be dominated by these bureaucracies since they will possess a near monopoly of information and expertise.

Both these political phenomena seem to create the conditions for policy convergence between and among postindustrial societies. If socioeconomic conditions are roughly parallel in postindustrial societies, it follows that the political agendas will be similar; similar social problems will arise and the state will be called on to address them. While similar agendas need not necessarily lead to the adoption of similar policies, the policy choices will always be limited. Furthermore, the likelihood of diffusion in societies closely linked by modern communications media is high. The existence of analogous problems therefore will pull political systems toward convergence in their public policies. Moreover, the policymaking process of postindustrial nations will grow more alike, as the dominance of bureaucracies becomes more common. As a result, it seems logical to anticipate the converging of the outcomes of political processes—public policies. Already pulled toward convergence by a similar set of postindustrial issues, bureaucratization will override the differing structural and cultural factors of modern political systems, and reinforce the tendencies toward convergence.

The evidence for the advent of a postindustrial economy seems indisputable. Whether viewed as godsend or curse, Western economies are witnessing a decline of their heavy industrial bases and the steady growth of the information and service sectors. The rates and the details are different, with the United States leading Britain on most measures, but the trend is easy to document in both. Moreover, it appears that there has been some shift in mass attitudes in several Western publics; values labeled "post-modern" have shown up in a number of societies and the percentage of people who hold them seems to be growing.[9]

In addition, there are studies demonstrating that there has been a convergence in the styles of policy formation. Richardson has detected such a convergence in Western Europe (with some allusions to the United States also) centered on sectorization.[10] That is, he argues that a large number of political subsystems have developed which are only loosely connected to each other. Likewise, Sharkansky has demonstrated that in many cases policy is made by bureaucracies that are virtually autonomous.[11]

My contention is not that either of these developments fails to pull contemporary Western political systems toward convergence; rather, it is that whatever commonalities are produced by the growth of similar political issues and converging policy processes must weigh in against strong forces endogenous to the political system. In the cases of Britain and the United States, at least, these forces are substantial. Important institutional and attitudinal factors still separate the two countries, and, most important, each has a different policy inheritance. An examination of Table 2 will help sharpen the point.

TABLE 2:   *Why Convergence or Divergence?*

Policy	Major Reasons
Industrial Policy	Policy inheritance; political culture
Labor market	Policy inheritance; institutional framework
Taxes	Ideology of decision makers; constitutional structure; policy inheritance
Energy	Technical requirements
Consumer policy	Technical requirements
Pensions	Subsystem autonomy and identity; technical requirements
Health care	Policy inheritance
Housing	Policy inheritance

NOTE: The term "institutional structure" refers to the various agencies, boards, commissions, and so forth that are involved in a policy area whereas "constitutional structure" refers to the broader structures of executives, legislatures, etc.

Consumer policy is a good example of the power of postindustrial issues in shaping policy. The nature of the economy dictates from what a consumer must be protected. Of course, there may be, and is, more or less regulation of given industries and variation in the legal remedies. But the fact that there is no difference in spoiled American or British meat or in fraudulent Ponzi schemes pulls the systems toward similar substance in their consumer policy. Energy policy reinforces this conclusion in that the only pressures toward convergence flow from the fuel bases. Absent a similar fuel base, even the parallels discussed by Rudolph would seem unlikely.

Pensions policy, on the other hand, illustrates subsystem autonomy with bureaucratic dominance. In both the United States and United Kingdom, the formulation of pension policy has been largely in the hands of autonomous bureaucracies, at least since the early years. The structure of the two countries' bureaucracies and the "working assumptions" of those who staff them are remarkably similar. In this case, convergence results therefore from the parallel methods of making policy decisions. Moreover, the fact that the "technical requirements," here that both nations have an aging population, are similar adds to the pressures for convergence.

However, in the other areas, internal factors assume a primary place, as shown by the table. Postindustrialism is a stage of economic development that is layered on top of each society's past. It does not alter that past nor people's perceptions of it. There will be pressures pulling political systems toward similar policies, but in many aspects of political life they will remain at a very general level. Just as the period of industrialization did not produce identical policy responses throughout Western Europe, much less North America, we should not expect all postindustrial societies to be in concert. Significant national differences will continue to exist.

Turning to policymaking, I believe Richardson is correct. What sectorization can do, though, is raise the importance of cultural, institutional, and constitutional factors. It may produce convergence, as it did with the case of pensions; but it will do so only when there is an autonomous subsystem dominated by a technically oriented bureaucracy. Sectorization may well have the opposite result: the subsystems are, after all, British subsystems or American subsystems, and the presence of attitudinal variables and the fact that the political maneuvering occurs within a presidential or parliamentary system and within a federal or unitary state are highly significant. The power and autonomy of subsystems may be similar, but the nature of political processes within the subsystems is different, often sharply so.

Health care is a good contrast to consumer and pensions policy. Presumably, British broken arms call for treatment identical to American ones. Furthermore, health care policy is a substantially autonomous subsystem in both nations. Yet the institutional and financial web in which an American has his arm set is quite different from the pattern in the United Kingdom. Thus, the similar technical requirements of modern medicine cannot "overcome" political culture and considerable interest group activity. Moreover, the subsystem phenomenon accentuates the differences rather than bridges them, and precludes the sharing of policy information. While, therefore, there is a large amount of sharing in the technical aspects of medicine, no one is much interested in policy information from the other country. How to bargain in a governmental budget game shares little with the complexities of third-party payment.

In each of the other policy areas, the story is much the same. The policy inheritance, and usually its attendant institutional framework, has made the subsystem different from its counterpart in the other country. After a certain policy is established, an institutional web of agencies, boards, commissions, and interest groups grows up around it. Issues may be similar across countries and the power of government bureaucracies may be great in all modern nations, but neither is guaranteed to be the most important factor when political battles are fought out and decisions made within each subsystem. The way previous policies shape the balance of forces in the subsystems militate against such converging tendencies. If previous policies were different, therefore, there is a high likelihood that current policies will be also.

What of the policy influences of Margaret Thatcher and Ronald Reagan? Elections have little point if they are not for policy reasons; and most research has indeed shown that elections do have important policy ramifications.[12] With so much emphasis in the popular press of both countries on the desire of these leaders to effect change and their similar proclivities, why has there not been a closer convergence?

One explanation is that it is easy to overdraw inferences on policy specifics from general ideology. True, Thatcher and Reagan touch the same notes and invoke the same virtues and images, but the accents and nuances of their actual policy ideas are often not the same. Peter Riddell, for instance, stresses this point while analyzing the Thatcher record.[13] In economic policy, the best specific example is the fact that neither Thatcher nor Geoffrey Howe ever contended that tax cuts would create enough growth to cancel out the deficit caused by income tax reductions. Thus, one would have to read the record very carefully before putting forth a determinative argument based on the two leaders' ideologies. Nevertheless, they do share more in common than any other pair of postwar leaders, and it does not seem unreasonable to believe that their preferences would lead to a good bit more convergence than has occurred. I, for one, and I think most of the other authors, predicted far more convergence, at least in the sense of movement in the same direction, than we uncovered.

A major offsetting element is surely the fact that they faced different situations within their parties. Not only do the offices carry different party responsibilities, but the coalitions they had to build to gain and keep power were different. The Tory Wets and the allies of Representative Jack Kemp posed different threats. Another is that the realities of parliamentary and presidential government require a different political calculus. Reagan, after all, had to deal with a Democratic House and midterm elections, while Thatcher could ignore Labour leaders except in debate and could call her own election time.

The foregoing points are obvious to anyone with even a textbook knowledge of the two political systems; however, the contrast goes beyond that to what might be called the "operational realities" of political life. Thatcher, for instance, may be able to fashion parliamentary support more easily, but at the same time she has been hemmed in by a number of semiautonomous bodies. In labor market policy, for example, she had little choice except to work through the established instititutions. Reagan, on the other hand, has had much more ability to direct the executive branch, as Graham Wilson's study of his regulatory policies shows.[14]

In the final analysis, however, we are led once again to the role of the past, the policy inheritance. The policies in place when each came into office shaped the givens. Even if they were identical in outlook and disposed to adopt identical policies, neither could have remade the political system's policies within his or her time in office. The corpus of governmental actions that make up "public policy" in the modern state is too complex, too far flung, and too interwoven to be made over even in a decade.

This is not to say that there has been no convergence resulting from their tenures. Certainly if the Labour party had won the 1983 election there would be markedly less convergence than there is. The point is to stress that political change in modern democracies occurs at the margins, and the baseline for the margins is handed down from the past. It is a testimony to the strength of these policy inheritances that there has not been more convergence. Both Reagan and Thatcher desired to do more in a shorter time than most other presidents and prime ministers. What may be remarkable is not what they have done, which is significant in both countries, but the degree to which the resulting policy universe is decidedly recognizable.

In discussing the structure of administration, Hugh Heclo recently wrote, "Compared with other nations, Britain and America certainly resemble each other in terms of their skepticism about political authority, particularly as such authority might extend into spheres of personal liberty, civil rights, family life, and so on. But these family resemblances notwithstanding, we are not the same people."[15] Much the same can be said of our public policies, economic and otherwise. The past is different in dozens of ways in the two countries. The lineage of policy development deviates substantially in virtually every area. Moreover, views of the acceptable role of the state and the institutional structures of administration are still noticeably different. Pressures for convergence notwithstanding, then, specific policies in these two democracies continue to diverge more often than they converge.

NOTES

1. See, for example, Donley Studlar, "Conclusion: A Crisis of Participation?" in Donley Studlar and Jerold Waltman, eds., *Dilemmas of Change in British Politics* (Jackson: University Press of Mississippi, 1984), esp. 238–41.

2. Louis Hartz, *The Liberal Tradition in America* (New York: Harcourt, Brace, 1955). See also Donald Devine, *The Political Culture of the United States* (Boston: Little Brown, 1972).

3. The literature is immense. See, inter alia, Edward R. Tufte, *Political Control of the Economy* (Princeton: Princeton University Press, 1978) and Douglas Hibbs and Heino Fassbender, eds., *Contemporary Political Economy: Studies on the Interdependence of Politics and Economics* (Amsterdam: North-Holland, 1981).

4. Hugh Heclo, *Modern Social Politics in Britain and Sweden* (New Haven: Yale University Press, 1974).

5. See David Howell, "Conservative Revolution: Keeping up the Momentum," *Political Quarterly* 54 (December 1983): 338–45.

6. In the following analysis, I am collapsing the first and third reasons cited above into one category. The reason is that forces making the party systems more similar are normally traced to the social system. Thus, whether policy convergence is a direct consequence of social and economic convergence or institutions acting as intermediaries, the causes for convergence are the same.

7. A.F.K. Organski, *Stages of Political Development* (New York: Knopf, 1965).

8. John K. Galbraith, *The New Industrial State* (Boston: Houghton Mifflin, 1967); Karl Mannheim, *Man and Society in an Age of Reconstruction* (London: K. Paul, Trench, Trubner, 1940).

9. Ronald Inglehart, "Post-Materialism in an Environment of Insecurity," *American Political Science Review* 75 (December 1981): 880–900.

10. Jeremy Richardson, "Convergent Policy Styles in Western Europe?" in Jeremy Richardson, ed., *Policy Styles in Western Europe* (London: Allen and Unwin, 1982), chap. 8.

11. Ira Sharkansky, *Wither the State?* (Chatham, N.J.:Chatham House, 1979).

12. Richard Rose, *Do Parties Make a Difference?*, 2nd ed. (London: Macmillan, 1984).

13. Peter Riddell, *The Thatcher Government* (Oxford: Martin Robertson, 1983), 14–15. His point, though, is limited largely to taxes (and the absence of a Moral Majority in Britain).

14. Graham Wilson, "Social Regulation and Explanations of Regulatory Failure," *Political Studies* 23 (June 1984): 203–25.

15. Hugh Heclo, "Washington and Whitehall Revisited: An Essay in Constitutional Law," in Richard Hodder-Williams and James Ceaser, eds., *Politics in Britain and the United States* (Durham, N.C.: Duke University Press, 1986) 116–17.

Notes on Contributors

Richard S. Flickinger is professor of political science at Wittenberg University and Research Associate at the Mershon Center, Ohio State University. His work on consumer policy and defense policy has been published in *Policy Studies Review* and *Peace and Change*.

Gary P. Freeman is associate professor of government at the University of Texas in Austin and a member of the editorial board of the *Journal of Politics*. Before embarking on the study of comparative pension policies, he published *Immigrant Labor and Racial Conflict in Industrial Societies*.

Jeffrey B. Freyman is associate professor of political science at Transylvania University, Kentucky. His research on the British Labour Party has appeared in the *Southeastern Political Review*.

Beth Fuchs is on the staff of the Special Committee on Aging, U.S. Senate. She received the Samuel H. Beer Prize of the British Politics Group for her Ph.D. dissertation on comparative health policy.

David B. Robertson is assistant professor of political science at the University of Missouri-St. Louis. The author of a prize-winning article in *Policy Studies Review*, he has also contributed to the *Historical Dictionary of the New Deal*.

John D. Robertson is associate professor of political science at Texas A&M University. A member of the editorial boards of the *Policy Studies Journal* and the *Journal of Politics*, his articles have appeared in the *American Journal of Political Science*, the *Journal of Politics*, *Comparative Political Studies*, and elsewhere.

Joseph R. Rudolph, Jr. is professor of political science at the Towson State University. Among the journals publishing his work have been *Comparative Politics, Western Political Quarterly, Polity*, and *Canadian Review of Studies in Nationalism*.

Nathan H. Schwartz is assistant professor of political science at the University of Louisville. His studies of housing have appeared in *Comparative Politics, Local Government Studies*, and edited books.

Donley T. Studlar is associate professor of government at Centre College, Danville, Kentucky. The author of some two dozen articles on British politics, he coedited *Dilemmas of Change in British Politics*.

Jerold L. Waltman is professor of political science at the University of Southern Mississippi. His previous books are *Copying Other Nations' Policies, The Political Origins of the U.S. Income Tax*, and *Dilemmas of Change in British Politics* (coeditor).

Index

AFL-CIO, 88
Alliance, 121
Alternative economic strategy, 51
American Medical Association, 224
Atomic Energy Commission, 122, 126

Bank of England, 35, 36
Beer, Samuel, 3, 49
Bevan, Aneurin, 210
Beveridge, William, Beveridge Report, 188, 191, 196
Bretton Woods Agreement, 31–34, 53, 59
British Medical Association, 210, 211, 215
British Technology Group, 50
Brzezinski, Zbigniew, 6, 10
Budgets, Budgeting, 20, 37, 50, 70, 74, 77, 78, 79, 82, 83, 88, 91, 98, 101, 102, 103, 104, 105, 106–9, 114, 115, 122, 140, 194, 198, 208, 209ff., 215, 218, 219, 220, 221, 222, 223, 226, 227, 234, 237, 238, 239, 249, 250, 251, 253, 262, 267
Bureaucracy, 5, 47, 77, 184, 193, 194, 195, 197, 262, 263–64, 265, 266, 267

Cabinet (UK), 25, 35, 160, 214
Callaghan, James, 47, 75, 238
Carter, Jimmy, 54, 83, 129, 130, 131, 133, 134, 156, 158, 159, 165, 220, 227, 237
Castle, Barbara, 197, 198

Central Policy Review Staff, 214, 215
Chamber of Commerce, 156
Citizens of Advice Bureaux, 160
Common Market, *See* European Community
Community Development Block Grant Program, 86–87
Comprehensive Employment and Training Act (CETA), 72, 74, 84–85, 89
Confederation of British Industry, 77, 81
Congressional Budget Office, 37, 52, 110
Conservative Party, 47ff., 63, 75, 88, 98, 103, 108, 112, 129, 189, 197, 198, 209, 211, 214, 215, 247
Consumer Product Safety Commission, 155, 159
Consumer's Association, 162, 163, 167
Consumer's League, 152, 161, 162
Consumer's Union, 152, 161, 162, 168
Co-operative Movement, 153, 157, 162, 163, 167
Corporatism, 10, 11, 62
Council housing, 235, 236, 238, 240, 241, 242, 243, 244, 245, 248, 254, 255, 256, 262
Council of Economic Advisers, 37, 159

Deficit (US), 26, 30–31, 105, 106–8, 115, 218, 239, 250

For UK *See* Public Sector Borrowing Requirement
Democracy, 5–6, 48, 146, 185
Democratic Party, 29, 57, 83, 86, 104, 129, 167, 168, 221
Department of Energy , 129, 134, 136
Depreciation, 105
Depression, 20
Diagnosis Related Groups, 216, 224–26, 227
Diffusion, 6, 10, 170, 264
Donovan, Raymond J., 83, 92
Drug Safety Tests Act, 155

Earned Income Credit, 100, 106
Economic Development Administration, 56
Economic Recovery Tax Act of 1981, 104, 106, 107, 111
Emergency Jobs and Recession Relief Act, 86
Employment Acts, 1980, 51, 75; 1982, 51, 75
Employment and Training Administration, 72, 73, 83, 85–86, 86–87, 90
Enterprise Allowance Scheme, 79–80, 90, 92
Enterprise zones, 50, 56
Environmental Protection Agency, 130
European Community, 91, 141, 172, 260
Excise taxes, 100–1, 102, 103, 104, 105, 107, 261
Export-Import Bank, 56

Fair Trading Act of 1973, 157
Falklands War, 80, 107
Federalism, 35, 62, 83, 86, 91, 99, 124, 130, 168, 185, 219, 266
Federal Reserve Board, 26, 27, 36, 37, 90
Federal Trade Commission, 155, 159
Finance Act of 1977, 100
Fiscal policy, 18–19, 25, 38, 44, 77, 101
Friedman, Milton, 72, 208

Greater London Council, 91

Gross Domestic Product, 16–17, 25, 28, 77, 83, 99, 100, 102, 103, 106, 107, 109, 186, 190

Health Services Act: 1976, 210, 212; 1980, 212, 213
Healy, Denis, 27
Heath, Edward, 34, 47, 48, 157, 168, 209, 215
Heclo, Hugh, 9, 196, 197, 262, 268
Heritage Foundation, 74
Howe, Geoffrey, 25, 75, 79, 101, 103, 112, 113, 115, 158, 198, 214, 261, 267
Huntington, Samuel, 6, 10

Ideology, 6–7, 9, 10, 28, 29, 48, 57, 63, 64, 69, 70, 73, 77, 78, 98, 183, 185, 194, 198, 209, 215, 223, 227, 228, 248, 261, 262, 267
Income taxes, 98, 99, 100–6, 108, 109, 112, 113, 114, 218, 240–41, 261
Industrial Reorganization Corporation, 48
Industrial Training Boards, 77, 89
Inflation, 21, 24, 25, 26, 28, 29, 34, 37, 47, 49, 59, 60, 70, 73, 74, 101, 104, 164, 168, 169, 192, 193, 199, 218, 221, 227, 259
International Monetary Fund, 32, 34

Jenkin, Patrick, 212
Jenkins, Roy, 167
Job Corps, 83, 85, 87, 88
Job Training Partnership Act, 56, 81, 84, 85, 86, 88, 89, 90, 91
Johnson, Lyndon, 164, 165, 194
Joseph, Keith, 72, 74, 75, 76, 197

Kennedy, Edward, 85
Kennedy, John F., 153, 165
Keynesian economics, 4, 19–21, 23, 38, 51, 57, 58, 59, 60, 72, 74, 98, 194
King, Anthony, 9, 62, 114, 171

Labour Party, 29, 47ff., 75, 77, 103, 121, 129, 130, 137, 138, 140, 158

163, 188–89, 197, 210, 216, 227, 238, 243, 247, 268
Laffer, Arthur, 72
Laissez-faire, 18, 63, 83, 90, 136
Lawson, Nigel, 26, 75, 104, 113
Lowi, Theodore, 183

Macmillan, Harold, 167, 209
Manpower Services Commission, 72, 74, 75, 76, 77, 78, 79, 80, 90, 91
Marshall Plan, 47
Marx, Karl, 5
Medicaid, 219, 222, 223, 226
Medicare, 188, 220–21, 222, 223, 224, 225, 226
Molony Committee on Consumer Protection, 156, 157, 167
Monetary policy, Monetarism, 18, 19, 21–23, 25, 38, 44, 49, 59, 64, 74, 75, 90, 113, 208, 218

Nader, Ralph, 155, 162, 165
National Coal Board, 123, 126, 129, 130, 138, 139, 141
National Economic Development Council, 47
National Enterprise Board, 48, 50
National Health Service, 207, 208–218, 220, 227, 262
National Insurance Act, 188
National Research Development Corporation, 50
New Deal, 152
Nixon, Richard, 33, 53, 90, 130, 132, 133

OECD, 34, 70, 72, 108, 150, 151, 159, 170
Office of Management and Budget, 37, 83, 85, 86, 87, 159, 221
OPEC, 34, 122, 124, 126, 135, 142, 143, 144
Organski, A.F.K., 263, 264

Pensions, 184–200, 262, 266
Phillips curve, 21
Plowden Report, 36
Political parties, party systems, 3, 4, 7, 31, 37, 62, 63, 185, 194, 195, 196,
198, 244, 246–47, 248–49, 254, 259, 267–68, *See also* names of particular parties.
Postindustrialism, 7, 10, 54, 259, 264, 265, 266
Powell, Enoch, 77
Prior, James, 75, 77, 78
Privatization, 51, 140, 160, 207, 209–218, 221, 222
Productivity, 31, 34, 44, 46, 48, 50, 51, 57, 59, 73, 98, 101
Professional Service Review Organizations, 222, 223
Public Sector Borrowing Requirement, 51, 64, 102, 103, 104, 107, 115

Reagan, Ronald, 4, 10, 11, 23, 26, 27, 38, 54ff., 57, 58, 62, 63, 64, 65, 69, 70, 71, 73, 81, 82, 83, 87, 88, 89, 90, 91, 92, 98, 102, 104, 105, 109, 112, 113, 114, 115, 128, 130, 131, 135, 136, 141, 142, 143, 144, 145, 146, 151, 158, 159, 169, 171, 173, 192, 199, 200, 218, 219, 220, 222, 223, 226, 227, 228, 233, 234, 237, 238, 239, 240, 249, 250, 259, 261, 262, 263, 267, 268
Reconstruction Finance Corporation, 57
Reich, Robert, 57
Republican Party, 29, 63, 82, 83, 85, 86, 87, 88, 98, 108, 129, 194, 218, 220, 221

Sale of Goods Act, 152
Section 8 Program (Housing and Community Development Act of 1974), 235, 236, 249
Seldon, Arthur, 211
Separation of powers, 35, 62, 185
Small Business Administration, 56
Smith, Adam, 18
Social Security, 22, 99–100, 106, 108, 109
Stockman, David, 82, 83, 84, 85, 88, 220, 221
Supply-side economics, 22–23, 38, 57, 58, 82, 98, 101, 105, 113, 128, 218

Tax Equity and Fiscal Responsibility
	Act of 1982, 105
Tax Reform Act of 1984, 105
Taxation, taxes, 11, 19, 22, 23, 24,
	32, 44, 50, 52, 53, 55, 56, 58, 64,
	70, 82, 98–115, 132, 136, 140,
	188, 194, 199, 208, 213, 221, 234,
	242, 247, 250, 251–52, 260, 261
	See also specific types of taxes.
Tebbit, Norman, 75, 76, 77, 79
Thatcher, Margaret, 4, 10, 11, 24, 25,
	26, 27, 38, 49ff., 55, 56, 58, 61,
	62, 63, 64, 65, 69, 71, 73, 74, 75,
	77, 78, 79, 80, 82, 88, 89, 90, 91,
	92, 98, 101, 103, 109, 112, 113,
	114, 115, 120, 121, 128, 129, 131,
	137, 139, 140, 141, 142, 143, 145,
	146, 151, 159, 160, 161, 169, 171,
	173, 192, 199, 200, 207, 208, 209,
	210, 211, 213, 214, 216, 217, 218,
	219, 222, 227, 228, 233, 234, 237,
	238, 240, 241, 245, 247, 248, 255,
	259, 260, 262, 263, 267, 268
Three Mile Island, 128, 137
Titmuss, Richard, 196, 197, 198
Truth in Lending, 153

Truth in Packaging, 153, 155, 166
Thurow, Lester, 57
Trade Union Act of 1984, 51, 75
Trades Union Congress, 78, 79, 81
Treasury (U.K.), 35, 36, 47, 62, 107,
	188, 198
Treasury (U.S.), 37, 62, 194, 195, 198

Unemployment, 17, 20, 21, 25, 26,
	28, 30, 31, 32, 34, 54, 59, 60, 69–
	90, 101, 102, 103, 199, 260
United Kingdom Atomic Energy
	Authority, 123, 126, 129, 138

Value Added Tax, 25, 100–1, 102,
	104, 107, 112, 114, 261
Volcker, Paul, 26

Wilson, Harold, 27, 47, 157–58, 168,
	198
Work Incentive Program, 87
World Bank, 32

Young, David, 75, 76, 78, 79, 80
Youth Training Scheme, 77, 78, 80,
	81, 89, 90